Journey *to* Tobruk

~ Dedication ~

I DEDICATE THIS BOOK TO MY LATE PARENTS, DR JOHN OLDHAM AND MARGARET (NEE MURRAY) OLDHAM. THEIR LIVES WERE INEXTRICABLY TIED TO THAT OF MY UNCLE, JOHN MURRAY, THE SUBJECT OF THIS BIOGRAPHY.

I WOULD ALSO LIKE TO PAY TRIBUTE TO MY MATERNAL GRANDMOTHER, LAURA CONSTANCE MURRAY GLANVILLE — A CONSTANT SOURCE OF INSPIRATION TO HER FAMILY. SHE WAS FORTUNATE IN HAVING FOUR HEALTHY, LOVING AND SUCCESSFUL CHILDREN — LORRAINE, PETER, JOHN AND MARGARET.

IT IS THE LETTERS JOHN MURRAY WROTE TO HIS MOTHER, MY GRANDMOTHER, BETWEEN 1931 AND 1960, THAT INSPIRED THE WRITING OF THIS STORY.

Journey to Tobruk

John Murray — bushman, soldier, survivor

LOUISE AUSTIN

PIER
9

~ Foreword ~

by HER EXCELLENCY
Ms QUENTIN BRYCE, AC
GOVERNOR of QUEENSLAND

STORIES OF HEROISM STIR IN EACH OF US A PROFOUND ADMIRATION, A SENSE OF WONDER AT THE SHEER DARING OF THE HUMAN SPIRIT, UNLEASHED AGAINST ADVERSITY. OUR HEROES INSPIRE AND BLESS US, URGING US TO NEW STRENGTHS AND GREATER FEATS IN OUR OWN PATHWAYS.

TO CALL JOHN MURRAY a hero is no trite exaggeration or colloquial commonplace. His life is a truly extraordinary one, and deserves the attention of everyone who has looked into Australia's past to find our identity, our purpose, our character.

All three beat strongly in the heart of this Australian, driving his contribution to land and country, shaping a journey across the world, into great suffering and profound wisdom.

In the story that unfolds in these pages, he rises from inauspicious origins to test his mettle against the harshness of the Australian bush; to embark with his comrades on the gruelling venture of the second Great War; to return undiminished and build a family, a livelihood, a career in politics, and a growing legend.

Beyond the bones of his narrative, John Murray emerges as a warm heart and a keen wit; a generous son, an open and attentive learner, ready to engage and absorb the hard lessons of the wide world. His energy and *joie-de-vivre* shine in the letters and fragments of his own hand,

and his integrity radiates from the careful inscriptions of a loving and respectful editor.

In collecting and recording his life, Louise Austin has captured not only the soul of a great Australian, but the spirit and saga of a time that made Australia great.

This book, destined to be a family treasure, is also a gift to our nation and our community. It will teach us about who we are, where we've come from, and the heroism that will always stir our national story.

8 May 2008

- Contents -

3 Barlow Street
Clayfield Qld, 4011
25.9.99

Dear Louise
These are most of the letters I wrote to Mother from 1931–60.
It was a surprise to find that she had kept them. I've put them
together in sequence as far as possible—many are undated—and
of course location was not always allowed during the war for security
reasons. I have pencil numbered each page for reference.

Number one was written by the bookkeeper at Manfred
homestead, W.A. Woods, a very fine ex Major of Light Horse
from the 1914–18 war. Your father worked with him for
the time he was at Manfred. He was also my 'guardian' for the
first year or so of my six years there. He was a friend of Ben
Chaffey and reported to him by phone most nights to Melbourne
on the daily doings on the station. He was extremely strict with
me but it was very much for my benefit.

Please bear in mind that I turned fifteen a few days after
arriving at Kilfera, and then on to Manfred, which joined.
The homesteads were about 60 miles apart and the total area
was about one and a quarter million acres.

So I do ask you please to make some allowance for the very
immature writings and thoughts expressed in my letters to the
family, particularly until about the second year of the war. From
then on I started climbing the ladder of rank, and attended some
schools and courses, finding myself associating with intelligent
and interesting men. I was very fortunate indeed.

There are a number of time gaps in my letter writing, mostly
during action. You will also find a few I wrote to your mother.
She wrote often and sent parcels. Ruth was also very good. But
she of course was just like a sister then.

If you do find the time and curiosity to have a glance at this pile
of ramblings, and want some clarification, I will help if I can.
Uncle John

~ *Preface* ~

LOU DARLING — FOR ONCE AND FINALLY — I LOVE ALL YOUR
QUESTIONS — LITTLE ONES — BIG ONES — ANY ONES —
ROLL THEM IN ANY TIME DAY OR NIGHT — IF THERE COULD
BE A LOT TO AN ANSWER AND I SEE THAT I'M GOING TO
PRATTLE ON A BIT — SUCH AS THE START OF THE TRIP WITH
THE CATTLE — I'LL ADVISE YOU AND YOU MAY LIKE TO
CONNECT UP TO A RECEIVER OR SOME DEVICE TO RECORD —
ENTIRELY UP TO YOU. I'LL DO ANYTHING TO HELP YOU GET
THE RECORD STRAIGHT AND KEEP IT STRAIGHT.

Monday, 10 July 2006 2:17 PM

DURING THE RESEARCH for an autobiography I published in 2003—*Secrets and Silence: A Family Memoir*—my mother's brother, John Murray, presented me with a series of letters, discovered in a cupboard upon his mother's death. He had written regularly to my grandmother through the entire period of World War II—from his enlistment in 1940 until his final return to Australia in late 1945. A few letters before and after those years also survive.

The night I began reading the letters was a sleepless one. I was fascinated not only by their personal and historical content, but also by how each letter built upon the last, showing the growth of my uncle—from a young boy to a mature man. Six years facing bullets, bayonets and bombs had undoubtedly accelerated his personal development. It occurred to me that the letters offered an excellent starting point for another view of my family. I approached my uncle for permission to write his story, using the letters as a basis. He was wholeheartedly enthusiastic from the start, agreeing also to allow me to interview him for supplementary material. Without his passionate support the book would never have been written.

For the story of his life I depended on three resources: my uncle's letters, his willingness to tell me anything and everything I wanted to know, and for background data, books on World War II. Knowing that the letters had been censored, I interviewed John Murray for more than thirty-five hours. My uncle showed remarkable tenacity in getting the job done. Not once did he complain, even though the interview sessions were at times gruelling. Since his correspondence barely touched on his pre- or post-war life, he willingly gave me details about that part of his life as well.

As far as possible I have retained the flavour of John's spoken narrative. When the words are his, I have merely used indentation or inverted commas, without a specific footnote. Some of the words and sentiments he expressed might now be considered politically incorrect, but I was reluctant to change them as I wanted to preserve authenticity. The letters remain unedited except for when length or repetition necessitated cuts. At rare times I have used poetic licence to describe an emotion for him or others in the story. However, his life is presented almost entirely as he told it to me.

A word about veracity. Commenting in the introduction to E.H. Carr's book, *What is History?*, Dr James Vernon claims that historical writing always includes a subjective element; that historians cannot escape the constrictions of their own era that influence their ideas and assumptions.[1] Historical anecdote may be similarly viewed.

The recorded story about Constance Murray, John's mother, is an example. Retold to the author more than fifty years later, the story was doubtless subject to time and subjectivity in its retelling. It may be that Constance Murray was intent on distilling her past, putting the best light possible on a family history she did not care her children to inherit. It could be that her older son embellished his mother's story for similar reasons or unknowingly retold the story with some inaccuracy. Two versions in the endnotes have thus been recorded.

I must point out that the descriptions of preparations, training, defence tactics, attacks, withdrawals, defeats and victories form an incomplete and unbalanced microcosm of a limited part of World War II. This is not a war book and I do not pretend to cover in detail the progress of the war. Nor is it a history book. Though I carried out thorough research, it is possible that the text contains errors of perspective or fact. These are my fault entirely.

Because of my biographical emphasis, I have not covered the extraordinary contributions of many fine fighters from other Australian military units or indeed from other countries. My story spotlights the actions of one man within his own unit—the 2/13th Infantry Battalion (one of the three battalions in the 20th Brigade). Often the unit focus is even tighter. It zooms in on his B Company, 11 Platoon and sometimes to an even smaller group of men, eight to ten of them in 6 Section. When John Murray becomes Intelligence Officer for his battalion and later for his brigade, the focus is on that role.

John demonstrated unswerving loyalty to his battalion. He often referred to their extraordinary morale. When he was allocated his military ID before he left Australia, it was neither his division (of more than 10,000 soldiers spread over three brigades) nor his brigade (of more than 3000 soldiers spread over three battalions) that captured John's imagination. It was his battalion—the 2/13th—that elicited his steadfast allegiance.

It has been claimed that the Roman way of separating a military division into smaller and smaller units contributes to untold victories. Every soldier feels part of a team. Though part of a larger division, most veterans will nominate their battalion if asked where they fitted in.

John belonged to all of the following—each unit smaller than the one above:

9th Division
20th Brigade
2/13th Battalion
B Company
11 Platoon
6 Section

The writing of this book has opened my eyes to war. I am a pacifist. Nevertheless, I acknowledge that war is inevitable. When I started to write I had no idea that I would become engrossed in the minutiae of war; that I would search out books about a particular unit, individual battles and that I would develop such great regard for the 2/13th Battalion. Those who served in World War II have my ceaseless admiration for the brave service they performed.

John's wife Ruth died during the writing of this book. The loving force she was in John and his family's lives had already become abundantly clear to me. Ruthie was John's love and his muse: without her he quite simply would not have been able to realise many of the achievements described in this story.

I would like to pay special tribute here to John Murray. He generously gave me so much of his time that throat lozenges were his constant companion. He opened his soul to me.

We shared laughter and tears, which I will always remember and for which I will always be grateful.

Chapter One

Childhood cut short

PERHAPS I SHOULD NOT WRITE THE SORT OF STUFF I WRITE
TO YOU ... BUT DARLING, YOU ARE MY MOTHER, AND WHEN I
WRITE I FEEL THAT I AM TALKING TO YOU, NOT WRITING.

—John Murray, December 1942

JOHN MURRAY NEVER forgot his fifteenth birthday, which fell six days after Christmas Day, on 31 December 1930. He became a man that year.

Only a month before, he was boarding at the King's School in Parramatta, in western Sydney, in a stately colonnaded home that had been Australia's first Government House. At the age of fourteen he was still wearing the regulation uniform for juniors—short black pants with a red stripe down the side, a white shirt and a black tie. 'A dear little boy John was,' his older brother, Peter, said of him—affectionately, proudly.[1]

At the end of that school year, John's chest swelled with pride on the day he was presented with the Junior House Cup, awarded annually to the boy who was considered 'an outstanding Gentleman, Scholar and Sportsman'.[2]

'There is no money for you to continue,' his mother Constance Murray said matter-of-factly, shortly after the ceremony. 'You will join Peter at *Manfred* ... become a jackeroo. As you know, a man called Ben Chaffey owns the property.' There was no room for argument.

John (centre), captain of the King's School Junior cricket team, 1926.

John knew from his brother Peter that *Manfred* was a half-million hectare (one-and-a-quarter-million acre) sheep property situated approximately 65 kilometres (40 miles) south-west of Ivanhoe, in western New South Wales. He had heard about its monster paddocks, its immense flocks of sheep and its vast numbers of out-stations. More than forty men worked on the place.

Within weeks, short pants were exchanged for tough long dungarees, polished black leather shoes were replaced by brown riding boots, and the King's School army hat decorated with a red puggaree became an Akubra. The classroom, where well-aimed paper planes had flown at low altitude, became the hot, red earth.

At first John was unaware that the owner of *Manfred* had more than a passing interest in him; for weeks he did not even set eyes on Ben Chaffey. Over the years though, he and his brother gradually pieced together details about their 'employer'. Still, the picture remained blurry. It was not until many years after Ben's death that John learned the full truth about this most unusual relationship.

When Chaffey died on 3 March 1937, John had already been working at *Manfred* for just over six years. The newspaper clippings announcing the date, time and place of the funeral were always kept in his mother's possession. 'So young,' she had said to John when he referred to Ben's death. She knew his age—and furthermore had read that 'floral tributes from all over the Commonwealth filled three cars in the funeral procession'.[3]

Then in July of that year, Constance sat down on the cold sand of a Sydney beach with her first-born son Peter. At last, when he was twenty-three, the jigsaw would come together for Peter; the random pieces gathered in his youth were about to fit into place.

He listened quietly as she spoke 'between sobs and tears', her face creased and drawn as she struggled with her disclosures. 'Never mind,' Peter attempted to console her. 'No,' she replied, resolute, 'I want to tell you all of this. When it's all over, we'll never talk about it again. I feel the time has come that I should tell you everything. Tell the others—when you feel it's right.'

The first confession to Peter was that her name was not Constance: it was Laura. Her son did not immediately ask the reason. This would be revealed as the story unfolded.[4]

Laura's parents, William Treweek and Rebecca Dean had met after William arrived from South Australia to work as a contractor on the Darling River in the west of New South Wales. They probably first made contact while working at *Moorara*, an immense property that spread along the banks of the Darling north of Pooncarie, with its homestead located on the river. William and Rebecca married in 1888, at *Peaka Station*, 'in the bride's home', also a dwelling on the river.[5]

William's work, mostly digging wells, meant that they were regularly on the move. Accompanying him around the river properties, Rebecca stuck by her husband as he sought work to support their growing family.

Continuing her story to Peter, Laura stopped every few minutes to brace herself against the unexpected physical effects of her revelations. Choked with sobbing, she divulged more, told her eldest son of her fate.

She was born on 4 October in a tent at *Moorara*, on the banks of the river during the great flood of 1890—within a year of older brother Samuel. Three more Treweek siblings were registered; another boy and two girls. Within twelve days of the birth of the youngest baby girl, still unnamed, Laura's mother was dead. Complications from the pregnancy had left Rebecca Treweek with a fatal fever.[6]

In August 1897 William Treweek became a widower. Laura was motherless at the age of six.

Understandably, William Treweek was keen to see his children settle in proper homes rather than live in makeshift camps, as he had done. He encouraged them as teenagers to seek employment in the homesteads of some of the larger properties around the Murray–Darling Basin. Since much of his contract work had been centred on *Moorara*, a station that had been added to well-known pastoralist Ben Chaffey's extensive holdings in 1904, this was most likely the first property to employ William Treweek's oldest daughter, when she was about thirteen.

Laura's father would have been happy with this development. After all, the 'innovative' Chaffey had 'increased the men's wages and rations' on his purchase of the station; he was 'ahead of his time'.[7] Over the years, Laura worked not only at *Moorara* as a domestic and companion, but also in two other homesteads that belonged to Chaffey: *Cuthero* and *Moorna*.

When Ben Chaffey purchased *Cuthero*, around the middle of the year 1909, he retained the station's manager, Mr Donohue. The manager's wife, an educated, motherly figure, treated Laura very much as a daughter, rounding off her education with lessons in music, literature and all manner of things to do with the home. Peter recalled: '[Mother was] wonderful at preserving, making jams, sewing and making clothes … She was Mrs Donohue's favourite.'[8]

On his inspections of the property, Ben Chaffey was entranced by the beauty and talents of young Laura, conspicuous for her fine features, upright carriage, porcelain skin and sharp intelligence. She was about eighteen or nineteen at the time. An instant meeting of minds and a strong attraction ensured more regular visits to *Cuthero*.

There was, however, a severe obstacle to the development of any lasting relationship. In 1898, aged twenty-one, Ben had married Cowra Crozier, who came from one of the respected pioneer families in the district.[9] Their only child, Mavis, was born two years after the wedding, but the marriage had not produced the longed-for sons.

Laura had also borne a daughter, at the age of nineteen. Little is known of this pregnancy apart from the father's surname—Byron. Peter was reluctant to probe: 'I didn't have the heart to ask more when she was telling me this. She was sobbing and crying and getting it off her chest. We sat there quietly on the beach … I just sat there and listened to what she told me.'[10]

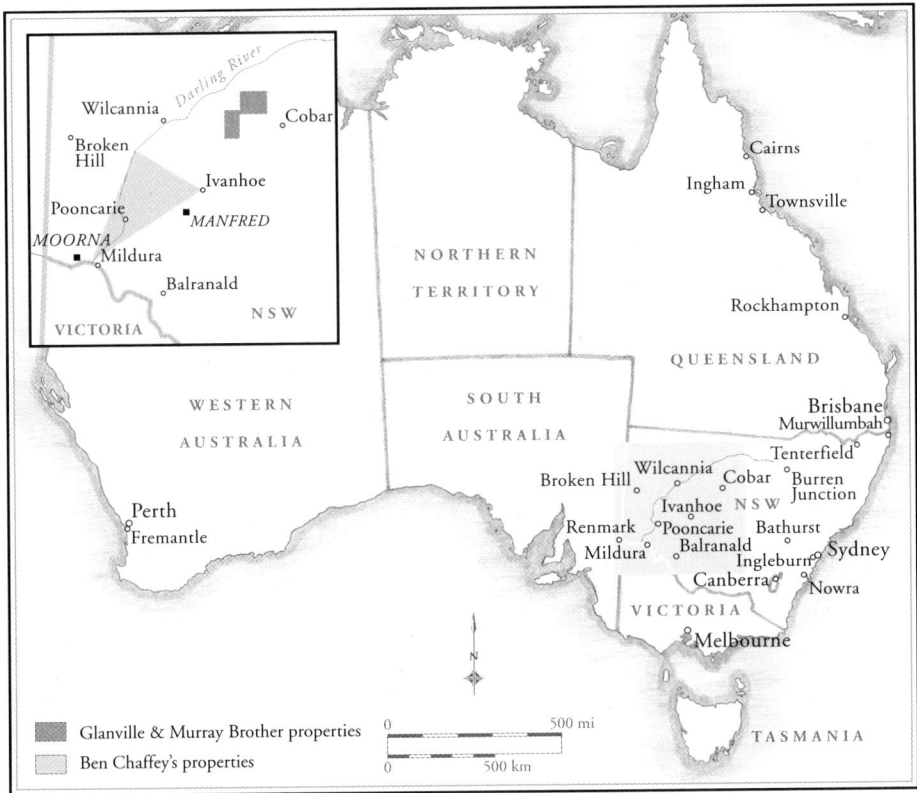

John Murray's pre-war and post-war world in Australia.

Laura endured a secret confinement at St Joseph's Refuge in Adelaide, South Australia, in January 1910. Baby Laurinna—the name later changed to Lorraine—was immediately adopted out to a childless couple, the Sellars. Peter had no idea if Ben Chaffey knew of the pregnancy, birth or adoption.

Following Lorraine's birth Laura returned to New South Wales—first to *Cuthero* and later to Ben Chaffey's new property, *Moorna*. He purchased this station in 1911, 'an extensive property with Anabranch and Murray frontage ... perched in a bend of the Murray, downstream of Wentworth, with the river winding around three sides of it ... It was a beautiful homestead ... a magical place, with its white walls seeming to float on the green grassy slopes that run to the Murray.'[11]

Rebuilt on a large scale by the new owner and 'lit by electric light and every modern convenience', the property provided work for over thirty men.[12]

John's father, Ben Chaffey, about 1917 – about the time he bought *Woodlands*.

Chaffey, a 'generous and loyal employer' also engaged numbers of women there for domestic duties—including twenty-one-year-old Laura.[13]

At *Moorna* Ben and Laura's feelings for each other intensified. To overcome the seemingly insurmountable problems that faced their desired union, Ben suggested a solution. He asked Laura to allow him to establish her with a home in Melbourne if she would return his love and give him children. Laura accepted the unorthodox proposal and made immediate plans to leave.

Chaffey purchased a home for Laura in 1914, in the Melbourne suburb of Malvern under an assumed name—registered as 'Mrs Constance Murray (owner)'. Some time later, probably before John's birth, Laura moved to a lovely old Victorian home with tall, leadlight windows and high ceilings in the adjacent suburb of Armadale. Located at 6 Huntingtower Road, *Hillington* was a much grander home.[14]

Shortly before the birth of her first son, Laura made a trip to Adelaide in 1913 to reclaim her daughter, Lorraine, now almost four years old.[15]

No registration of Peter's birth or details of his birthplace have been found, but it is known that Ben and Laura had three children together: Peter, born in November 1913; John on the last day of December 1915; and a daughter, Margaret (Margie), in May 1917.

In the same year as their daughter Margie's birth, Ben added yet another property to his holdings. *Woodlands* was situated in a rural area, at the northern end of Melbourne's present Tullamarine Airport. Being closer to Melbourne than any of his other properties, the dwelling was within easy travelling distance of his second family.

As usual, Ben set about designing alterations and new structures; all of his properties shared the same features. Over a decade after Ben purchased it, John would visit *Woodlands* and admire the highlights his father had added: 'Motor garages, tennis courts, use of identical piped watering systems to feed his homestead gardens and orchards, similar plantings of roses in garden beds, the same variety of trees, the use of one particular colour of paint (duck egg blue) on verandah ceilings, the inclusion of skylights in homestead verandahs, circular driveways and even the use of identical T Model Fords.'[16]

Ben was particularly fond of his rose gardens; on every property his instructions urged the various managers to take great care of them. One of his exhaustive lists of managerial duties ended with the directive: 'Don't forget to water the roses.'[17]

Much closer to major racetracks, *Woodlands* became a place of entertainment for Ben Chaffey's many friends and a suitable venue for celebrations as he continued to enjoy racing successes—in the Caulfield Cup, and the AJC and Victoria Derbies.[18]

While the new property allowed Ben to concentrate on one of his obsessions—racehorses—it also enabled him to extend his visits at *Hillington* in Melbourne, where he could see Laura and observe the development of his young children.

He watched his sons with a father's eye. Already they showed signs of physical and intellectual aptitude. Though just a toddler, John's ability to manoeuvre and manipulate his surroundings resulted in Ben's growing paternal pride.

However, with every month that passed tensions were growing in this second home, creating pressures that would eventually crack the harmonious family arrangement.

Chapter Two

Laura's dominion

THERE WAS NEVER A MOMENT THAT MOTHER WASN'T
THINKING HOW TO ENCOURAGE US TO DO MORE ... JUST A
LITTLE BIT OF PRESSURE ALL THE TIME. IT WAS NEVER
OVERWHELMING. HER ENCOURAGEMENT WAS NEVER-ENDING.

– John Murray

THE ROMANTIC LIAISON between Ben Chaffey and Laura Treweek was
kept entirely secret. As the son of a pioneering family, Ben could not
afford a scandal. After all, his father, engineer George Chaffey and uncle,
horticulturist William Benjamin Chaffey, were well-known figures in the
Mildura district—even 'famous'.

In the 1880s the Chaffey duo had been invited to develop an irrigation
settlement in Australia on the Murray River by Alfred Deakin, minister in the
Victorian Government and, later, Prime Minister of Australia. The politician
envisaged a 'Chaffey colony' situated near the junction of the Murray and
Darling Rivers. It would be similar to those the brothers had already set up in
both California and Canada, with wide sculptured thoroughfares, fountains,
avenue frontages, an agricultural college and shopping centres. And of
course—the basis for the settlement—irrigated orchards.[1]

After a difficult beginning—shelved government plans for the promised
railway to the capital city, a falling river level, leaking irrigation channels
and angry accusations from investors—the superb fruits eventually reaped
success for their owners in both Renmark and Mildura.

In time the Chaffey brothers were feted as founding fathers of the district. Alfred Deakin spoke of them as 'lion-hearted men of great knowledge, judgement and experience'.[2] However they would be horrified to learn that with the over-expansion of their original ideas, growing salination problems now besiege the once mighty Murray–Darling Basin.

Ben Chaffey was his father's son. Even before completing school at the renowned Geelong Grammar, he had developed a strong interest in the land, closely observing the clever use of water, as had his father and uncle before him. His passion for racing horses and expansive pastoral holdings resulted in a full life, conducted at breakneck speed.

Years before, aged thirty, he had written to a friend: 'I have been overhauled by several doctors and they say that my brain is simply tired out for the present and will not work anymore until it has had a thorough rest.'[3]

Sometimes Laura was involved in Chaffey's whirl; sometimes not. Socially isolated, she remained on the periphery of his life. With her attention focused on household matters and the rearing of her children, she became more and more concerned about her unconventional situation. She wrapped herself and her family in gossamer, fabricating an elaborate scenario to protect their reputation.

With the move to Melbourne, the name Laura Treweek disappeared into distant crevices. In its place she had adopted the name Mrs Constance Murray, metamorphosing into the wife of an imaginary solicitor, Mr Chester Byron Murray, who enlisted late in World War I. Having reportedly produced his last child before departing for France, this soldier, her 'husband', supposedly died of Spanish flu in the pandemic of 1918, which killed some 50–100 million people worldwide in just eighteen months. But his identity was never extinguished. By then, all the children had taken on the family name of Murray, which they kept for the duration of their lives.

Despite this façade, complications multiplied for Laura. Lorraine was confused by the domestic arrangements, being shuffled backwards and forwards between convent and home when Ben visited; Peter was approaching school age; and John and Margaret would perhaps also be facing awkward questions about their paternity. Perhaps even Ben was beginning to feel the pressure of his second family so close, with the conflicting demands it entailed.[4]

With the future of her children uppermost in her mind, Laura made the momentous decision to leave Melbourne forever. She planned her flight meticulously. In the winter of 1918, while Ben Chaffey was in America on

John's mother, Laura Treweek, around 1912—about the time she moved from *Moorna*.
After the move she became known as Mrs Constance Murray.

a business trip, the twenty-seven-year-old woman stepped onto a train in the dead of night with her four children and a nurse. Being eight years old, Lorraine was able to help with the little ones: Peter almost five, John two-and-a-half years old and Margie a babe at breast. For Peter, the trip was unforgettable: 'I remember it well … arriving at Albury Station on the old steam train with Aunty Joan [companion and nurse], getting out and walking miles in our little short trousers … and then walking onto the New South Wales train and getting into an old-fashioned sleeper … it was freezing, at midnight.'[5]

Despite her conflicting interests, Laura was a practical and intelligent woman, and thus quite efficiently managed the long trip to Sydney. However, little is known of the emotional toll this episode exacted on her young life.

A photograph of Ben Chaffey remained on her dressing table in whichever house they lived. 'Who's that, Mummy?' asked John one day, child-like, innocent. 'It is a man I knew very well,' was his mother's enigmatic reply.

John was able to recite from memory the poignant verse in his mother's small journal, which he had come across in his teenage years. He would never forget the words in his mother's handwriting; they had a startling and distressing effect on him:

> The thorns which I have reap'd are of the tree I planted:
> They have torn me, and I bleed:
> I should have known what fruit would spring from such a seed.[6]

On arrival in Sydney, Constance soon settled in the northern suburbs, first in *Hillview*, a roomy flat at Turramurra, then in various locations around the suburb, including a ground floor flat, *Koorara*, opposite the St James Anglican Church. 'Mother never wanted to settle too close to anyone; the neighbours would become suspicious. We moved and moved and moved,' said John.

Laura's fabricated name and circumstances continued. Away from the immediate pressures of her nonconformist existence, Mrs Constance Murray began an extended period that was difficult and lonely, but immensely rewarding. The church was a point of contact. Through Reverend Cameron, Constance met members of the Emery and Glanville families, who were related by marriage, some of whom operated successful dairy farms on the Shoalhaven River, 160 kilometres (100 miles) south.

Over the years the Murray children spent many a school holiday at *Wogamia,* the farm belonging to Basil and Marla Emery. None of the Emerys was aware of Constance Murray's mysterious background.

Laura was a stern disciplinarian. 'She only had to say "John" to me at the table, or to any of the family, and we would freeze.' When Peter announced he was leaving home at the age of ten, packed suitcase in hand, she ignored the wailing of his siblings. 'Don't worry. He'll be home when it gets dark and he's hungry.' She gave away John's scooter to a less fortunate boy because he ignored her instructions. She insisted on apologies when they were due; expected and received respect. However, her strict persona hid a devoted parent intent on providing a rich upbringing. 'My mother was the most wonderful mother ever,' claimed Peter. John described Laura as an affectionate and loving mother whose commitment to the welfare of her children was constant and absolute. 'Darlings,' she said. 'Never worry, there will never be anyone else in my life until you grow up.'

And how did Laura cope with maintenance for her young family? At the age of ten, John felt tense when his mother dressed up in her finest clothes once a month to visit 'the trustees', the mysterious fount of all money for the family. When she returned, she appeared 'different—not herself'. The children believed at the time that their 'father', Chester Byron Murray, had left money for their support, but much later John thought it was possible on those occasions that his mother was visiting Ben Chaffey, that she was still in love with him and he with her.[7]

Despite Laura's move, Chaffey did not renounce the family. He continued to provide her with a considerable allowance. 'As far as I remember,' Peter said, 'it was two hundred pounds a month,' the equivalent to around $13,000 per month in 2009. 'That went on for years and years and years … until the Depression came.'[8]

This financial support eventually enabled Laura to move to *Colchester* in Warrawee, next to the public school on the Pacific Highway, within walking distance of the railway station. It was the several acres of adjoining paddocks there that most attracted John. At dusk, when he was roaming in the bushland, the nurse wearing 'a uniform with big linen straps and a cap' would call him in for dinner. Reluctantly he would return from 'the wild'.

The children were privileged: they played tennis and attended elocution classes; a beach or mountain resort was their destination during the school holidays. Laura taught them impeccable manners, disciplined

The Murray family on their horses at *Colchester*, about 1927. From left to right: Laura, Lorraine, Peter, John, Margie.

them, encouraged them in their education, insisted on clear enunciation, read to them and steered them towards horses and country life.

John's expert horsemanship began with the dappled pony of his childhood. His mother's early indoctrination worked; John and his little sister became 'obsessed with the idea of horses'. When they moved to *Colchester* where there was a shed to store riding paraphernalia, John's mother deemed it time for important purchases—a chestnut for Peter named Copper, Merrylegs for Margie and a mottled grey pony for John: 'I called him Dapple. This was absolute heaven … I've never forgotten him—my first real possession.'

Dolly, the next addition, was very soon put to work pulling the newly acquired phaeton, the family's only means of transport. The children learned to manage the horse and buggy through trial and error. One day, members of a road repair gang agreed to their request for help and had 'a good old laugh' when they saw the reason for the horse's stubborn refusal to budge; Dolly's collar was on upside down. At other times, much to Constance's embarrassment, the bay mare headed directly for the pub; her previous owner, a real estate agent, had spent most of his time there. 'Mother was mortified.'

Horse-riding and training became a priority. Molly Lance, 'a splendid horsewoman and family friend from the country', had an insider's knowledge of the equine world that allowed her to arrange trained ponies for the two younger children to ride at shows and gymkhanas. Brother and sister won plenty of awards and ribbons.

John and Margie rode to a little private school at Pymble each day— about an hour each way—rain, hail or shine. 'Yes, Mother was determined we learn to ride.'[9]

Laura was also intent on her children learning to read. She would gather them around her at night, they in their pyjamas at her feet and she in her rocking chair, 'conveying the sensitivity of what was happening' in each story she read aloud. *Oliver Twist* was their favourite and, at times, so moving that their sobbing could be heard throughout the house. 'She would always make amends,' however, ensuring they were smiling and laughing before they went to sleep.

Her children inherited a library of books: *A Short History of England*; a complete set of Dickens; works of Cowper, Wordsworth, Keats, Tennyson. And countless others.

Ben Chaffey's generous allowance enabled the children to continue their education in private schools. Soon Miss Christie's Turramurra kindergarten and the small primary school at Pymble were to be superseded by more formal schooling. In 1926, ten-year-old John joined his brother Peter at the Junior House of the King's School.

Years later John realised that his father had arranged an inspection of his youngest son, and probably of Peter, during their junior secondary school years. When John travelled from King's into the city one day to meet his mother, her greeting took him by surprise. 'Hello darling,' she said, 'raise your hat to your mother.' It was only later he discovered that his father was standing amongst a few other people in the background, close enough to scrutinise him.

Ben had attempted to meet his daughter Margie in a different way—at *Colchester* in Warrawee. On seeing his daughter rush in for a glass of milk, he asked Laura if he could talk to Margie. Always protective, Laura remained firm. With quiet determination she refused him permission.

When John arrived at King's aged ten, Peter was already making his mark as a sportsman—an excellent boxer and athlete. In 1929 Peter represented King's in the 100-, the 220-, and the 440-yard individual sprints and the 440-yard relay at the GPS[10] athletics carnival, a competition between a group of Sydney private schools. His records held for seventeen years. Boys from another school were heard to comment after one handsome win: 'Look! There's that King's boy—Peter Murray—that's him. Impossible he's under sixteen.' He was already the size of a man.

Though not as big and tall, John quickly followed in his brother's sporting footsteps. A leading athlete, he was soon made captain of the junior cricket and football teams. In his third year he was appointed House Monitor in charge of a dormitory and by his fourth year he was Captain of the Junior House.

The invitation to captain Thomas House for thirteen- and fourteen-year-olds came as a surprise to him, as it was extended on the heels of a memorable prank. Being the ringleader of an out-of-control pillow fight, John had received 'six beauties on the backside in front of everyone'. When summoned into the housemaster's office the next day, he was stunned: 'Murray, I've made a re-arrangement through the House,' Mr Blaxland announced. 'As from this moment you are Captain of the House. I'm sure you can do it.'

Later, reflecting, John believed that in addition to his mother's stern but loving influence, school activities further instilled in him the discipline necessary for future military life: morning and evening prayers; long practice routines for his soprano singing voice; strict study routines; team activities and the captaincy of junior sporting teams and boarding houses.

But those enjoyable formative years were not to last. Less than three years after his commencement at King's, a shock wave spread inexorably from America to the rest of the world.

Few were unaffected by the crash of the Wall Street stock market and its aftermath, the Great Depression. Within two months of the first sign of trouble on Black Thursday, 24 October 1929, the share prices on New York's stock exchange fell by approximately 40 per cent; within three years Australian exports such as wool and wheat had halved. Exceeding 30 per cent, Australia's unemployment rate was one of the highest in the world. Some hopeful workers headed for the country where hundreds joined long queues to apply for one job. All manner of breadwinner would camp in local showgrounds in their relentless seach for employment.[11]

Ben Chaffey's circumstances plummeted. He was obliged to sell off many of his large rural holdings. A significant number of King's School families suffered a similar fate, finding there was no longer money for private school fees.

In John's case, despite the headmaster's urging and the offer of a scholarship, his mother withdrew him at the end of 1930. With the benefit of hindsight, John was convinced that her action was a matter of 'fierce pride'. He concluded that the thought of being beholden to more than one benefactor was too much for his mother to bear. Whatever the reason, John had not yet turned fifteen 'when the axe finally fell'.

Chapter Three

Early training

YOU WERE ON YOUR OWN; YOU HAD TO MAKE IMMEDIATE
DECISIONS. YOU HAD TO GET CRACKING EARLY ... EARLIER
THAN 5.30 AM ... I LEARNED FASTER DOING ALL THIS ...YOU HAD
TO THINK FOR YOURSELF ...THAT WAS AN EDUCATION FOR ME.

—John Murray[1]

CONSTANCE WAS NOW without an allowance. While she encouraged Lorraine
to continue work as a newspaper cadet and the study of French at the
Berlitz language school at night, Constance found herself penniless, with
little chance of gaining employment. The church and the kindness of
friends saved her from the humiliation of the Depression. Her meeting
with the Emery family through Reverend Cameron at Turramurra led to a
kind offer. Being invited, together with twelve-year-old Margie, to live in
the old *Wogamia* slab house on the banks of the Shoalhaven River, was
'the family salvation'. Margie was offered the additional advantage of
attending the private tutoring classroom of the Emery boys, who later
noted with admiration her photographic memory.

Peter helped with the move: 'We had to sell our car, our horses—everything.
We kept one good horse—Laddie. I rode him to Nowra. I went from
Turramurra through Parramatta and Liverpool to Campbelltown and out to
Appin in one day—48 miles. The next day I rode 82 miles from Appin and
arrived at the other side of Nowra, at *Wogamia* farm. After a couple of days
there I went back [to Sydney] and from there John and I went to *Manfred*.'[2]

Undoubtedly there had been conversations between Ben and Laura about the course of their younger son's future, when the money dried up in 1930. The decision taken seemed natural given the circumstances. By then Ben Chaffey had decided to throw all his energies into just one property.

Manfred, in fact, comprised two stations, *Manfred* and *Kilfera*. The principal homestead, *Manfred,* sat at the south-western end of the property; and the *Kilfera* homestead, 113 kilometres (70 miles) away, was located at the eastern end, 24 kilometres (15 miles) from the township of Ivanhoe. Out-stations, including *Beilpajah*, *Darnick*, '*A' Well* and *Prince's Lake,* were sprinkled over the immense area to help with the property's administration.

Running along about 48 kilometres (30 miles) of the eastern boundary of *Manfred* was the Sydney–Broken Hill railway line, which would soon deliver fourteen-year-old John almost to the gate of this huge landholding.

Manfred would play a hugely significant role, physical and emotional, in the next six and a half years of John's life. It would provide harsh, sometimes draconian, training for his future. However, at this stage, he was not thinking much of the decades ahead.

Throughout much of the long, rattly train trip John asked Peter plenty of questions about the property, but eventually he succumbed to exhaustion. On reaching the railway siding for the little town of Ivanhoe in the middle of the dark night, the two boys trudged to the village, rolled out their swags and slept until the dawn birdcalls awakened them. After a satisfying hotel breakfast, they set off in a Chaffey vehicle for *Kilfera*, where Peter was working. John felt the nervous anticipation rise a day or two later as the same vehicle delivered him towards *Manfred*—alone.

The long trip between the two homesteads allowed the newcomer to appreciate the immensity of the property, which would employ his waking hours for the next six and a half years. 'It was a vast empire … about 1.26 million acres …140,000 sheep … sixty men permanently on the books.'

Billy Woods was the first employee John met—the *Manfred* bookkeeper/ accountant who was to be his boss. Woods then introduced him to his young assistant bookkeeper, John Oldham, soon to become a medical student at Sydney University.

John Murray had no idea as he shook John Oldham's hand, that they would be so closely connected in the future. Only a couple of years later the jackeroo would receive medical treatment in Melbourne from Oldham's father—a physician—and some ten years on, his sister, Margie, would marry the young doctor. John Oldham had already seen a photo of

Margaret Murray—a schoolgirl in plaits—on top of Peter's cupboard and had quipped, 'I'll marry that girl!'

There was no meeting with Ben Chaffey.

As the years went by, for each of the Murray brothers there was a gradual recognition of the familial relationship with Ben Chaffey.

Peter had put together his unusual heritage in a piecemeal way, beginning with a memorable incident at *Colchester*. His mother was listening to the old crystal wireless set—'one where you could put a cat's whisker on a crystal and listen with earphones'. When he complained that he couldn't hear properly, his mother chastised him. 'Now sit still and listen,' she scolded, unusually flustered. Laura had a good reason to insist on silence. Ben Chaffey's horse, also called Manfred, was streaking ahead to win the Caulfield Cup.[3] It was 1926; Peter was twelve years old.

Once Peter arrived at *Manfred* in 1929, to become a jackeroo, his boss Ben Chaffey felt strangely familiar. Ben's daughter, Mavis Chaffey, contributed more to the mysterious unravelling. One day, some time towards the end of that year, Peter heard a familiar laugh—loud and hearty. He stopped in his tracks, expecting to see his sister Margie come around the corner of the homestead. But it was Mavis Chaffey, singing out to somebody inside. 'She sounded *exactly* like Margie—her voice was the dead same as Marg's—no difference at all.'[4] Margie and Mavis had never met.

Yet another incident added a piece to the confusing jigsaw. When Charlie Sullivan, an old stockman, was reminiscing about the earlier days working for Ben Chaffey at *Moorna*, he mentioned a beautiful young girl helping the manager's wife—a girl they all loved. They were puzzled by her sudden disappearance. Peter's heart missed a beat. Without question that girl was his mother. Old Charlie Sullivan remained none the wiser. Peter commented: 'It [the knowledge about his father] happened so gradually … I was working things out and it suddenly became a fait accompli … what I suspected. It wasn't a surprise when my mother started to tell me, because I knew …'[5]

Younger brother John was fascinated but confused about the relationship. Peter had discussed his suspicions about their paternity in general terms, but subsequently had revealed nothing substantial, having determined that details of his mother's disclosures on the beach were better left unspoken. 'I didn't tell John much until the other day [1989].'[6]

Though John suspected Chaffey was his father, the picture had always been hazy. Always wanting to know more, he had been overly interested in any gossip around *Manfred*. Ben Chaffey was a man to be reckoned with, they said. A bit reserved; a bit of a loner. A good boss. Later John was to assess him as, 'a born manager, with a wonderful presence' who would 'liven everyone up when he was around'. He was big, broad-shouldered, good-looking and intimidating.

John would never forget their first meeting on the property. One day, after he had caught sight of Ben Chaffey and Billy Woods sitting outside having a late afternoon drink, the bookkeeper walked over and told him that 'the Chief' had requested a meeting. When Woods warned the boy that he had about five minutes to get dressed, the fifteen-year-old felt his stomach lurch.

John had been given no time to prepare. He began to sweat. Rushing around his tiny room, he threw clothes into a couple of large, old kerosene tins that served as a cupboard, and kicked dirty boots under the shearer's stretcher. Then he waited, 'feeling like a shattered wreck'. As he was taking yet another deep breath, he heard heavy footsteps. Suddenly the little doorway was filled with a massive man—about 190 centimetres (6 feet, 3 inches) tall.

'Are you John?'

The Chief had a strong, tanned face, a big body and an air of authority. The boy leapt to his feet.

'Yes, Sir,' he replied, his throat tight. He could not think of what else to say.

'Are you settling in?'

'Yes, Sir,' he repeated.

'I want you to work hard. I know you can do it.'

Giving a brief smile, Ben Chaffey turned to leave. John lowered himself onto the stretcher and tried to control the shaking.

The hard work John was assigned at *Manfred* tutored him for survival. An essential quality for the boy on this huge property was resourcefulness, though the first letter Constance received from Mr Woods gave no hint of this:

Dear Mrs Murray,
I just want to send you a line to say that your young son John is here with me, and seems very happy and contented. He came down from Kilfera on Tuesday. Yesterday I let him go out with Mr Mariner—where they were doing some sheep work, Peter

being there also. John seemed thrilled with his day out, Mr Mariner said he hopped into all that was going on. I think I will arrange for him to go out on the lamb marking camp next week—he wants to go, so he will get a taste of camping-out life and with Peter with him I am sure he will be quite all right. You may rest assured Mrs Murray that I will look after him and do all in my power to make him happy and contented. Today he is doing his bit on the lawns, etc. He sends his love to you and will write on Sunday.
Yours very sincerely,
W.A. Woods
8 January 1931

John's first major job was looking after the property's store—'a massive supply room the size of a workshop with shelves of provisions'—keeping it tidy and filling up orders from the various out-stations, whose managing couples or overseers rang in to Billy Woods when they needed to re-order supplies. To avoid costly mistakes it was essential for John to develop administrative skills rapidly.

The rations—some 10 to 12 tonnes—came by rail from Melbourne to *Manfred Pastoral Company* twice a year. John ensured he was always on the spot for their arrival. At the *Manfred* railway siding he watched the teamster with his eleven pairs of horses collect and load the goods into massive wagons. Once back at the store, one of his many regular tasks was to sort through and record the boxes of jam, four dozen tins to a case. He would find the occasional tin of strawberry, marmalade or gooseberry, but mostly it was plum. 'There was light plum, dark plum, medium plum—plum, plum, plum.'

His own supply was always plum jam and treacle—'occasionally golden syrup, but mostly treacle'. The welcome bounty also included 'a wonderful thing called powdered milk'. However, treacle and milk did not compensate for hardship.

Loneliness was a hurdle. Peter was rarely able to visit his brother; *Kilfera* was too far away and his job too demanding. John Oldham had soon left for university; there was no one his own age—and no family.

Once his duties were done, John sneaked away from Billy Woods' store to the men's quarters in search of company. Depression-affected professionals—out of work engineers, barristers, accountants—mixed with the regular farm-hands, and John relished all their stories, sometimes prurient and off-colour.[7] He found the atmosphere 'pretty powerful'— ribald yarns, guffawing, foul words—but that was of no concern. 'Peter had warned me and guided me extremely well.'

One night, Scotty Bloomfield, a wrinkled old Scotsman with a broad brogue, turned to him squatting in the corner, and said, 'Jack … what religion are you, boy?' They almost always called him Jack. He hesitated, caught unawares and not sure how to answer. Scotty stared at him with piercing eyes, pointed and said, 'Jack, speak the truth and shame the devil.' Those words stuck with John for the rest of his life.

Some of the men took advantage of his youth and inexperience. When Ben Chaffey built a new shearing shed on the property, John was put under the care of a bullying wool classer named Jack Salter, 'a brute of a man'. Fortunately another man, Dick Taylor, only in his twenties, kept a watchful eye on the boy. It was a useful lesson for John—'seeing a man having the courage to protect'.

John always made sure he melded into the background to escape the watchful eye of Mr Woods, who forbade him to go anywhere near the 'bad company'. His boss would stand on the store verandah and whistle him up like a dog. 'Where's that boy? Where's that bloody boy?' As time passed, the young worker learned how to concoct foolproof excuses to explain his absences, developing avoidance techniques of the finest kind.

'Setting rabbit traps' was John's alibi if questioned on his whereabouts.

John was a fast learner. As well as being responsible for store provisions, he was soon assigned another job. Given a saddle for the night horse, he was told to muster twenty to thirty horses each day from the 405-hectare (1000-acre) horse paddock. The job meant getting up before dawn to bring them back to the home yard for the stockmen. By 9 am it could be close to 50 degrees Celsius (122 degrees Fahrenheit) in the shade—far too late and hot for the men to start their day's work.

Riding out to collect the horses, John learned to make use of the leader of the mob, yelling out orders and cracking a whip if necessary. He had to be on the lookout for rabbit warrens that could be 'the size of a room', although it was almost impossible to see the ground as he galloped in the dark. Sometimes his horses would falter and at least one stumbled and broke a leg. There were times when he had rotten horses—'a stinker of a night horse who would want to buck'—occasioning many a bad fall.

While riding out in the vast paddock, John learned to read the night sky for survival, especially using the Southern Cross. Occasionally one of the horses would have a bell around its neck. Because it was dark, the only indication of the horse's whereabouts was the sound of the bell. Instinctively John lined it up on a star for extra guidance, steering towards it all the while. This experience would help him later. 'In the desert the stars meant everything.' The North Star, 'fixed in the firmament', was their salvation.

John claimed that the moon was also invaluable in the desert. At *Manfred*, it allowed travel at night; he developed night sight. Apart from this advantage, time and time again he noticed how the moon 'gave comfort to some of the old fellows', who used it for forecasting the weather. Their meteorological forecast, looking at the angle of the moon, was too accurate to ignore. When the moon was lying on its back in the shape of a saucer it was holding moisture and was a dry moon. If tilted slightly it meant rain.

Being naturally curious, John took advantage of opportunities to learn, offering assistance whenever he could. One day there was no one to collect the mail for *Manfred*, delivered weekly at *Clare Station* about 25 or 30 kilometers (15 or 20 miles) south. John was asked to collect it in the T Model Ford. 'I've never driven one of those,' he was loath to admit, in reply to the request. His limited driving experience had been in his mother's Nash, which, from the age of ten, he had driven backwards, to park in her garage. He had not been allowed to drive it forwards.

Mr Woods assured him that the groom would show him the ropes. However, the instruction to just crank it and push the pedal was the only help he got. John set off slowly. 'That thing's running a bit rough by the sound of it,' an old codger muttered when he arrived. 'Look under the bonnet for a loose wire.' He did, and with an almighty surge a shock sent John flying back about 3 metres (10 feet). Though everyone had a great old laugh—'the bloody mule's kicked him'—he had learned to drive a T Model Ford.

However, there were many things he had not yet learned. Once, when Peter arrived with his favourite dog, in the middle of a searing summer, the brothers decided to take off in the Ford to check a well, about 10 kilometres (6 miles) from the *Manfred* homestead. Before long the engine seized up. Too late they discovered that their only water bag had developed a slow leak and was empty. John's tongue soon became so swollen he could not speak as they dragged their feet towards home in the scorching heat.

Peter carried the listless, dehydrated dog. Fortunately another worker spied them way out in the distance and saved all of their lives by administering small doses of precious water. The boys learned a lesson that day that they remembered for the rest of their lives—that heat can be deadly. There were plenty of gravestones around the area attesting to that grisly fact.

After working for a couple of years in the store as well as mustering and horse-tailing around the main homestead, it was felt that John was responsible enough to be moved to the outer reaches of the property. He spent the summer, autumn and winter of 1932 at the *Beilpajah* hut mostly on his own—moving stock, riding the boundaries and looking after vast tracts of land.

Beilpajah was a 9 metre (30 foot) long hut with a fireplace at one end— just one room. It had a wood slab floor and pine log walls with mud worked in to close the gaps. Bags attached to the logs served as makeshift wallpaper, but there were always cracks that let in the cold air. With night-time temperatures dropping below freezing point, the hessian ceiling, even though weighed down with sand and dust, offered little protection. John collected water in a bucket scooped from a dam about 90 metres (100 yards) away. Bathing was as simple as swimming in the dam when the weather allowed it or sponging when it was too cold. In drought conditions he got used to surviving on no bathing whatsoever.

Once a month the manager dropped in with rations: onions, potatoes, flour, sugar, tea, powdered milk, baking powder, currants, sultanas, plum jam and treacle. John killed his own meat, which he butchered and stored in a lean-to out the back, using a Coolgardie safe with water dripping down hessian bags to cool it. He had neither green vegetables nor fresh milk.

As usual, John painted a rosy picture for his mother:

> *Everything is going along just the same up here ... there has been good rain to fill the tanks and grow nice young green grass for when the lambs arrive. The ewes are starting to lamb now and if things turn out as expected there should be about 33,000 lambs reared this coming winter ... I have a new mate out here at* Beilpajah, *an old chap of 65 named Jock Page, and he's not a bad old stick if taken the right way. We have moved out of the shed quarters down to the old boundary rider's hut, about half a mile from the shearing shed.*

The old hut is really a cosy place … We cook in the camp
ovens and at night sit around the fire and smoke our pipes …
Also we have an excellent variety of meals. For seven days a
week (sometimes I'm sure it's eight), our menu consists of:
  Breakfast: tea, meat, damper and jam (or treacle).
  Midday: (mostly eaten somewhere in the paddock) tea and
brownie, which is a kind of cake with a couple of handfuls of
currants and sultanas thrown in.
  Dinner at night: hot meat (roast mutton) with any amount of
roast spuds and onions and plenty of black tea. After which we
wash up, tie our dogs up and then smoke.
  It's not very often we have visitors, and our nearest neighbours
are 11 miles away. But in spite of that one never gets lonely; there
is always so much to occupy the mind; the thought of the doings
for the next day—whether this or that may happen, etc—all help
to turn the mind from running into the personal groove, which
never does any good, in my opinion anyway.
1 May 1932

Old Jock Page, generously described to Constance Murray as 'not a bad old stick', turned out to be 'a miserable, spiteful old bastard'. John discussed the problem with one of the property managers and succeeded in having him removed from the hut. However, he was lonelier than ever after the old man's departure. Occasional respite came in the form of travelling swagmen, often escaping the ravages of the Depression. They provided John with longed-for company and he would always invite them to stay.

John particularly looked forward to the shearing season when suddenly the whole property was teeming with workers, giving him company 'for a couple of months'. Twenty-six shearers and about forty roustabouts dealt with over 4000 sheep per day. Over a period of six weeks approximately 120,000 sheep were shorn—roughly 20,000 per week.

The chef, Charlie Still, who every year juggled his holidays from one of Melbourne's nightclubs to coincide with the shearing, arrived at *Manfred* about two weeks before the season started. He stayed with John in the hut and from the first day they went out together shooting rabbits, which ended up in a large pot, cooked 'in some delicate way, with a spice or two'.

Charlie prepared three meals a day for the shearers, roustabouts and swagmen, in two sittings—and baked scones and lamingtons as well.

Shearing always came to an end far too soon for John.

When John was not working in the paddocks, in the shearing shed or on the boundary, there was an additional activity that had to be fitted into his day. Before he left the city, he had made a promise. While packing 'boyish things' in his bag, his mother announced her plan for his further education. She had arranged to have books sent to him by an elderly gentleman from the Sydney Book Club. A pledge was extracted from her son. She would supply the books; he would read them.

Sure enough, a bundle of eight books arrived several times each year. Initially the old gentleman sent him a sprinkling of romance, historical narrative and thrillers, accompanied by a note asking him to indicate what he had enjoyed. In the first pack he received a mix of D.H. Lawrence, Tolstoy, Georgette Heyer and 'an unforgettable book', *And Quiet Flows the Don* by Mikhail Sholokhov. After about six months there was no need for the survey. The old man sent a good range of books each time, trying 'conscientiously to send books that would benefit me'. This unusual form of education lasted for at least three years.

John took great care to protect the books when he was on camp—quart pot on one side of his saddlebag and books on the other. When the temperatures soared to 50 degrees Celsius (122 degrees Fahrenheit) in the shade and the old blokes were at smoko in the middle of the day, he would pull out a book: 'I used to take books instead of lunch in my saddlebag. I'd have a bit of damper. And during the long, long hours when you had to camp with the stock, early in the morning until evening, I'd read under a tree. While they snored their heads off, I read and read and read.'

Even in the shade, John was constantly squinting because of the glare. If he wanted to read at night he used a hurricane lamp. Though his eyesight was weakening he understood that his mother 'had her good reasons' and kept his side of the bargain.

In later years as he recalled the coloured covers of those books and the scorching temperatures, John bit his lip. Tears welled in his eyes: 'I was fourteen when I made that promise to my mother. It was a hell of a thing for me to do, to have to read those books. I did … um … fulfil my part of the bargain … I really did … I did …'

It was not until much later that he appreciated the benefits. When he earlier concluded that his lack of education had disadvantaged him—

'I don't understand English. I never did,'—he did not realise that he was learning English in one of the best possible ways: through reading. Despite the dust, heat and loneliness, John was gradually learning about ideas, writing styles, words, history and the world.

Chapter Four

Woodlands

[WOODLANDS IS] A RARE AND POSSIBLY UNIQUE EXAMPLE OF
A VERY LARGE, PORTABLE HOUSE IMPORTED TO VICTORIA IN
1842 ... THE HAND-PAINTED INTERNAL WALL DECORATION
OF THE WEST WING IS UNUSUALLY RICH, AND EXTREMELY
RARE IF NOT UNIQUE IN VICTORIA.

IN TERMS OF SETTING, THE HOMESTEAD IS IMPORTANT
FOR ITS SURVIVING COURTYARD GARDEN WITH THE EARLIEST
RECORDED EUROPEAN PLANTINGS (MAGNOLIA GRANDIFLORA)
AND FOR RETAINING ITS RURAL, WOODLAND SETTING OVER
150 YEARS.

—Department of Conservation and Natural Resources, Victoria[1]

IT WAS MID-1932. John, now sixteen, was heading back to the hut at
Beilpajah after an exhausting day. His first face-to-face meeting with Ben
Chaffey at *Manfred* over a year before had never left his mind. Dutifully
following his father's instructions, he had worked hard. While the
intervening time had forced him to mature at speed, the demanding work
and inadequate diet had left their mark. His rapidly declining health was
obvious; he had sores all over his body.

As John reached the hut, he was startled to discover the identity of the
occupant of a utility parked outside. He was even more taken aback when,
after a brief greeting, Ben Chaffey immediately examined the whites of
his eyes.

'Hello, John. You're not well.'

'No, Sir. I'm not.'

'Gather your swag and your dogs. I'm taking you back to *Manfred*, then we'll go to Melbourne. You need to see a doctor.'

Despite his attire—dirty flannel shirt and dungarees—John was quickly transferred to Chaffey's Humber Pullman and in no time was heading towards Melbourne. As they journeyed south he made many a surreptitious glance towards his father, who sat in front with the chauffeur.

On arrival at *Woodlands*, Ben arranged an immediate consultation with Dr Edward Percy Oldham, the father of John Oldham and a physician in Collins Street. Oldham chided his good friend: 'Ben, what have you been doing to this boy? He's not too good. I think you've been treating him a bit roughly.' John was sent directly to St Vincent's Hospital, where he spent two weeks recuperating.

The day after his discharge John was chauffeured to the department store Myers—where Chaffey was a director—to be fitted out with suits, work clothes and 'anything else you need'. He was met at the main door 'by quite a gathering and whisked away for royal treatment'. *Have all my Christmases come at once,* he thought to himself as they directed him inside, still with his 'dreadful old clothes' on. Fitted out with two beautiful suits, shoes and socks and some rather more respectable work clothes, John left the store animated.

He would wear the work clothes while helping Ben with the horses and assisting with general work around the property. But just when would he wear his beautifully tailored suits and polished leather shoes?

One day soon after the shopping spree, John was instructed to get 'dressed up to the nines'. Once suitably attired he was whisked away to the Moonee Valley Racing Club in north-west Melbourne where his father, as chairman, was hosting an official luncheon. To John's amazement, he was seated next to Lord Huntingfield, the Governor of Victoria. As the decked-out youth sat down, thoughts raced through his head. *Surely my father wouldn't put me here if he didn't believe I could behave properly? My father has shown perfect trust in me and in the way Mother has brought me up. I'll have to prove to him I can do it.*

The boy was instructed to call the Governor 'Your Excellency' and did so periodically during the lunch. While the Governor spent time chatting to him John could feel Ben's slightly worried eyes upon him. The jackeroo wondered if he might be boasting too much about *Manfred*, with its vast numbers of stock and sales. However, he also felt strongly that his father was proud of him. And justifiably so.

The 'very good yarn' he'd had with the Governor earned a tribute from His Excellency. 'Thank you! I've enjoyed our conversation very much!' The Governor's words rang in his ears.

Over 'the next couple of months of idyllic idleness' John very much enjoyed the more relaxed routine at *Woodlands*. He keenly sensed Ben Chaffey's continuing interest in his welfare and training. Though their true kinship was not discussed and his father had 'never ever raised the subject', a close rapport was developing, an unspoken acceptance of their relationship.

Every morning at dawn Ben knocked at the young jackeroo's bedroom door to ensure he was up and about. After a quick meal in the breakfast room, they walked together from the homestead to the stables. While the grooms went about their daily tasks, John and his father would start the same drill with every horse—'look at his front, his rear, lift his tail and have a look at his backside'.

John particularly looked forward to the days when they would travel further afield, chatting together and finally arriving at country properties to inspect Manfred or Whittier, his father's prize racehorses, famous for their wins in major races including the Victoria Derby in 1925 and the Caulfield Cup in 1922, 1925 and 1926.

The inspections were a must, as the stallions were now fully occupied in siring programs. One comment from a stud owner during one such visit was unforgettable. 'I knew your father well! A Mr Murray from South Australia!' he exclaimed to Chaffey's assistant. Taken aback, John nervously replied, 'Did you, Sir?' Ben Chaffey chipped in immediately, adroitly steering the conversation back to horses. Though now aware of his paternity, John's lack of certitude about his background and his careful diplomatic nature prevented him from ever bringing up the subject. He was sure his mother would not want him to probe, and Ben Chaffey certainly did not encourage it. The exchange on that day was never discussed.

Nevertheless, John strongly felt his father's interest. He even occasionally accompanied Ben into his Collins Street office in Melbourne, where they laughed and joked together. 'They were happy times.' One memorable day when they travelled to the city together, Ben left John to spend some time window-shopping on his own, while he conducted work meetings. Fascinated by the drawcards of the city, John decided to visit the Tivoli Theatre. He had been to the Tivoli with his mother in

Sydney, but had never seen such a magical performance as he saw on that day.

Dressed in oriental long silks, Arthur Bourne came waltzing out with his piano accordion, playing a classic, 'Over the Waves'. John listened intently, spellbound. Staring at the musician, the program and the 'beautiful accordion', he determined there and then that he would own one. It was a quick calculation once he discovered the price. He could buy a Wurlitzer using the wages of more than a year already sitting in his account, plus an additional six months' earnings he could save.

Often when Ben had business meetings, John stayed behind to work with Mavis Chaffey's husband, Albert Campbell, the manager of *Woodlands*. Unaware that the jackeroo was her half-brother, Mavis would invite him to join them for breakfast. John returned the favour. He helped groom her West Highland Terriers, keeping them snow white and taking 'armfuls of white terriers and spaniels' to innumerable dog shows, where he was inevitably smothered in white chalk.

At one of the shows John sat mesmerised by the performance of a border collie rounding up sheep. 'How can I get a dog like that?' he asked the owner, after a spectacular act. He had soon arranged for a female paddock dog to be sent to him at *Manfred* for the purchase price of five pounds. Later he bought Lady Blue—a grey-haired bitch for thirteen pounds. 'That started my love affair with collies.'

Ben's increasing pride in his son caused John some embarrassment. One night in the 'trophy room' at *Woodlands*, where the Caulfield cups were displayed in a glass cabinet draped with winning ribbons, Ben, his wife Cowra, and her companion and housekeeper, Bess McPherson, had gathered in evening dress for pre-dinner drinks.[2] John was standing in front of the fire when Ben asked him a disconcerting question. 'Eleven-and-a-half stone, Sir,' he quickly replied, aware that all eyes were on him. The work as a jackeroo had played its part in his rapid physical development. Though only seventeen, he was now over 180 centimetres (6 feet) tall and well-covered.

John felt uncomfortable and flustered by the attention. He flushed at the thought of Cowra's presence in the room—a strong, positive woman who was kind, but quite formal and polite with him. 'Mrs Chaffey was very kind to me but I tried to keep out of the way.' He often wondered if she guessed the kinship. His observation that 'at times she looked right through me' suggested that she did. The distinct likeness between him and his father 'was never mentioned'.

Cowra was indeed kind enough to provide John with a variety of activities at *Woodlands*. A couple of months into his stay with the Chaffeys, her niece arrived for a week's holiday. Colleen Crozier was great fun. When they were racing over the paddocks one day John's gentlemanly instincts were rewarded. 'Let me help you,' he offered at the barbed-wire fence, intoxicated by the glimpse of her red bloomers.

Once his health improved, more and more John was able to enjoy the familial atmosphere. He ate with the family and regularly went out with them, mostly to race meetings, sitting up proudly in the back of the Humber Pullman. When they arrived at their destination, Tommy Byrnes, the horse trainer, would look after John while Chaffey, having checked to see that the young boy had money, would settle himself in the box. 'He would give me a pound, so I could easily put five shillings on a horse if I wanted to. I was treated like a son.'

Where the Chaffeys went, John went. Cowra quietly acquiesced.

Eventually John's enjoyable stay at *Woodlands* came to an end. If reluctant about the return to *Beilpajah* he kept it to himself. Despite the isolation, there was now something, albeit inanimate, that brought some pleasant company into his life. The accordion that soon arrived from Melbourne became a constant companion. Whenever he was on his own, teaching himself to play the instrument filled the lonely hours: 'Night after night on my own before I went to bed, particularly on a moonlit night … I'd play and practise my accordion, practise my simple tunes. There was a log or a stump—not far, ten yards out from the gateway into the hut—and I could go and sit out there. The accordion and the tuition book … It was a bit of a lifesaving thing really, a bit of a lifesaver.'

Some time after John's visit to *Woodlands*, another incident laid him low. While he was working at *Darnick*, one of the out-stations of *Manfred*, a sharp knife he was using to cut a sheep's throat slipped and severed a tendon in one of his fingers. The chief boundary rider took him in a sulky to the railway siding in the middle of nowhere. 'Wait here until the train comes. You've got to get to Ivanhoe.' There, about 110 kilometres (70 miles) away, he could get medical attention.

John got out at the siding and waited. It was dark and cold. His finger throbbed. When exhaustion overtook him in the dead of night, he lay down on the track to make sure he would hear the approaching train. Suddenly the vibrations woke him from a deep sleep; the train's glaring lights were bearing down on him. He jumped up and waved frantically, only to be met by a gruff question from the driver as the train jerked to a halt, 'What the bloody hell do you want?'

John explained his predicament. Freezing, he then huddled around the brazier in the train's cab for what seemed like hours, until he was let off at the town's siding. He trudged about 1 kilometre (half a mile) towards the lights of Ivanhoe and waited for morning.

Finally the bush nurse appeared. After inspecting his finger, she poured carbolic acid onto his wound, hoping to prevent infection. She could do nothing for the severed tendon. When he eventually got back to the *Manfred* homestead, he instinctively knew that Billy Woods' advice was correct. 'You've got to get down to Sydney for that. Back to Ivanhoe with you and onto the train.'

John needed his family; he wished the women in his life were closer. Lorraine was impossible to reach. While working as a multilingual journalist in Sydney, she had been spotted by the Japanese ambassador to Australia and had accepted his offer to become governess to the children of Prince Tokogawa—an admiral in the Japanese Navy and cousin of the Emperor. After twelve months in Sydney teaching the children English, she had been transferred with the family to Canada, where she continued her French study, and from there to Japan, where she became fluent in Japanese.

To reach his mother and Margie, John had to travel to Nowra. The last time he had seen them was in 1932 when he and Peter had visited *Wogamia* to build their mother an access wharf for the old launch that chugged up and down the Shoalhaven River. Since then, 'when a dribble of money came in', his mother and sister had moved to the outskirts of the town.

The local doctor was direct with John; he would have to have his finger off. The thought of amputation galvanised the family. John's mother insisted her son visit Sir Charles Blackburn, a prominent Sydney doctor who had given her children annual check-ups when she was living in the city. 'You're not eating, and you're smoking,' Dr Blackburn admonished John.

Following an operation and plenty of remedial exercises, John regained part use of his finger.

After the stay at *Woodlands*, John had more than occasional contact with his father. Perhaps the criticism by physician Edward Oldham directed to Ben for his 'rough treatment' had been noted: 'Several times when he came up to *Manfred* from Melbourne … Ben would have one or two of his grazier friends staying there and would tell Billy Woods to bring me in.

Billy would say, 'You're going to eat with us tonight so tidy yourself up.' 'They had a lovely big dining room in the main building … I would sit there at the table like a quiet little boy and if anyone spoke to me I would answer, but I didn't speak otherwise. I just listened to their conversation … talking about the Melbourne races or finances.'

John was convinced that it would have been impossible for Ben to extend similar hospitality to Peter, who was never invited to the dinner table at *Manfred* or at *Woodlands*: 'The physical likenesses were very obvious. I don't think Ben could ever have [invited Peter to dinner]. Features much the same. Yes—they had the same manner of walking—big men … I think Ben would have only just got away with it with me and that's all, if in fact he did.'

Peter and John related to their father in different ways. Peter himself confessed that he occasionally approached Ben Chaffey in a confrontational manner and was openly critical. In mid-1934 he had a run-in concerning the administration of the property and left *Manfred* in a huff. He had become fed up with the irritating interference of the bookkeeper Billy Woods, 'tattling tales and making mischief', and the way his father ran the property from his Melbourne office, 'managing the whole thing on the telephone'.[3] The catalyst was the loss of 19,000 sheep. Ben asked Peter for his opinion about suing the manager, Jim Fitzgerald, for the disaster. Losing his temper in reply, Peter criticised his father for trying to manage from afar. He backed the manager to the hilt.

The argument widened and Peter's criticism reached deeper, into the way his father had relinquished his responsibilities to his mother and the family once the Depression hit. Ben retaliated. He had spent 'thousands and thousands' on his second family and had plans for his older son's future. Peter was not impressed: 'I don't think anything of your plans. I won't be here for very much longer. I'm leaving for Western Australia. I want you to understand that.'[4]

Later Peter discovered that his father had arranged a job for him before he travelled west—a paternal gesture that may have acted as a salve. Before his departure, he took Margie to meet their father at his office in Melbourne. Peter was twenty; Margie, seventeen. The visit was a way of apologising to his father for his recent outburst; he was 'pretty sorry about it' and advanced some conciliatory comments. When Ben explained his financial decline and inability to continue his support of the family—'Things have happened'—Peter acknowledged his difficulties. 'No worries.'[5]

Margie had not seen Ben Chaffey since the day he walked into their home on Sydney's north shore when she was a small girl. Now in his office they talked and talked. Margie was animated, and all the while Ben studied the face of his daughter.

Neither child realised it was the last time they would see their father.

Just before this visit, Constance had moved with Margie to Sydney. During her time at *Wogamia* one of the local bachelors made it his business to re-establish contact with the alluring widow to whom his family had so kindly offered help. At that time much of Charlie Glanville's working life was spent away from his home area, having joined the Army Survey Unit after his return from the Great War. However, he was taken by Constance's charms, proposed to her soon after their reunion and by March 1934 had married her and moved to the city. The couple lived together with Margie in Killara, and relocated in early 1941 to Dee Why, on the northern beaches.

'He was such a nice man,' Peter Murray recalled of the outstanding horseman and kind gentleman who had been awarded a military medal for 'initiative and valour' in the Great War.[6] John later wrote of the stepfather who had fitted so closely into their family, 'I know I feel that he has always been there.'[7]

With her children now seemingly settled, in 1935 Constance made a trip to England to visit her first daughter who was temporarily living in London. Despite Lorraine's ill health at the time of her mother's visit, Constance received every attention. She wrote to her daughter just before her departure from the Rutland Hotel, on the day of her return to Australia:

> *When I think of you being ill … and getting meals and shopping for an extra person, I don't know how you did it … I have so appreciated all you did for me to make my stay enjoyable. You deserve a Life Peerage for all your sweetness and loving kindness … Goodbye Sweet and God bless you.*[8]

Meanwhile, John continued to work for Ben Chaffey, with his responsibilities extending to *Kilfera* over the next year. Always the bearer of family news, John wrote to his mother while she was in London:

I do hope you receive this before you leave England as I don't know whether Peter has written to you recently or not. Perhaps you know that he has left the West and is in this district once again with a good position.

He was offered the overseer's job on Albemarle Station *close to Menindee, about 70 miles from here and he accepted 150 pounds per year for a start. This job is a good one and I think he will make the most of it … the manager of* Albemarle *had only met Peter once for a few moments and judged him on that one meeting … Peter has been there only a few weeks and I managed to see him about a fortnight ago. He looks wonderfully well; so big and clean looking and so respected that I am very proud to have him as a brother.*

However, this change of his has made your suggestion of all meeting in the West impossible now, darling, much as I would love to. Perhaps I may be down for Christmas, I really don't know yet, as things are getting a bit better for me here now, with sometimes more responsibility, so I just have to watch my step.

Life could be a lot worse for me, and although this waiting is trying at times, I am still only twenty so life is before me, with any amount of opportunities … a few mistakes are bound to come, and it only remains for me to profit by them …
31 August 1935

Early in 1937 John decided to go to Melbourne. He had heard rumours that Ben Chaffey was suffering ill health. Once in the city he was forced to confront an unpleasant reality. His father was dangerously ill, much sicker than originally thought.

John felt helpless and confused. As his father lay dying in his bedroom at *Woodlands*, one leg amputated from the effects of thrombosis, he rang from the Federal Hotel to ask Cowra if it would be possible for him to come and see Mr Chaffey.

'No, I'm sorry it's not,' she said.

The curt reply led him to wonder again if Cowra suspected their true relationship. He was 'pretty sure' she did. *If only there was a chance to talk as father and son*, John thought. But propriety had always influenced his behaviour and he decided to let it be.

When asked about the most upsetting moment in his life, John replied: 'I don't know … I don't know the worst moment. You know one of the most upsetting things … [was] my father dying … It was a crushing blow … not to be able to go out and see Ben when he was dying. I felt terribly disappointed I couldn't go and see him. It left me rudderless. Awful feeling.'

Ben Chaffey was buried in the Bulla Cemetery, very close to *Woodlands*, with no members of his second family in attendance. It would be over sixty years before John visited the grave.

For a while, life was meaningless: 'I went back—drifted back up there [to *Manfred*] and just went into—pulled out of—got what money was owing, gathered my few possessions and went into Ivanhoe. I never went back.'

While obituary notices outlined his father's achievements, one later report, published by the Victorian Government in relation to *Woodlands*, was more revealing. It outlined his fall into severely reduced circumstances: 'Ben Chaffey died on March 3, 1937 … He was buried in Bulla Cemetery …At the time of his death he was still chairman of the Victorian Amateur Turf Club, an office he had held since 1930, as he was considered a capable administrator and advisor on improvements in racing. He was also Chairman of Directors of United Distillers' Pty Ltd, and managing director of Goldsborough, Mort and Co. Ltd. [wool brokers]. However, his own business affairs were in a mess and his probate papers showed that he had debts totalling 266,000 pounds.'[9]

Reflecting on Ben's financial decline many years later, Peter gave details of Chaffey's rural consolidation, suggesting that it was part of the reason for his father's decline: 'Oh, he was a pretty good man, a very clever man, a brilliant man. But his empire fell to pieces. You see he had—he'd sold all his other interests—he bought *Manfred* and *Kilfera*, and went out on his own. He spent hundreds and thousands of pounds, which would be millions of dollars today [1989], making *Manfred* into a good station … He had over 150 windmills on the place … built homesteads … He had a huge pumping station that came off the Mildura irrigation scheme … a steam engine was pumping water out of the well—the Eureka Well—pumping it 7 miles up into the hills and gravitating it further—miles and miles—he opened up country that had never been watered before.'

With hindsight, John agreed that in addition to Ben's passion for horseracing, his father's concentration of *Manfred* and *Kilfera* had contributed to his financial woes and decline in health. Both sons acknowledged however, that no one could have predicted the intensity of the forces Chaffey had been compelled to face, the three antagonists that conspired against him simultaneously—the continuing Depression, a prolonged drought and plummeting wool prices.

John reflected further on the property consolidation. Had his father not centralised, he knew that he himself would not have had the opportunity to work there for all those years. Right through his life he would look back to the 'strengthening' he had received at *Manfred* and *Woodlands*. 'It was a wonderful start for me.'

Chapter Five

Australia at war

WELL FOR ME, I SUPPOSE, I DON'T KNOW IF YOU CALL IT
PATRIOTISM OR WHAT, BUT I JUST FELT YOU NEEDED TO BE
PART OF YOUR COUNTRY'S DEFENCE. AND AT THAT TIME SEE,
WAR WAS COMING ON, AND I SUPPOSE LIKE SO MANY OTHERS
I THOUGHT IT WAS A BLOODY GREAT ADVENTURE THAT WAS
GOING TO HAPPEN AND I WAS GOING TO BE IN IT. BECAUSE
WHILE PATRIOTISM IS DEFINITELY MIXED UP IN IT, THE FACT
THAT IT WAS THE BIGGEST THING GOING AROUND THE PLACE
AT THE TIME AND YOU COULD BE IN IT WITH A HELL OF A LOT
OF OTHER BLOKES YOUR OWN AGE, NOTHING BEATS IT.

—Caulfield, 2000[1]

IT WAS NOW mid-1937. In his own words, John had felt 'rudderless' after his father's death. There was little purpose to his life. He became a knockabout: jackerooing on a distant property 'way out west' near Wilcannia; mustering; and, in the end, after some discussion with his brother, setting up a business with him, shooting and skinning kangaroos and foxes. 'We always worked well together. Peter was good in the bush. I was reasonable, but Peter was excellent.'

The brothers' venture ranged over thousands of square kilometres from the edges of Queensland, out to South Australia, down to the Darling River on the Victorian border and inland to Ivanhoe. They worked hard, unafraid of travelling huge distances overland through isolated areas:

'Two shoots a day, daylight and evening, when they were feeding. There was always a roo from the mob who was watching; if you could pick that one there would be utter confusion. You tried to shoot humanely … you had to shoot in vital parts without damaging the skins. We employed a young fellow to help us skin. We got 1000 in ten days at one stage. Then we took off to Sydney with the skins and sold them.'

Foxes were a nightmare for the farmers. They would stalk the weakened pregnant ewes, 'clean them up in a few bites'. Showing one reluctant grazier the contents of a fox's stomach (undigested baby lamb) was enough to ensure the continuation of the fox trade on many properties, where the scavengers were poisoned with strychnine in tobacco cans—up to eighty on any one night.

While the slaughtering served the brothers well in the post-Depression years, they soon became 'sick of being smothered with blood and always handling dirty, smelly animals'. With little need for persuasion, they decided it was time to join the mines at Broken Hill, in the far west of outback New South Wales. All cleaned up, fit, presentable and well spoken, the young men were ensured of immediate employment by the owners of the mines, even though the employment queues 'were miles long'.

However, soon the dangers of working in the mines long-term became all too obvious to John. Shovelling sand down chutes to secure the denuded mines and taking draft horses down hundreds of metres in cages so that they could drag the skip trucks of ore along dark passages were not activities for the weak-hearted. Unclear instructions from Yugoslav supervisors presented an added danger. 'I had to learn a bit of their language—all sorts of phrases for my own safety.'

There was, however, one memorable event that relieved both the danger and the tedium. Emerging dirty and exhausted from the cage one day, lamp affixed to his head and his old blue dungarees saturated with sweat, John suddenly heard his name being called out by the manager. He squinted in the bright light: 'Lo and behold, Lord Huntingfield in his second term as Governor, came over and said, "Don't I know you?"'

'Yes, Your Excellency, you do. We met at the luncheon at Moonee Valley.'

'I'm delighted to meet you again. Good luck!'

All the other miners were flabbergasted. Their jaws dropped as they saw the Governor of Victoria extend his hand. They knew well enough that their mate's hands were filthy.

Even though the money was good, within eighteen months, twenty-three-year-old John had decided to quit his job at the mines. After a series of calamities, 'the final straw' was when three miners were killed in a cave-in. 'We worked and helped to get them out. Then I thought, to hell with this.'

He had volunteered to stay on for the four days needed to extract their mangled bodies from the mine, but then it was goodbye.

John began making arrangements for a droving trip. The Tibooburra Mail would take him to the remote settlement of the same name—Tibooburra—an Aboriginal word meaning 'pile of rocks'. The small town was in the far north-west corner of New South Wales—red-earthed, scattered with large boulders and reputed to be one of the hottest places in Australia.

On joining the droving team he would head for south-western Queensland. Around 560 bullocks were due to be rounded up there, for the beginning of a three-month trip. The team would move the cattle south on the hoof towards Adelaide in South Australia, where greener pastures would fatten them for market.

Due to start his travels in a little over twenty-four hours, John placed into his swag the final necessities—pipe, tobacco and wax matches. He paused, satisfied. Droving was a physically tiring job, but smoking was a pleasure that filled the endless hours. Momentarily distracted by his own planning, he reached for the flat, round British Tobacco tin and his Briar. It was just after 9 pm on the evening of 3 September 1939. He would listen to the late news and savour the last pipe of the night.

When he heard the familiar voice of Robert Menzies, the Prime Minister of Australia, crackling over the airwaves, John leaned closer to the old wireless. Words were cutting in and out, so he quickly bent over to fine-tune the station and turn up the volume. Hearing the word 'war', he stopped dead: 'It is my melancholy duty to inform you officially that in consequence of a persistence by Germany ... Great Britain has declared war on her and ... as a result, Australia is also at war.'[2]

John was shocked to hear the announcement. After all, it was only a little over twenty years since the end of World War I. Of the 300,000 Australians who enlisted in the Great War, 61,919 had been killed and around 156,000 wounded, gassed or taken prisoner. Devastating numbers for a population of fewer than five million.

John's stepfather, Charlie Glanville, had sometimes spoken about his experiences in the cavalry. John himself remembered the brass band celebrations of war's end. He was almost three years old when he and his mother walked in Cronulla with the rejoicing crowds. Looking up he had seen tears streaming down crumpled faces as 'The Last Post' was sounded on a single gleaming bugle. The images were fixed tight in his memory.

Despite the horrific statistics from two decades before, the Prime Minister apparently had no hesitation in his support for Britain in this new war. He beseeched 'God in His mercy and compassion' to deliver the world 'from this agony'.[3]

For many Australians, including John's mother Constance, this early spring broadcast was unbelievable. In fact, Menzies' description of the 'struggle that we must at all costs win' was not taken too seriously at first. In the months following the German invasion of Poland on 1 September 1939, the war was soon tagged 'phoney'. Neither France nor Britain responded as Germany and Russia divided Poland between them.[4]

Australia's Minister for Air, James V. Fairbairn, returned from France with an important announcement: the Maginot Line, a powerful French line of defence along its border with Germany, was impenetrable. No German army could breach it.

In the few months to follow, Australians found it difficult to believe the Empire was in danger, especially as Menzies showed such 'cheery optimism' in public. 'The summer of 1939–40 was a hot one, post-Christmas sales were a bonanza for retailers, and Donald Bradman made his 90th century and 34th double-century at the Melbourne Cricket Ground ...'[5] There was no sense of urgency. Everyone went about their business.

If Constance had any concerns about her son joining up, John was able to put her fears to rest. The day after the Prime Minister's announcement, he wrote to his mother to reassure her. The custom of young girls throwing a white feather to pacifists, or 'conscies', held no fear for him:

Tomorrow morning, I leave by the Tibooburra Mail and will pick up the rest of the droving plant somewhere along the road. We take delivery of the cattle on the 15th. There are a few horses to break on the road back, so our time will be well filled 'til the 15th.

All this war business sounds rather bad alright, but whatever you do, don't worry about us [John and his brother Peter]. I'm not going to do any enlisting even if the lasses hand me a white feather or two; in fact it will take more than a white leghorn chook to make me even consider it.

However, this trip will take at least a couple of months, and after that if I don't get another trip with the same plant, I'll probably go well out and have a good look about, perhaps out towards the Territory. That country out there should be safe enough …
4 September 1939

Two days after Menzies' fateful broadcast, John joined three men, a wagon and twelve horses. He had been approached by drover Bob Thomas, the owner of the wagon. The two men already employed would act in turn as driver, cook and horse tailer. As the third hand, along with general droving routines John would also be responsible for twenty-five to thirty horses, unwanted animals picked up from stations along the way. He had a name as an experienced horseman and a 'rough rider': 'It was up to me to see what I could do with them. Not a nice thought. It kept me awake a bit. They'd been broken in to some degree—but there were one or two proper outlaws we had to discard. Remember, we were working with these horses in the open—no yards most of the time, caught, hobbled, saddled, mounted and then mostly a bush buckjumping spectacle.'

The real work would start in south-western Queensland, when they picked up the 560 bullocks. Returning through the 'Warri Gate' to Tibooburra—the Gate was on the Dingo Fence—they would make their way slowly down the stony ranges to Broken Hill, then skirt around the mining town and head south towards Adelaide.[6]

The patterns of droving were familiar to John. By 4 am he was up. Supplies in the wagon were checked: flour, tea, sugar, jam and coarse salt. The last item was most important; it would preserve the perishable meat they killed along the way. After a quick wash, a cup of black tea and breakfast, he would roll up his swag and join in discussions on the day's movements with the boss. The cattle were on the go by the time the sun lit the horizon.

John had learned early at *Manfred* that, whether sheep or cattle, the principles were constant. Pace was crucial: the lead 'should never be allowed to walk faster than the comfortable pace of the tail of the mob'. The stock were allowed to fan out and graze in the open spaces but were always brought back together at the end of the day.

Comfort was not uppermost in the minds of the drovers: it was safety. Vitally important was to choose a good night horse—'close to your swag and fully ready to fly aboard, either to lead front or flank of the mob if you needed to get control'. The night horse had to be of the right temperament. If the rider rattled all his gear, there would almost certainly be trouble. 'Until the cattle settled down I did not take my boots off, except for a bit of an airing during the camp dinner, perhaps.'

At the end of each long day, there was one absolute essential: lighting the campfire and then keeping it going strongly all night. Every evening the men gathered the stock up near the big fire—directing the cattle to one side and placing wagon, the horses and themselves on the other. There was a good reason for this arrangement. If the mob was disrupted and began to panic in the middle of the night, they would split *because* of the fire—and the drovers would survive.

Many a life had been lost to frightened cattle stampeding at night.

As John travelled along with the drovers, snippets of worrying news concerning early war casualties were filtering through. This was not the normal talk of weather, stock sales or commodity prices. Would Hitler be content with his invasion of Poland or was further aggression planned?

It seemed that everyone was talking about becoming a pilot—the ultimate in glamour and daring. John began to think of a way he too could contribute to the war effort. A single episode involving pilots was the catalyst.

The droving trip was well underway, the cattle settled so nicely that John could almost allow himself to take off his boots when he turned in for the night. However, when they reached the clay pans around Broken Hill things changed. Unusually, it was pouring with rain. While attempting to skirt around the town, the drovers and their horses were sliding on the greasy ground and the cattle were slipping in the wet mud. John was desperately trying to help keep all of the animals in a tight herd.

Then there was a sudden roar in the sky that broke the pattern entirely. When John saw Tiger Moths in the distance he knew they belonged to the Broken Hill Aero Club, subsidised by the mining companies. Bob Collins, an instructor, had been training 'keen young pilots' for some time. Back in Broken Hill before the droving trip, John had noticed the eager interest these men were showing in the exotic pastime.

That the cattle became agitated on hearing the noise was not a surprise, but what happened next was quite unexpected. Suddenly the Tiger Moths zoomed down very low and in a flash 'the valiant young fighter pilots had dropped dozens of small paper bags of flour on the herd'. In a trice it was over, but this unique bombing practice frightened everyone and spread out the cattle and horses for miles. 'Some horses were down; some getting up; and some with pack saddles on their sides. It was a terrible mess.'

John sat on his horse and thought: *You bastards. What chaos. If I had a rifle now … I'd bloody well shoot you.* Then, after the initial shock and some time to restore order, he began to reflect. For the first time he felt involved in the war. Those young fellows were training; they were doing something for the war effort. The paper bags of flour were bombs. Even if their action had been irresponsible, their practice was serious.

For the rest of the trip John thought long and hard. By the time he got back to Broken Hill he was convinced. To join up was the right thing to do.

Leaving his bike and a few other possessions with Peter, who was still working in the mines, John hauled his swag over his shoulder and took the next train to Sydney.

He would visit his family first and then attempt to enlist. Apart from his brother, the rest of John's family were now living in Sydney: his mother with Charlie Glanville in Lane Cove, a northern Sydney suburb; his older sister, Lorraine, near the centre of the city in a flat at Potts Point; and Margie, his newly married younger sister, with her husband Dr John Oldham, in Wollstonecraft, near Lane Cove. Being a close family they often got together for evening meals.

On this occasion, even when the conversation turned quickly to the European conflict, John did not inform his mother of his intentions. *Wait until it's done*, he thought. Much to his disappointment the quota for the first round of recruits for the 6th Division had already been filled.

Meanwhile, Lorraine offered to put him up. At the time she was living in a spacious apartment with the influential editor of a scandal rag *Smith's Weekly*, Bill Rodie, who was almost certainly working for the government. Conspiring together, the pair had already plotted John's future. They wanted to get him into Intelligence, but first he needed to gain some experience in the traditional police force. When John expressed a preference for the Mounted Police, Rodie set about using his contacts to arrange it. He rang the Commissioner of Police whom he knew personally. Send the young man out to the Bourke Street Barracks was Commissioner McKay's advice. A Sergeant McKeachy would be in charge there.

McKeachy gave John two orders: to pass an exam and to ride Sailor, a buck-jumping horse in a Sergeant Windsor's care. Much to his surprise John passed the exam, commenting that McKay had probably already said, 'Pass him!'

Then he had to ride Sailor whose trainer, Windsor, was 'an aggressive kind of a bloke'. By the time he appeared with his horse, all the police cadets were coming out of the woodwork, eager to see the new boy on the block get thrown off the infamous trick horse. John tried to mount but did not even get his foot in the off-side stirrup before he was thrown onto his back.

This was the opportunity for Sailor to attack him, to dig his teeth into his victim's flailing left arm. When John grabbed the ear of the animal, Windsor objected. 'I'm not going to let him savage me,' John shouted back, smacking the horse on the nose. This upset Sergeant Windsor even more. As John managed to climb on, Sailor threw everything at him, obeying signals from his trainer. John held on tightly like he used to when the horses were tearing through the rabbit warrens at *Manfred*. He felt the power and speed of the horse, but clung on hard.

'Get off! Jump off!' shouted Windsor. John landed on his feet and got a cheer from the men gathered around. Sergeant McKeachy was delighted and congratulated John. 'You're in! In one or two months you'll be hearing from me.'

Biding his time, John looked for other employment and found a suitable position immediately, as an assistant for the shearing season on *Bugilbone Station*, a beautiful 2000–2400 hectares (5000–6000 acres) of river country at Burren Junction, a few hundred kilometres east of Bourke.[7] He got on well with his employer, and despite the bossy maid who yelled out to him to answer the phone, life was 'extremely pleasant'. In the letter to his mother there was no reference to war:

> *The job is going very well indeed, much easier than any job I have had to date ... The family are a splendid lot; seems to be perfect harmony ... Living with a family like this has made me do things that I have never had to do before [on the other stations]. I have to shave every day and dress every night for dinner ...*
>
> *You are quite right about slipping into bad habits ... It may interest you to know that I have started a course of Pelmanism,*

and I think it is going to be a wonderful thing for me. I've only been at it for about a week … There are numerous thought exercises to practise every day and they don't take long to bring results.[8]
April 1940

Waiting for the next call-up, John now made it his business to follow all news of the overseas action. The war clouds in Europe were becoming thicker and dirtier. Germany continued its bold, surprising and aggressive incursions.

In April 1940, Denmark and Norway were attacked. On 10 May 1940, Hitler invaded Luxembourg, the Netherlands and Belgium in one great thrust forward. By the end of May the German army was advancing into France; Paris fell in June 1940.

Australian families rallied to the cause as pressure mounted for all suitable candidates to join up. Many thought of Britain as the Mother Country, having repeated every Monday morning at school assemblies as students, 'We honour our God, we salute our flag, we honour the King.'

After some discussion, Peter and John had already decided that only one of them would leave Australia in the event of a call-up. The two had agreed that it was much more sensible for Peter to stay behind. By then he was married to the attractive, fair-headed pianist, Jane Moore, and managing a property. They both knew that it was the government's firm policy to discourage those with essential occupations such as his from joining up.[9]

For his part, John also felt a growing support for King and Country. When the 7th Division advertised, he immediately began application procedures for enlistment. Then he sat down to write to his mother.

As Constance Glanville started to read the letter from John, dated 17 May 1940—written from *Bugilbone* one week after the latest devastating German blitzkrieg—her eyes darted ahead. One sentence in the middle of the letter stood out; her heart dropped. She saw the initials AIF and knew they signified the Australian Imperial Force:

Now, darling, I want to tell you now that I have just made application to join the AIF. This was quite a sudden decision, but I really can't keep out of it any longer Mother dear. The news of the last week or so has been really shocking, and as they want men badly now I'm not going to keep out of it any longer …

German territory in Europe by the end of May 1940.

Now, darling, I know this is rotten news for you. But I definitely want to do my bit now, things are really too serious. So although you must think me very changeable, I must ask you darling to get accustomed to the idea as soon as possible. I know that any other young man in my position would do the same ...

It is hard to say just how long it will be before I will be down Mother ... It depends on how many applications are ahead of mine. I even may be too late to be included in the 7th Division. However, I really will feel better if I get a chance to do my bit ...
17 May 1940

Constance needed to pause for a while and quietly reflect. Since stoicism marked her personality, she would accept her son's decision to join up. But the thought of his departure brought up a confusion of emotions. Though she would not admit to it, fear was mixed with pride.

Chapter Six

A new kind
of training

My husband was a miner at that time ... He had that
adventurous spirit, and he went through the line, and
they said, 'What do you do?' and he said, 'Coalminer'.
So they said, 'No, you're restricted, you're not to come
through,' so he went back and got in another line
and when he went through it he said, 'unemployed'
and was straight in.

—Penglase & Horner, 1992[1]

Despite the fact that John told his mother he would wait until summoned, he was impatient to join up. He left *Bugilbone Station* for Sydney in late May 1940 and on arrival headed directly to Martin Place, in the heart of the city. The place was abuzz with bands playing and swarms of people crowding around registration booths on every block. Officials were readily accepting volunteers and then delivering them in trucks to Victoria Barracks, an army base in the inner-city suburb of Paddington.

John barely had time to look around when an old bloke in full World War I uniform approached him, explaining that a certain Lieutenant Colonel Fred Burrows was a friend of his and had been given a battalion. If he wanted a good war, that unit was the one to join. 'You couldn't get a better man than Fred Burrows.'

Colonel Burrows had been awarded a medal for bravery during World War I. After the war he had commanded a citizen battalion and then, from its inception, the Recruit Training Depot, which had trained the 6th Division. Now this formidable figure was to command the 2/13th Battalion. From the day of his appointment in late April 1940, Burrows focused intently on finding recruits, putting together a small team known as 'The Talent Scouts', led by Captain Les Dawson.

In no time at all John found himself packed into a truck headed for Victoria Barracks. There the volunteers lined up for medical tests, vaccinations, enrolment and posting to various units. During his medical examination John's concern that the wound in his index finger would go against him was unfounded. 'If you were a bit lithe and from the bush, you were accepted.'

When pressed to join the artillery John said he wanted to join the 13th Battalion. 'Did you say the 13th? You're my boy!' It was Captain Les Dawson. 'Don't you let anyone talk you out of it!'

Without even collecting his gear, which was still at Central Railway Station, John went straight from The Barracks to Ingleburn, part of a large military reserve around Liverpool and Camden, about 50 kilometres (30 miles) south-west of Sydney. In the midst of all the excitement, the rough conditions there did not appear to matter. The long huts held about thirty men each but there were no beds, just piles of hessian and bales of straw that were offered as rough mattresses. Boots or scrunched-up trousers served as pillows.

John learned that the Australian Army was made up of two or more corps, each with around 30,000 men, and commanded by a general. He would soon appreciate exactly where he fitted into the pattern of each corps:

> DIVISION—made up of 10,000–20,000 men in three
> brigades and commanded by a major general.
> BRIGADE—made up of 2500–5000 men in three
> battalions and commanded by a brigadier (general).
> BATTALION—made up of 550–1000 men in four
> companies and commanded by a lieutenant colonel.
> COMPANY—made up of 100–225 men in three platoons
> and commanded by a captain or major.
> PLATOON—made up of 30–60 men in three sections and
> commanded by a lieutenant.
> SECTION—made up of 9–16 men and commanded by
> a corporal or sergeant.

Almost immediately he was assigned his precise military identification. By the end of the day, Wednesday, 22 May 1940, John was part of the 7th Division, with a specific number that would head every letter he wrote home (NX20884) and precise identification for his Brigade (the 20th), Battalion (2/13th), Company (B Co.), Platoon (11) and Section (6). Each recruit in the infantry was also issued with his own numbered rifle for the duration of the war.

A surprising number of returned soldiers from World War I had re-enlisted, and young men were signing up in growing numbers, many of whom were under military age and had lied about their date of birth. John was delighted to see several of his old schoolmates at Ingleburn, though the recruits came from all over and ranged widely in age and profession.

The Army had a tough job, to 'turn civilians into soldiers'. Somehow they had to weld 'the full mix of rookies'—a disparate group of lawyers, schoolteachers, roustabouts, bank clerks, factory workers—into one unit.[2] However, trainers had one undeniable advantage. With the news of the devastating advances made by Hitler in Europe, every recruit was impatient, chafing to get on with the job.

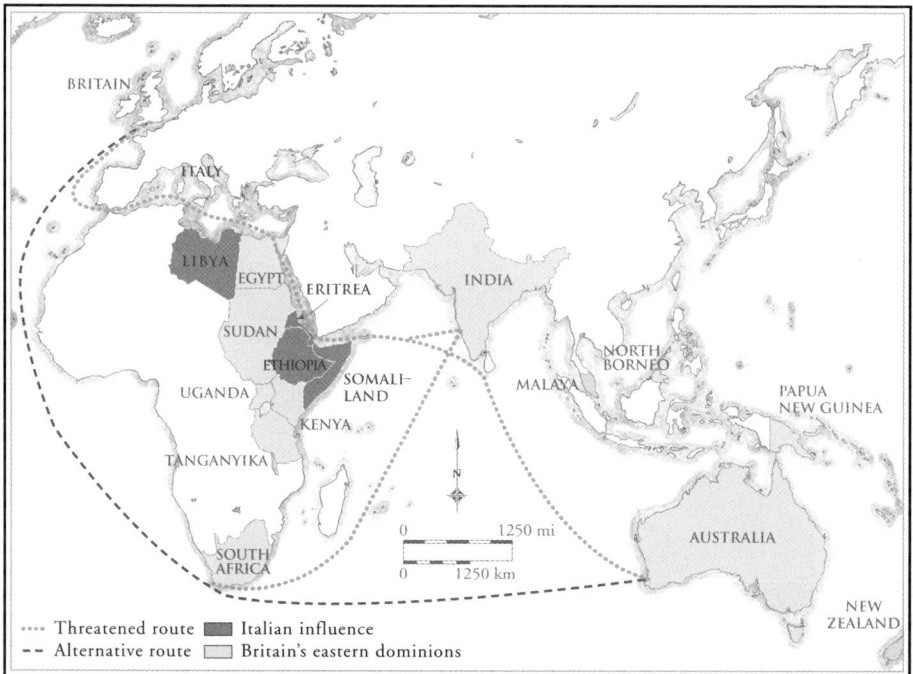

British and Italian spheres of influence.

For the Prime Minister of Britain, Winston Churchill, there was a sense of urgency. He saw very good reason for the troops still in Australia to begin their service abroad as soon as possible.

Benito Mussolini, Italy's Fascist dictator, now in alliance with Hitler, was bent on extending his 'empire' in North Africa and North-East Africa. This raised the terrifying possibility of an attack on Egypt and the British-controlled Suez Canal. His ambitions sent a shiver of fear throughout the Commonwealth.

How would Britain be able to efficiently continue trading if they lost control of the Suez? The alternative route around the Cape of Good Hope would add at least a month to their journeys. How would Indian and Australasian troops get through to the Middle East—fast becoming a vital theatre in the minds of the British? The oil wells there were indispensable to the war effort.

Britain was now under threat. In a daring rescue effort in late May and June 1940, hundreds of thousands of British troops had been evacuated from the beaches of Dunkirk and the surrounding French coastline and transported back to Britain to protect their increasingly vulnerable homeland. The loss of equipment and supplies was devastating.

Churchill's speeches inspired patriotic fervour. On 4 June, the British leader delivered a now famous speech in the House of Commons: 'We are told that Herr Hitler has a plan for invading the British Isles … we shall fight on the beaches, we shall fight on the landing grounds, we shall fight in the fields and in the streets, we shall fight in the hills; we shall never surrender …'[3]

So far away from Britain but so closely related, Australia was being inexorably drawn in. The threat of the invasion of Britain was virtually unbelievable to Australians; they quickly responded. By mid-year 100,000 men had volunteered for service and within a few months not only the 7th but an 8th Division had been filled.

By July 1940, the Battle of Britain had commenced. The German Luftwaffe was attempting to gain air superiority in preparation for a channel invasion. Churchill referred to 'a new Dark Age'.

John was more convinced than ever that he had made the right move.

Training at Ingleburn for the 2/13th Battalion soon began in earnest—instruction with elementary rifle exercises, infantry drill, bayonet training, sentry duties and night operations. Arduous marches began almost immediately.

The 2/13th Battalion marching through the streets of Katoomba in August 1940.
'… it is wonderful marching strictly to attention, company after company, with not a head turned to one side, and arms all swinging evenly'. John Murray is in the far (top) row.

Always dressed in immaculate uniform and demonstrating detailed knowledge of the daily program, Commanding Officer Colonel Burrows demanded high standards at all times. To impress on the men the importance of strict discipline in punctuality and dress, almost every day there was a battalion parade. A cane on the behind or a loud, sharp order told recruits they were not marching according to his standards. He quickly gained the nickname of 'Bull Burrows'. Despite this tag, the CO showed great pride in his unit, was fair-minded and had a genuine interest in every man. He soon gained the respect of the entire battalion.[4]

On 22 June 1940, the ex-members of the 13th Battalion from World War I gathered to hand over the flag to the new unit. Already there was a pride in belonging to the 2/13th. One of the platoon sergeants remembered the 'soldierly bearing, the absolute steadiness on parade and the general air of precision'. With a sharp eye he noted the 'newly formed band, with its spectacular array of shining instruments'.[5] Even in those early days Colonel Burrows had boasted that he would have the best band in the AIF.

Public marches in the surrounding countryside were soon introduced. For most of the soldiers these encouraged bonding; they were a pleasure rather than a duty. Probably the most memorable march for the 2/13th was the ten-day one over the Blue Mountains to a new camp at Bathurst. Along the way the battalion received wild applause and much publicity.

Pleased with all the community attention, John wrote to his mother during the march:

We left Ingleburn on Monday and have been plugging along steadily ever since and tonight we are camped at Hazelbrook and will be in Katoomba tomorrow night …

Being the first Battalion to come through is really a wonderful experience; the occupants of every house are lined along the roads cheering, clapping and waving little flags; the children madly excited … When not marching at attention, we cheer and wave to everyone and talk to all the kiddies. But when marching through the towns, then the band strikes up and our rifles come to our shoulders … company after company, with not a head turned to one side, and arms all swinging evenly.

So glad you saw my photo in the Herald. *It was quite a good one of our platoon really, although fixed bayonets would have looked better. We had movie films taken of our march over the mountains and they are showing already. They are only short but quite good …*

Yes darling, it's all very nice and a wonderful life. We get split up at night in the towns and are sleeping in schools and halls and even boarding houses … always on the floor, but are quite comfortable.
[Date indecipherable] 1940

Appearance was important for the soldiers, especially as the press always accompanied the marches. Photographs and films showed rifles and fixed bayonets gleaming in the sun. The 34-pound load carried by every recruit included a rifle, bayonet, web equipment and haversack. Inside the haversack were the essentials: a groundsheet, cardigan, hold-all, towel, spare socks, gloves, mess tin, plate, knife, fork and spoon. Each soldier also had to carry a respirator on his chest, in case of poison gas.

Understandably none of the darker side of war was publicised on the marches. Patriotism was everything:

> *Just a few more lines to let you know how our march is progressing … Coming through Wentworth Falls, there were women by the roadside with baskets full of wattle sprigs and as each man came past he was given one. They were put on our hats immediately, and it was a really wonderful sight to look right along the lines and see that colourful little sprig of Australia blending with the dark khaki …*
>
> *Three other NCOs and myself were fortunate enough to be the guests of the Family Hotel; in fact it was quite a shock to be wakened this morning at 7 o'clock by a charming little maid. However, tomorrow morning we move off once again, so will be back to reality again.*
> *[Date indecipherable] 1940*

Soon the march to Bathurst was over. On arrival at Glanmire Camp the men found spacious, modern facilities, a step up from the cramped conditions at Ingleburn. John reported that the countryside, where they could practise camouflage and deception skills, was perfectly suitable.

News of the war filtered through. France had now fallen; Britain looked even shakier. The thousands of newly trained recruits were keen to 'stop the rot', anxious to be overseas where the real action was.

Private Les Clothier was one such recruit. Though he risked punishment in keeping a diary—there was an Intelligence risk—he doggedly entered his thoughts and actions between 1940 and 1945. The boys called it the 'dixie' when asking him how his diary was going.[6]

John got to know Clothier well—they were in the same platoon. He was a smart young fellow with a bright personality and a great sense of humour— 'life of the party'. He gave the benefit of his perseverance to future generations, with meticulous diary notes that gave simple sketches of life as an ordinary soldier. One of Clothier's earliest entries on 17 October 1940, a few days before departing Australia, showed the pace of training: early morning parade in full dress, inspection, battalion drill, squad drill, fitting of equipment, 8-kilometre (5-mile) cross-country jaunt and jumping fences.[7]

As a country boy who had faced the bush alone, John found the more arduous activities easier than some of the city boys who 'had never been bitten by an ant and didn't know what to look for'. It is possible that his solid bushcraft experience was one reason for John's early promotion to Lance Corporal, the first rise in seniority as a non-commissioned officer (NCO).

As a prerequisite for this rise in rank John had attended a two-week training course near Campbelltown, about 55 kilometres (35 miles) south of Sydney, mainly with other GPS boys. They had been selected as most of them had had some basic form of military training as cadets. However, having left school early, John had not received any such benefit and knew far less about military matters. One day this became obvious.

While the trainee NCOs were being shown how to use a Bren gun, they were warned to take great care. These submachine guns had intricate internal parts that came from England. They could not be replaced easily. Much to John's horror he fumbled with a dismantled gun, which fell in the long grass. The next hour was spent searching, after 'this bloody Murray dropped it'.

In a letter to his mother from Bathurst soon after, John did not refer to his faux pas, but emphasised personal development as one important side benefit of his training. Hoping that she would see much that was good in his decision to join up, he highlighted the advantages it gave to someone like him, someone with little formal education:

As soon as we got back from our leave our advanced training started ... It's what we've all been waiting for ... Now, although there are set principles and certain rules of procedure, it's really more up to the individual and a very good test of qualities of leadership.

Every night now we go out into the hills and carry out exercises ... after each stunt we all gather round our officers and smoke and argue about the various points which might have been improved upon. Really, I think that this is the reason why the Australians are generally good soldiers; the opinion of any private is listened to and discussed when we are out like that, and the formality of the parade ground is practically forgotten. Of course, that is really what gives men confidence in their leaders ...

All the NCOs get lectures at night—at least on most nights— and we have to take notes and do a lot of study ... The lectures are also attended by all the officers and generally Col Burrows

comes along and adds a few remarks which are generally of great value. An NCO these days really has to know everything if he wants to get on at all, and not only Infantry work; it is so often that other units are attached with supporting weapons of various types that one has to know their work also ...
[Undated] 1940

Now that his mother was married to Charlie Glanville, John was not sure how much her financial situation had changed, though he guessed it was not rosy. Always concerned about her welfare, he continued to send her money, which he begged her to use for her own needs.

The reason for his attentiveness, he later conceded, undoubtedly lay in his remarkably unusual childhood, some details of which had been divulged only three years earlier, after his father's death and Peter's meeting on the beach with his mother.

His mother had coped for so long alone. He would do everything in his power to support her, and make her proud: 'There was nothing that could happen, that could be said or dug up from the past, which would have changed my views of Mother. Margie said the same thing.'

Soon the closeness between mother and son was to be interrupted. Though John had spent more than six years working on his father's property, it was his mother's Sydney residence that was home. With the time for departure drawing close, his mother arranged a small farewell party there. A feeling of gut-wrenching nervousness threatened John's composure as he opened the small gifts from family and friends. Was he really leaving his home and country?

And then, suddenly, it was goodbye. More and more young men were saying farewell to their families all around Australia. It wasn't easy, as departures were so constrained. Stiff upper lip, no crying, no fuss:

Your sweet letters arrived today and I read and re-read them dear, they were wonderful. Saying goodbye was the worst thing I have ever been through, darling; I realise now that I have not really faced much before ... I felt just like a little boy again, very small and helpless and it took me hours to adjust myself. I'll even make this confession to you dear ... I went back into the empty house and just wandered around aimlessly for about half an hour looking at pictures, picking up books and opening the piano; I even knelt down in the drawing room and said a prayer; strange thing for me to do actually, but you must know how I felt.

At North Sydney, I met Ken [Ken Forrester, a friend and fellow recruit] in the car and I just put my gear in, got in myself and neither of us spoke until we got right into town. He felt just the same.

The party on Friday night was marvellous, the first I have ever had like that. And it made it nicer still to have the little gathering of old friends. Wonderful of you to get me the watch, dear, but you must promise me to use the money you will receive each week for your own comfort; it will give us both pleasure and comfort if you do that.

Somehow I think that we leave here next Tuesday and go on board ship Tuesday night and perhaps sail on Wednesday. There will be 6000 of us on board and as to our destination, well we can only speculate. And what speculation it is. Rumours are just flying around the camp all day. It's Kenya today, India tomorrow, etc ... we are having all sorts of pre-embarkation stunts, packing all our gear in the correct manner and learning how to do all sorts of things ...
[Date indecipherable] 1940

The departure of John's battalion (along with his entire division) was expected around 13 October. While an unexplained delay did not not allow another reunion with his mother, it gave John the opportunity to provide her with some last minute information:

Just a hurried note dear, to let you know we had our sailing date put back for about a week ... Our outgoing mail has been held up so I'm taking the chance of Ken posting this in town tomorrow ...

Darling, the watch is wonderful, and now I've got it in a proper covered wrist strap ... All the parcels arrived and thanks so much for sending them. I now have everything I want, plenty of woollens and lately we have been issued with khaki shirts, cotton underclothing and long sox, and soon will be issued with shorts.

For the last 24 hours, I have been on Brigade Guard at the entrance to the camp …That duty finished at five tonight and I was just feeling like bed when orders came through for me to take my accordion and play some numbers in an open air concert held in the camp … I played three times and it's a funny feeling standing up on the back of a truck under a light with 1000 or more soldiers gathered all round.

Last week I was a bit lucky … Lieutenant McMaster (of 'Dalkeith'), the Brigadier's aide-de-camp … asked me if I would assist at the dance … Next day I was at the Brigade again and Mr McMaster paraded me before the Brigadier. The old Brig was very nice and thanked me very much for doing a generous service and said they remembered those things … Anyhow, he ought to remember my name—it's the same as his [Brigadier John Murray] which is quite handy!

Wonderful of Ruth to say she'd write. I'd simply love that; she's such a sweet kid. I'll settle down and write to everyone soon, I just can't yet. Things are too unsettled at present.[8]
[Undated] 1940

Parades, photos, gifts, farewell dances and concerts. There was an upbeat mood to John's letters, a strong current of anticipation. Excitement and a good dose of unreality spread through the crowds of young recruits as they waited. Most of them thought of their trip overseas as an adventure— seeing places they had never seen before and having a merry old time. One of them stated what many were thinking: 'I was frightened the war would be over before I got there'.[9] Being sports-minded, many thought they would benefit in more ways than one—plenty of action and lots of fun as well.[10]

Singsongs at Bathurst were popular. It seemed there would be time for singing and buffoonery on the ship also. Colonel Burrows had seen to that: 'Murray—your squeeze-box. What are you doing with that? You're not leaving that at home. From now on it belongs to the battalion. It's yours of course, but it's battalion stores now. We'll transport it for you and make sure it's handled properly. But of course you will play for the troops.'[11]

John was pleased. By that time he had completed a stint of professional training. While in Broken Hill, by chance he had come across the inspiring accordion player Arthur Bourne. Lessons with the master resulted in learning 'all the tricks and techniques'. Though he was unaware of it then, John would be invited to join the Regimental Band in the Middle East—a thrilling acknowledgement of his musical efforts.

For now, John was more than happy to obey Lieutenant Colonel Burrows; his accordion represented a link with home. He would be nervous but honoured to entertain his fellow recruits, especially on board what was reputed to be 'the second largest ship afloat'—one of the world's greatest ships: 'The *Queen Mary* was waiting to take us on the first stage of our great adventure.'[12]

Chapter Seven

Getting started

By the end of 1940, few Australians had been in action and the Australian homeland had not been touched directly by war ... In the Middle East, however, the AIF divisions were preparing for action ... Australia's relative insulation ... would not last into 1941.

—Penglase & Horner, 1992[1]

THE MEN OF the 2/13th Battalion set off on their final march on 19 October 1940, out of the Bathurst camp to the train station—eager young men bound for Sydney, taking their last look at brown paddocks, old wooden fences and straggly gum trees.

On their way they paid ninepence in advance, for a meal of one pie and a cup of coffee at Mount Victoria Station. When the train ploughed straight through the stop, there were howls of outrage. An official explanation for the blunder was not offered. Throughout the years to follow, 'What about our bloody pies?' and 'Where's our bloody ninepence?' became stock questions at any get-together, resulting in loud guffaws. Play-acting united the members of the battalion even more closely.

The dawn of 20 October 1940 was fine and clear. Over 6000 men were now aboard the *Queen Mary*—formerly a glamorous cruise ship for the wealthy, recently converted to a troop ship. John's battalion made up about 1000 of those aboard. The *Queen Mary* was just one of a convoy of three

The *Queen Mary*, a cruise ship converted into a troop transporter.

immense vessels, ready to accept the entire 7th Division from various ports of call along the coast of Australia.

Crowds lined the harbour foreshores and hundreds of small craft were gathered on the harbour to wish them godspeed with whistle blasts and frantic waving. But even this last link with Australia was fading fast.

As the convoy slowly followed its escort HMAS *Perth* towards the open sea, John felt a kind of inner turbulence. There were few who were not feeling tug-of-war emotions. Private Les Clothier wrote in his diary, 'It was blowing a bit, and at 11.30 am we lost sight of land.'[2] The sergeant of 11 Platoon, G.H. (Tim) Fearnside, felt that the *Queen Mary* had reached the Heads too quickly. Suddenly they could see only the 'blue infinity'. Beyond the ocean lay 'high adventure, foreign climes, excitement and fear and glory and death'.[3]

Though John was keen to absorb new information, he soon learned that much of it was not transferable. Every recruit received instructions on what could be included in outgoing mail. All letters were 'sanitised'. The list of banned subjects was as endless as the ocean: names, places, times, personalities, leadership qualities, weapon performance. Each of their letters was read and signed by a senior officer. Then a stamp was clearly pressed on the envelope: 'Passed by Censor'.

One of the few ways to give confidential information to family or lovers was to 'spirit it away' with someone returning to Australia:

I hope this reaches you safely, as I'm not sending it through the proper channels; one of the crew of the Queen Mary *is going to post it in Sydney when the ship returns …*

Soon after leaving Fremantle the weather gradually got tropical. Yesterday we crossed the equator and are now heading straight to Bombay … We have been issued with textbooks on Hebrew and Arabic so it's possible we may be going to Palestine afterwards … Life on board is very happy, there is plenty of drill and physical culture and all sorts of lectures, but with so many men confined together there is also trouble at times. There are wet canteens and lots of men get very drunk—there was a pretty serious riot the other day and three or four officers and men were lucky they weren't killed or thrown overboard …

The Perth *left us the other day with quite a little ceremony. The troop ships got one behind the other, and then the* Perth *came racing back past us with a band playing and all the naval ratings lining the decks in their white uniforms and holding their caps above their heads and cheering. I'll never forget the sight …*

When you reply to this, don't let on that you know where we are or that I have told you these things; there could be trouble from it. All our mail is censored by our platoon commander and naturally he would never let this letter go …

Have you been receiving the allotment of one guinea per week yet? That worries me quite a lot … When I get my two stripes I'll make it more straight away, and don't forget I'll also be very worried if I thought you were not using it.

Hope you are well, darling and happy and never worry about me; remember that I'm coming back to you bigger and better than ever, and I know that you're thinking of me just as I am of you and all the family.
October, 1940

On 4 November 1940, two weeks and a day after departure from Australia, the *Queen Mary* anchored at Bombay. Before disembarkation, the troops were reminded of the lecture they had received about India—the currency, the religions, the dress and language. Once on land John was mesmerised

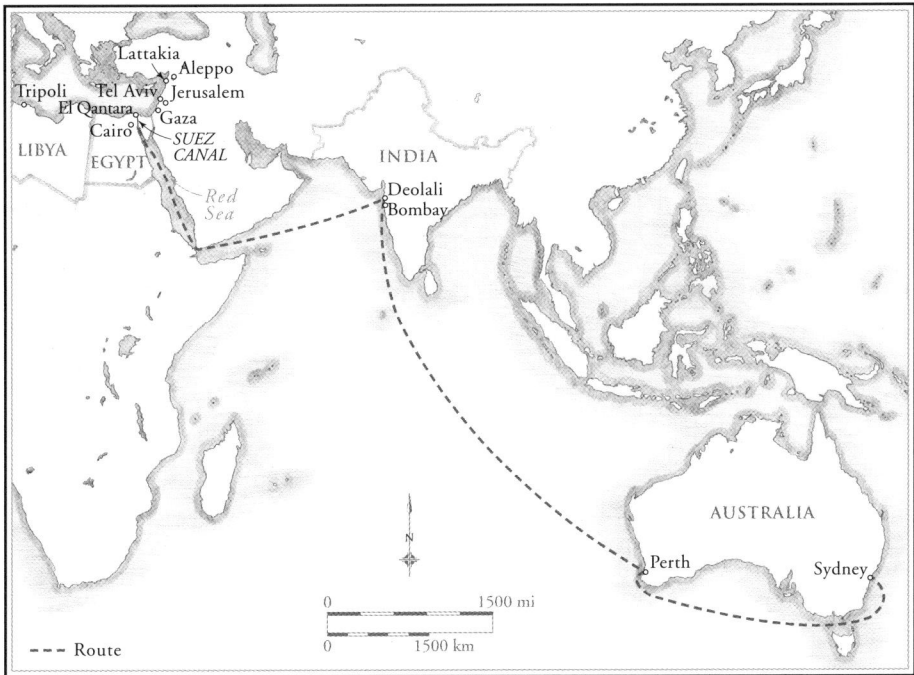

Route taken by the 2/13th Battalion from Australia to the Middle East,
20 October–25 November 1940.

by the contrasts: the palatial white buildings, unusual tramcars, pantaloons,
brilliantly coloured saris and hawkers selling their wares.

After a short time in Bombay the battalion headed for their camp
about 200 kilometres (125 miles) north-east, in Indian Army trains with
spartan carriages that 'you could really pack everyone into'. Though it
was a six-hour trip, not many of the men slept; they preferred to fool
around with cards or mouth organs or be entertained. 'Within the train,
Cpl. John Murray's accordion was never silent; 11 Platoon could be heard
singing throughout the whole journey.'[4]

The men were surprised when they arrived at the Deolali military camp.
John saw it as 'an old established English barracks' but with striking
differences: long native huts with woven palm-mat walls and earthen
floors; thatched roofs, *punkahs* (palm-leaf fans) and Indian cooks wearing
turbans. Though the facilities were generally rather primitive, there were
luxurious compensations and unusual diversions: Indian batmen would
clean boots, wash and iron clothes and bring shaving water to the door,

all for payment of just a few annas (cents); and hawkers, jugglers and acrobats seemed to materialise from nowhere each day to make some extra money.[5]

Once the arrival procedures at the camp were complete there was little to do, so John asked his platoon sergeant, Tim Fearnside, if he could 'disappear for a couple of days'. He quickly departed with 'a bit of tucker, a bit of gear and a few rupees', riding a bike out through the villages up into the cool of the hills, 610 metres (2000 feet) above sea level.

There was one encounter he would never forget. Silence except for the sharp sound of the wheels against the dirt—then the chatter of a small community, dogs barking. With smiling, arm-waving, head-shaking and nodding he managed to communicate with the surprised villagers, whom he found to be gracious, generous and kind-hearted. When he saw an elder with a shiny drinking utensil, probably handmade with furnace and anvil, John offered him a large amount of money for it. It has always sat on his bookcase. 'I have treasured that always.'

On the last day a church parade was held at Deolali, in the Garrison Church. Inside, John gazed at the stained-glass images of Christ and the cross, so familiar yet so far away from home. For no apparent reason he felt close to tears. He swallowed hard when he heard the old English regimental chaplain's soft, consoling words: 'Please remember the "Soldier's Prayer" throughout the war. It will always be there to give you solace':

Lord I will be busy this day. If I forget thee, please remember me.

Despite his mother's strict routine for her children to kneel for prayers before bed, John's religion was a practical one: influenced by the wide open spaces of the outback rather than the Church of England religion of his upbringing. He could therefore not understand the surge of emotion or why the stark message of the chaplain's prayer made him shiver. He always remembered the words exactly, but was puzzled by their effect. Was it homesickness, the lofty architecture of the Garrison Church, the straightforward plea to God, the acknowledgement that solace would indeed be required? He was overwhelmed by the simplicity, the trust and the implication of a demanding future.

The next evening the troops left their camp in the hills, travelled overnight by train and arrived in Bombay at dawn. Leave was granted to spend time in the city before their departure. Too curious to obey the warning to keep away from Grant Road, most of them rushed down to see what all the fuss was about. John was not prepared for what he saw there. 'I felt quite sick.' There were women in cages. To him it was abhorrent; he was shocked by the degradation—'to be able to walk along, go in and point to the one you wanted'.

The hour of departure, impressed on all, came with a rush; all soldiers were impressively punctual in reporting back. Eight days after their landing in Bombay they were about to set off again. Early in the afternoon of 12 November 1940 the *Christian Huygens*, part of a convoy of eleven troop ships, set sail.

As the convoy ploughed through the Indian Ocean, the reality of war became more apparent. Daily air-raid drills, lifebelts and steel helmets were compulsory and the ship was blacked out at night. The men received warnings to be prepared for action as they approached the Red Sea; air raids launched from Italian bases in North-East Africa were a strong possibility.

Though apprehensive, John was ready for adventure. One soldier observed: 'Nearly all of us are silly enough to hope that we will see a bit of action soon, a wish that no doubt will alter once we do.'[6] Private Les Clothier expected 'at least one air raid'.[7] Like Clothier, many of the men were disappointed when no bombs were dropped.

Once the convoy reached Port Tewfik waiting to enter the Suez Canal, hawkers in rowing boats appeared in their dozens, moving from ship to ship angling for sales as the vessels anchored. Their selling antics provided good practice for the haggling techniques the men would soon require on leave.

A few days later, halfway along the Canal, they disembarked at El Qantara, the departure point for the next leg of their journey, this time by rail. On 26 November, John clambered into one of many cattle trucks forming part of a train. He could hear animals bleating as they rattled through the Sinai Desert towards Palestine.

The dusty desert, spotted with the odd gum tree, was soon replaced by fields of crops surrounded by prickly-pear hedges, as the land became more fertile on their approach to Gaza.

The 2/13th's first camp was situated a few miles north of the famous Gaza Ridge. The area had been captured from the Turks in World War I, largely by two regiments of the 4th Australian Light Horse Brigade. The camp itself was a suitable base for desert training, separated from the sea as it was by a sandy belt, varying from 1.6 to 4.8 kilometres (1 to 3 miles) wide. There was not a tree in sight.

John wrote to his mother within days of arriving:

> *I received three letters from you yesterday and one from Ruth ...*
> *It was marvellous to hear from you dear and your little bit of*
> *news ... The trip was wonderful Mother. We saw some wonderful*
> *sights in India and also some horrible ones; that country certainly*
> *has two extremes in riches and poverty ...*
>
> *As this letter is censored I can't mention names of places and*
> *routes taken, but we are now in Palestine ... Charlie would be*
> *terribly interested as it's practically certain that we are training on*
> *ground he knew quite well.*
>
> *We've had so many changes in the last month and seen so many*
> *strange things that we could be sent anywhere at all now and settle*
> *down quite quickly. There is no doubt about Australians getting*
> *used to things quickly, after only an hour or two of changing money*
> *one could hear arguing and haggling of prices in an altogether*
> *strange currency; and some of it was as good as a circus ...*
>
> *Ruth wrote me a beautiful letter, one I'll always remember;*
> *what a sweet girl she really is; I must write to her soon ...*
> *Congratulate Charlie for me. I bet he looks well with a couple of*
> *stripes up ... Although promotion may be slow, I'll promise you*
> *as I have before that I'll do my best to get on and if I don't it will*
> *not be for the want of ambition.*
> *29 November 1940*

Soon the training marches began, tough and tiring for the unfit men after their long sea voyage. While they quickly regained fitness, nothing could hide the fact that the troops had little equipment. Their scarce supply had to be shared between companies.

Sentries kept a close eye on all weapons through the night and even chained the rifles to tent poles in an attempt to prevent pilfering by the Arabs. The kids also had to be watched. Stolen equipment fetched a good price in Tel Aviv.

The men eventually settled into the tedious training regime after 'the wise officers' introduced sport and other diversions. While rugby was a favourite for John, he was also interested in high jump, long jump and shot putt. Ridicule at a competition introduced for 'the best-dressed garden' soon changed to good-humoured rivalry when all platoons joined the fun. The winners, 13 Platoon, C Company, were dubbed 'Chilton's Carnations', named after the Company Commander, Captain Harry Chilton. 'The camp is being turned into a Botanical Garden,' observed Les Clothier.[8]

As relief from training, the men always had something to look forward to: leave. It was granted in small batches. Tel Aviv was the most popular destination, where cafés provided a good meal with wine or beer, and occasionally even a three-piece orchestra. Some leave-takers headed for the 'holier' destinations of Jerusalem and Jericho because they were reminders of Sunday school bible classes, treasure troves of history.

Back in the camp, entertainment at night—films or a visit from the Palestine Symphony Orchestra—kept boredom at bay. Some of the musicians, fugitives from Hitler's racial 'purification', provided bleak reminders of the war in Europe.[9]

Christmas was a challenge. Seated in the open air, the men were served by their officers with the traditional festive dinner of roast turkey, vegetables and plum pudding. When the parcels from home were opened, attacks of homesickness became painfully obvious, but were quickly overcome with boisterous joking. One comic interrupted a formal speech about loyalty and commitment made by a visiting government minister. 'Australia is behind you,' the politician encouraged. 'Yeah—6000 miles,' came the wisecrack.

It was now New Year 1941 in Palestine. Exciting news for the men filtered through during the month of January. The British troops in North Africa had decimated many Italian strongholds, with the Australian 6th Division infantry battalions in the vanguard. By 22 January 1941, Tobruk Harbour was in Allied hands. On its own the Australian division had taken approximately 25,000 prisoners.

On 3 February 1941, Hitler issued orders for German support to be rushed to North Africa. He was incensed by the humiliating defeat of the Italian Army. However, it was well known that the Italian soldiers had been at a disadvantage in the desert. Their tanks and armoured vehicles were light, their engines underpowered and their artillery left over from World War I.

To make matters worse, they'd had to face the most frightening of weapons—the bayonet. As the Aussies charged with their gleaming steel weapons the Italians surrendered in their thousands, or 'yelling and screaming for mercy … took off in the opposite direction'.[10]

When the 2/13th first heard about the 6th Division's victories in North Africa there was real concern that the desert war would fold up, leaving them with garrison duties only. While the jubilant 6th prepared to defend the newly won territory in Libya, the 7th continued what seemed by now to be their never-ending training in Palestine.

Even more frustrating was a major reorganisation of the AIF 20th Brigade. From early 1941 John's brigade was absorbed into the newly formed 9th Division under Major General Leslie Morshead's command. For a while all sense of unity was gone. The men soon realised, however, that they had an excellent leader. Morshead's military credentials were impeccable; he had fought on Anzac Beach at Gallipoli and led his troops into the trenches at Flanders.

While Morshead was determined to train the newly formed brigade afresh and re-establish morale, there remained a constant bugbear. Britain had not been able to supply the necessary numbers of weapons since the loss of most of their army's equipment in the evacuation of Dunkirk, back in May 1940. The British armaments industry was totally overwhelmed; factories were unable to keep up with demand.

John tried to keep up the regular correspondence with his mother, though with the increased Morshead-driven activity, Christmas 1940 and the New Year seemed to have come and gone in a flash:

> *Last week I received a lovely parcel from you, Xmas pudding and biscuits, etc, it was a very nice parcel, Mother, and thanks so much. Those home-cooked things made me very homesick for a while.*
>
> *The CWA at Burren Junction sent me another gift of a beautiful silver 'identity' disc and silver chain, with my name, number and religion, etc, stamped on it. A very nice gift indeed and also came at a time when I'd just lost my 'army issue' disc.*
>
> *Heavens! How I would love to be home again! We really have never appreciated Australia and just what it means to us. It's very necessary, I think, to see other countries to appreciate just how lucky we really are to have a home in Australia ...*
>
> *I find it very interesting. For some it has been for the better, it has developed individuality and initiative; others of course are just like lost sheep and have to be led about all the time ... So many of these chaps will never settle down if they get back after a few years of this show.*

Margie wrote me a sweet letter and sent snaps of Sueanne [sic]; that kid has certainly grown and must be very charming. So nice Marg has her own flat and little home now where she can entertain her friends and adjust herself properly.

Life is just the same with me, dear, I'm very well and happy and trying to get the best out of life. So glad you're going to DY [Dee Why]. I'm looking forward to a good holiday there when I get back.

In the same letter John referred to his mother's caution about his personal life. It was clear that she concerned herself with much more than his military activities. Dutifully John thanked her for the advice but kept discussion of personal matters to a minimum:

Received your letter concerning the plans for future marriage; don't worry dear, everything is well under control, but nevertheless I'm glad you mentioned it as there's no doubt that it is quite easy to write things when over here that one would never mean at home. It would no doubt be easy, as you say, to make a difficult situation for one to meet on arriving back home again.

I'm writing this sitting at a deal table in a big tent ... A full moon came up over the hills tonight and it was a beautiful sight. There is a little village very close and one can hear all sorts of mysterious sounds at night coming from there; donkeys braying and dogs howling, etc—all very weird. The moon is very bright here, everything is just like day and it makes guard work at night much easier ...

Moving around, one often picks up odd pieces of pottery with strange carvings and designs and it's hard to think just how old some of them may be.
2 February 1941

John's continuing education on matters Palestinian would soon be summarily cut short. The bush telegraph was humming with the role the men were about to adopt. The most persistent rumour was that the

20th Brigade would travel to Libya to support the 6th Division as an Occupation Force.

It was around this time that things started to go horribly wrong for the victorious Australian 6th Division. When the Germans headed towards Greece to support the disastrous Italian invasion there, Churchill promised to defend Greece, requesting Australian support.

Only three weeks after their stunningly successful North African campaign, the bombshell was dropped: the 6th learned they were to leave Libya to go to Greece, while a greater part of the 9th Division was warned to be prepared to move within twenty-four hours from Palestine to North Africa to replace them.[11] The 2/13th had no idea of the background machinations. John merely felt excitement, along with the others. No more training; action at last. Elated by the thought of involvement, the men were 'chafing at the bit'.

Menzies had apparently agreed to Churchill's plan, ignoring the advice of General Blamey, the Commander-in-Chief of the Australian Military Forces, who strongly counselled against it and, like the Australian War Cabinet, had serious reservations.[12] The decision, 'a controversial piece of Churchillian strategy', was considered by many to be a disastrous miscalculation.[13] Unbelievably, while the 6th Division was sailing north to Greece, German troops were landing, unopposed, in Libya.

The enemy ships had chosen a suitably covert passage. At the beginning of February 1941, they had sailed from Italy to France and then across the Mediterranean to French-controlled Algeria in Africa. All the while they flew French flags provided by German-dominated France, hugging the coast until they reached Tripoli, about 1050 kilometres (650 miles) west of Tobruk.

General Erwin Rommel arrived to take command of his men on 12 February. He was greeted by an eager, highly trained, battle-hardened contingent, ready for immediate action.

No one had predicted these moves. As late as 23 February 1941, even after the Germans had landed in North Africa, an Allied report indicated that the enemy would not be advancing and that their major efforts would probably continue to be made from the air![14] General Wavell, the British Commander-in-Chief of the Middle East, considered a German expedition to Africa 'most unlikely'.[15]

Circumstances proved this Allied assessment of enemy intentions disastrously wrong. From February to March the British Navy was working tirelessly to ferry troops and equipment to Greece. With all their attention and covering air support concentrated on this exercise, the German flotilla was able to slip through to Tripoli undetected. They were eager to begin their eastward advance.

It was 27 February 1941. Reveille was at 6 am.

There was great anticipation, noisy chatter and the 'usual mucking about' as the 2/13th prepared to leave their barracks in Palestine to march to Gaza and then continue the long trip across Egypt to Libya.

Morale was high. Because they were the forward unit of the 20th Brigade, expectations were especially buoyed. Without exact knowledge of the part they would play on arrival, they knew nevertheless that the balance of the 9th Division would be following them. Their role would be substantial.

Having crossed the Suez by punt, the men again piled into trains. Till now at every stop children had clamoured around the carriages with outstretched hands: 'Backsheesh!' But the luxuriant growth around the Nile River gradually melded into barren desert, which became 'miles and miles of blank-all'.[16]

The 6th Division had labelled the later arrivals in the Middle East 'deep thinkers', because of their apparent deliberation over entering the war. 'You bludgers should've heard the bugle call in 1939'.[17]

Now, at long last, was the opportunity to vindicate their name, their chance for action.

Chapter Eight

The first deadly experience

IT WAS ASSUMED THAT THE PREVIOUS SUCCESS OF THE
6TH AUSTRALIAN DIVISION IN LIBYA HAD REMOVED ALL
THREAT OF ENEMY IN THAT TERRITORY. INFORMATION ON
ENEMY FORCES IN NORTH AFRICA WAS VAGUE AND THE
MOST FAVOURED RUMOUR AMONG THE TROOPS WAS THAT THE
UNIT WAS ON THE WAY TO TRIPOLI [IN LIBYA], AS PART OF AN
OCCUPATION FORCE.

—Fearnside, 1993[1]

THE 2/13TH HAD now been travelling for almost two days.

By the time the men reached the end of the railway line in Egypt, about 190 kilometres (120 miles) east of the Egyptian–Libyan border, and disembarked in the bitter cold and rain, they were 'wet, miserable and tired'.[2] Their surroundings offered no joy. After a night on hard concrete in filthy barracks with thick layers of dust, they awakened on 1 March 1941 to see even more depressing sights.

The port township of Mersa Matruh had been bombed almost out of existence. Buildings were just shells, the town a mass of ruins. Each soldier struggled with his own emotions as he surveyed the scenes of chaos. Some knew that Mussolini had decided to invade Egypt about six months earlier to wrest control of the Suez from the British. Three months after that invasion, in the successful counter-offensive, it had come to this—devastation on an impressive scale.[3] Others were not aware of the area's recent past, let alone its millennia-old history. Centuries before, Marc Antony and Cleopatra had spent some romantic hours together in this Mediterranean bay, one of the most beautiful in the world.

The men stayed in the ruined town for one night. Trucks then took them into the desert. Their trip over the rest of Egypt to Libya would be slow, with very little variety in the arid countryside. Though the weather was freezing, John was well protected:

> *Don't think I ever mentioned to you before, that the balaclava old Mrs Duff knitted me and also Margie's scarf have up till recently been my most treasured possessions; they have kept me warm always and I can never understand why I've always been without one in the winters outback at home.*
> *March, 1941*

When the men reached Tobruk, in Libya, an almighty sandstorm blotted out the sun. As they sheltered from this *khamsin*, few of them could have predicted that a little over a month later this same place would turn into a fortress, which they would defend for a total of 242 days.

On 6 March the convoy of Australians from the 2/13th travelled in separate units across a wide area, heading through the bleak scrubby country towards Derna, about 130 kilometres (80 miles) west of Tobruk. 'What a laugh,' wrote Les Clothier, who was due to celebrate his 22nd birthday. All he could see were 'Eyetie' planes, tanks and abandoned 'ammo dumps'.[4]

Along the way the Salvage Corps were assiduously collecting Italian equipment—telephones, cable wire, motorcycles, anti-tank weapons and field guns, ammunition, camouflage sheets, tools—and stacking it into enormous heaps. John was lucky enough to find 'a beautiful Italian revolver', its magazine chock-full of sand.

The 2/13th continued to trundle along in their trucks, over the limitless stretches of desert sand. The sameness of the scene had quietened them down; they were weary; spirits were dragging. As they approached Derna something happened that would change their tired ways.

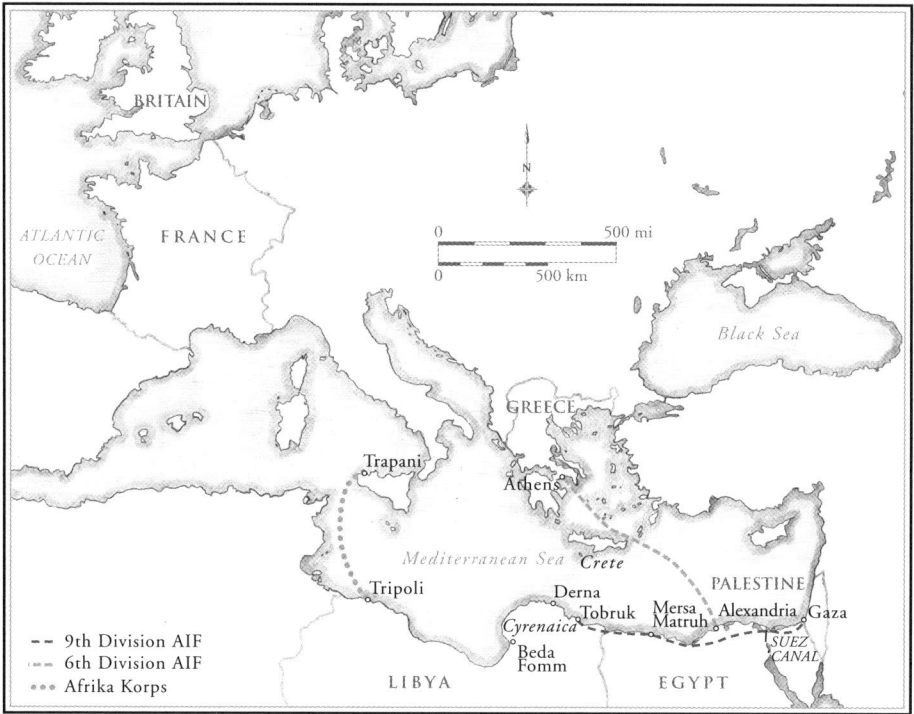

Troop movements February and March 1941.

At precisely 11 am, five Heinkel bombers swung in from the sea, their black swastikas clearly visible, the black-helmeted pilots in view. Taken entirely by surprise, the 2/13th Battalion suffered bombing and machine-gunning from an altitude of not more than 137 metres (450 feet).

The aircraft duty soldiers barely had time to give warning. When they yelled out to stop, thumping the panels at the back of the trucks, the drivers in convoy knew what to do instantly. Men poured out of the trucks, 'one out to the right, one out to the left', running in a fan-like formation as they had been trained to do. 'They knew the ropes. The big thing was to scatter.' The more distance between the men, the less damage one bomb could do. Some of the soldiers had a shot at the enemy planes but in return the whole convoy was strafed with yet more machine-gun fire.

For thirty torturous minutes the bombing continued, directed onto their section of the convoy. Fear, confusion, aggression, defiance. Then the planes droned away. There was a stunned silence. This was the battalion's first taste of war. 'It frightened the hell out of us. It sobered the battalion up a bit.'

Their commander, Colonel Burrows, restored order and then congratulated his men for behaving so commendably. They had the honour of being the first complete AIF unit in World War II to meet the German enemy. Quite unbelievably only two had been killed and one wounded, but the loss of those two soldiers was sad and unnerving. The whole of the battalion was unusually quiet after the sundown funeral at the Derna War Cemetery.

On 8 March, two days after the horrendous strafing, the 2/13th was detached from the main 20th Brigade convoy and put in reserve on the coast for two weeks, near Beda Fomm. Again, they salvaged Italian equipment scattered over several miles of country and put it into dumps.

The content of John's letters to his mother was now quite different. Despite his attempts to be nonchalant, there were hints of the battalion's changed conditions—for the worse:

We have moved from Palestine and are now well and truly in Libya, and under altogether different conditions. Instead of our comfortable tents we are now living in 'dugouts' just like rabbits. Every time we make a move we dig ourselves in at the rate of knots; it's quite fun really making these little underground homes. They are just deep enough to give protection, and they have to be covered carefully over the top so as to be camouflaged from above. When it's completed, you drag your gear in after you and look round with a sigh of satisfaction and wonder how long till the next move.

We are getting 'iron rations' now, which consist of bully beef and biscuits, with an occasional bit of jam or cheese. In the daytime, where possible, we boil our dixies and make our own tea. We make our own hot meals by frying up bully beef, biscuits and perhaps cheese all mashed up together in our dixie lids: quite a dish!

The dust and sand is a bit of a curse. The wind seems to blow from any direction and never seems to stop. What we miss now is sweet stuff to eat; chocolate, etc, anything sweet. Some of the lads in the Tobruk stunt were telling me that when they got there they just dived on cases of condensed milk and other sweet stuff after being a long time on 'iron rations'. There will be some great yarns to tell after we get home.

Received a nice letter from Margie today; first letter I've had for a few weeks. She seems to be doing well and mentioned that J.O. [her husband John Oldham] had left [for the Middle East] …

Only hope you are getting my letters, dear; I know I don't write very many, but I'd hate to think that those I do write are going astray … Did you get my letter telling you that I was only an acting sergeant? I still get letters addressed to Sgt. However, I'm now a full Corporal so that's another step up and makes all the difference in pay. Nearly double a Private's pay, so it will give me a good time next leave.

Well darling, I hope you are happy at Dee Why and getting things back to your own liking again. I'm looking forward to being with you when I get back, soon I hope.
Friday, 14 March 1941

From Beda Fomm John also wrote to his sister Margie, recording his impressions of the Italian defeat. In his letter there was no mention of the violent bombing they had suffered two weeks earlier, nor any reference to impending threats:

There's no doubt … [the 6th Division] gave them an awful thrashing. The wreckage of the Italian army is a sight worth seeing, certainly one that could never be forgotten. I don't think that the wildest accounts you would read in the papers at home could be exaggerated in any way.

God knows just what their whole army equipment would look like if it were lying around wrecked and broken. This was just their 10th army; one of many. It's rather sad and pathetic at times to look at such a mess and realise just what it meant to them and how so many of the individual soldiers feel about it. However much we are told that the majority of them were against Mussolini, they must have had pride in their units to a certain extent. It's the one thing a soldier gradually develops and it helps him to work as one of the team with the rest of the unit.

*In various parts one stumbles on heaps of undelivered letters
from Italy and other parts, and I'd give a lot to be able to
understand their languages ...*
20 March 1941

In reserve the men had the luxury of real conversation, albeit most often
focused on their immediate concerns. They had time to analyse their
position, to talk about the enemy. Soon they were to hear the name
'Rommel' mentioned constantly.

Lieutenant General Erwin Rommel was just forty-nine when he was
appointed to command the German forces in North Africa—a relatively
junior yet highly decorated commander who was an expert on infantry
tactics from World War I. He was apparently an inspiration to his troops,
not afraid to fight at the front. In his own words, a commander 'must try,
above all, to establish personal and comradely contact with his men, but
without giving away an inch of his authority'.[5]

General Wavell had underestimated Rommel; he did not perceive him as
an immediate threat. Lamentably, the general had no knowledge of Rommel's
personality: '... the exceptional drive, the bent for taking risks, the flair for
seizing opportunities and the penchant for acting independently of higher
information that would impel him to exceed his own personal authority'.[6]

When Hitler ordered Rommel to proceed to North Africa, furious that
the Italians had suffered such humiliation there, he also issued instructions
to wait for further advice—to adopt a cautious policy. But Rommel was
impatient, determined to recapture lost territory. Showing a strong streak
of independence, immediately on landing Rommel instructed his troops
to prepare for battle.

Still there was no real action from the Allied High Command in Libya,
based in the eastern province of Cyrenaica. Churchill was assured that no
dangerously large enemy force could have slipped through to North Africa
without the navy knowing.

Rommel's plans gathered momentum. The strength of his forces had
been seriously miscalculated. Though not a large contingent, by comparison
they were better equipped in every way. The Australians of the 9th Division,
in contrast, were seriously underpowered, being short of Bren guns,
mortars and anti-tank weapons. In the days before the Germans attacked,
they had only one Bren gun per Rifle Company.[7]

A slit trench with sandbags on top. To the right are dixies, for eating the bully beef with dry biscuits, and enamel cups.

It was by now quite clear to John that the 2/13th was not to be an occupying force as first rumoured. Instead of being in the relative comfort of a training camp, the men were now hiding in slit trenches. Lightning enemy raids from the air were common. Sometimes the awful sandstorms that swept off the Sahara were so vicious that neither side could make contact. Occasionally raging for days, these *khamsins* blotted out the sky, the sun and the landscape.

As early as 20 March 1941, a report to Allied Headquarters suggested that plans for a German attack were well advanced. With more than 200 German tanks now in Tripoli, it looked as though the campaign could possibly start before the end of the month.[8] But still the Allies were reluctant to believe it, expecting that several more months would be required to train the German soldiers in desert warfare.

When John wrote to his sister on the same day as this report was received, there was a jocular tone in his words:

> *It's five months today since we steamed out the good old Heads, so I'll celebrate by writing to you. Thanks for your letters, darling, and the snaps of Sue-Anne or is it Suzanne?[9] It's great to hear from you from your new address; you're quite settled now it seems*

as the wife of Captain Oldham. Sounds good to me, although I suppose your worries have just started.

If Suzanne can toddle a bit and has already started to swing on the tablecloths and look into paper bags and pull the lids off things, I can just imagine the fun you must be having. For Heaven's sake, don't let my niece do anything that I wouldn't have done at her age. You see, I desire she should be a model baby. See that she does all her howling now so there will be not even a whimper in her system when I get back. She must never scream at night, otherwise you'll find me diving under the house for cover, thinking there's a 'screaming bomb' on its way.

Any point like that I'll let you know from time to time and you could easily jot them down under the heading of 'Mothers' Modern Methods for the Post War Child'. Might be worth a few bob later on.

Anyhow, darling, don't forget to show her my photo now and again (not the one with the powder tin in my hand) and tell her that it is her Uncle John who will be coming home soon with a pocket full of lollies.

We're well into Libya now, darling and conditions are rather different to Palestine ... We're getting quite 'cave men' now. It's all underground living and digging yourself in after every move. Every time a plane comes near, the scene is very much like a rabbit warren when the rabbits have been out feeding and suddenly get a fright. Believe me, it's no disgrace to be the first rabbit down. We live two to a 'dugout' and I'm a little bit afraid that one of these days my mate and I will both get jammed in the hole with our heads down and —es up. Once down underground we wait and hope for the best ...

However, no complaints, Marg ... I'm even on very friendly terms with a village of fleas, which is in some part of the dugout yet to be found. They use me as a sort of playground every time I get settled down for a sleep, and they have some wonderful games, mostly some form of 'hop-scotch'. Anyway, they always seem to be a hop ahead of me when I start doing the chasing.

We often talk about the good old days at Ingleburn and Bathurst and we realise now just how lucky we were when we were there ... There are no canteens now; money is absolutely useless to us. We get an issue of five small packets of English cigarettes once a week and two boxes of matches. Sometimes we pick up a few packets of Italian cigarettes, vile things to smoke, but anything does. If that's all they have to smoke, no wonder they can't fight.

There's lots I'd love to tell you, but the censor would object ... fortunately one's memory can never be censored ...
20 March 1941

In a letter to his mother, John even became philosophical about his army role, able to step back and quietly analyse his function both as section leader and as an observer of the wider military entity:

Just received two wonderful letters from you, darling, have just this minute read them ... think this is the first I've written to you in pencil, but it's a case of have to now. Even the paper and envelopes are some I've picked up from Italian dumps. But I don't suppose you mind very much how they are written.

We've moved again since I wrote last and in our new position we are out of the sand, which is a blessing ...We can see the Mediterranean in the distance and it looks terribly inviting ... It really is an inconvenience to be dirty and to have fleas all over you. I've often been pretty dirty in the bush, but somehow it's different over here. After two or three days without a wash one feels rotten and if we can bathe our bodies once a fortnight then we're doing fairly well.

I've been in charge of nine men for some months now ... These men are actually my responsibility in nearly every way, and believe me some funny things crop up ...They fight under me and I'm also responsible for their protection. The men are such mixtures ... Some are very lazy and it's hard to get them to do their share of work. The trouble is you can't sack a man in the army if he doesn't suit you. A man has to be just about useless before anything can be done about it and even then he generally finishes up with an easy job somewhere away behind everything.

But any way, there's no glory in war, as Charlie always quietly tried to impress on me. He was right in everything he said. A man joins up and enlists with an overwhelming tide of manhood and a great satisfying feeling of confidence that he will do great things. Long months of training gradually level him out so that he just becomes one of the team and then he gets flashes of realisation that he, as a man, is a rather small unit controlled by someone else's brain. It doesn't take him long to realise that he can't just rush out of his trench with a machine gun or a grenade just when he feels like it and play hell with the enemy position. He also learns sooner or later that the army can get along quite well without him and so he sometimes wonders just why, after all, he did join up.

Wars are not won by individual heroism. It is the one big team working together that does the job. There is the one thing common to us all, and that is fear, that is the greatest leveller of all. In an air raid, for instance, when you are out in the open with absolutely no cover or protection, you can sneak a look around and see your leaders, men of high rank, men you look up to and respect, doing exactly the same as you are; trying if possible to get closer to the ground, wishing the ground would swallow them up. You know then that no one man is better than another.

I appreciate your advice on the 'thorough overhaul'. Very often my weaknesses are revealed to me stark naked; I think I know just about all of them, but it's only half doing the job to just know them. But it's hard, Mother, to adjust those same weaknesses at this stage. Nevertheless, it's worth trying and I agree that being honest to oneself is really the main thing …

Don't worry dear about me writing to any girls. The truth is that I've been away nearly 6 months and I've only written about three letters outside the family … So please, don't worry, darling.
[Date indecipherable] 1941

Rommel continued to refine his plans for a three-pronged attack: retaking the occupied areas in Libya, occupying northern Egypt and seizing the Suez Canal. Before the Allies had a chance to recover from the Greek campaign, he would begin his offensive—no later than 8 May 1941.

For the commander of the 9th Division, any imminent attack raised grave concerns, especially about the paltry numbers of weapons available. Major General Morshead was constantly sending urgent messages to the

Allied command in Cyrenaica for more equipment and air support, but getting no results.

The Italian weapons were considered dangerous to use but the armour-starved Australians continued to hoard them, despite instructions to the contrary. When Les Clothier went out shooting with an 'Eyetie' rifle, Captain Gillan 'went mad' and took it from him.[10] By contrast, the Germans were in an enviable position with better armoured cars, ninety Messerschmitt fighters, more than eighty bombers in North Africa—and back-up available in Sicily. The Allies' puny forces, with just thirty aeroplanes, seemed laughable in comparison.

On 17 March Morshead had requested that the un-motorised infantry be withdrawn. They had 'no hitting power at all'.[11] But it was too late. The Germans were already advancing.

In this pathetic state of un-preparedness, John Murray and the rest of the 2/13th Battalion prepared for battle.

Chapter Nine

Face to face
at Er Regima

ER REGIMA WAS A RAILWAY STOP WHERE THE ROAD AND RAIL
FROM BENGHAZI CLIMBED OVER THE STEEP ESCARPMENT ...
HOW WAS IT THAT A BATTALION OF THE NEWLY ORGANISED,
PART-TRAINED AND ILL-EQUIPPED 9TH DIVISION SHOULD
MEET THE VICTORIOUS GERMANS IN SUCH A PLACE?

—Wartime Magazine, Australian War Memorial[1]

THE IMMEDIATE GOAL for Rommel was always Tobruk and its harbour.
He needed it as a base for supplies, to attack two vital targets in Egypt: the
rich Nile Valley and the Suez Canal—the gem of transport, still under
British control.[2] The biggest challenge for the German leader was how to
make this crucial harbour site his.

The Germans had first amassed their army in Tripoli Harbour, over
965 kilometres (600 miles) west of Tobruk. Now relentlessly approaching
along the coast, on his way to Benghazi, Rommel was heartened by how
easily the Allied positions were capitulating. Town after town was falling as
the Germans bombed the roads from 30 metres (100 feet). The Benghazi-
El Agheila road was so severely strafed that it became known as
'Messerschmitt Alley'.

Out-manned and out-gunned, the British abandoned Benghazi on
3 April. Despite instructions from Germany that no operations were

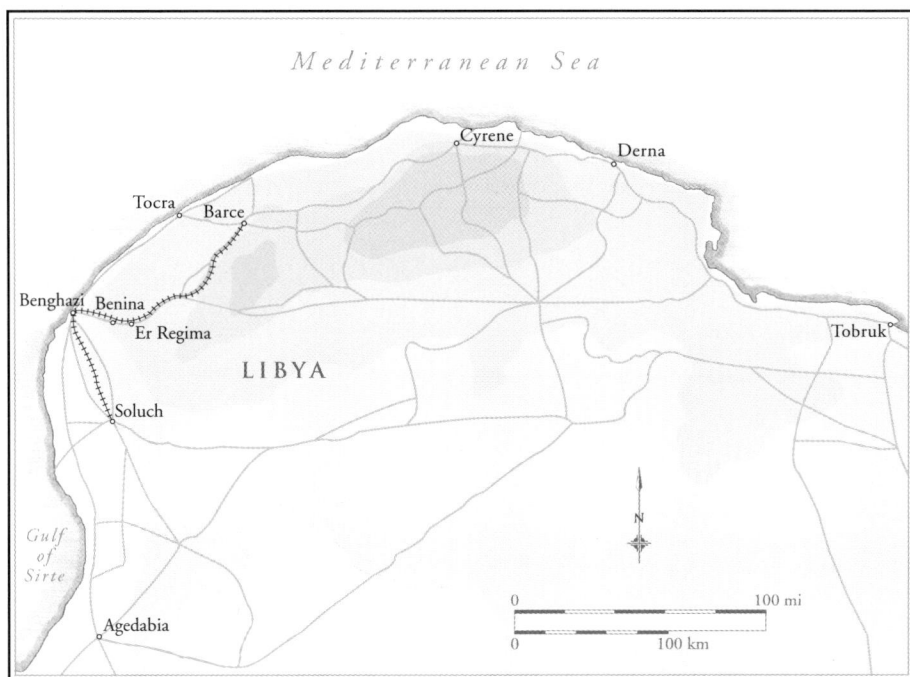

The first ground clash between the AIF and Germany was at Er Regima, on 4 April 1941.

to be undertaken before the end of May, Rommel chose to continue with his advance.[3] After taking Benghazi, he planned to charge inland towards the escarpment—a wall of hard shaly rock that rose some 122 metres (400 feet) feet above the plain, with a 100-kilometre (62-mile) front. This escarpment had important passes, one at Er Regima and one near Tocra, with both leading directly towards the gem he now coveted—Tobruk.

The most pressing job for the 9th Division was to defend the escarpment and its passes in order to deny the enemy access from the plain. The escarpment was to be held by just three Australian battalions. Protecting Er Regima, the main pass and most direct route inland, was the responsibility of the 2/13th Battalion—and that was despite the unit being short by one entire company. There were no reserves to support the action that was developing.[4]

Unbelievably, 'discipline and morale was at its highest'.[5] This was fortuitous, as Er Regima was the first face-to-face confrontation the battalion would face.

With nerves on edge, the men prepared their defensive positions. As they dug in, John was frustrated at the ungiving nature of the ground. With the usual inadequate equipment, practically nil Intelligence and without reinforcements of armoured troops, the men on the thinly held front knew they would be hard-pressed to withstand an all-out German attack.

The atmosphere was tense. The troops prepared with the grim knowledge that they were severely under-manned. Tension mounted by the minute.

On 3 April, air reconnaissance reported a German armoured column approaching from Benghazi, using the railway line as their guide. What John and his men feared soon became quite obvious. That afternoon, from their elevated positions, they could see the Allied vehicles retreating, first in small numbers and then as a torrent, each stirring up enough dust to attract enemy aircraft 'as surely as the smell of blood will attract sharks'.[6]

The German forces were vastly superior. Fortunately the 2/13th did not know exact enemy numbers. The combined Allied forces had less than thirty tanks; Rommel had nearly 300. With the comparatively vast number of German Stuka dive-bombers, Messerschmitt fighters and long-range bombers it soon became obvious that there was little hope of putting up an adequate resistance. Finally it was considered that the odds were too great.

Late on 3 April there was an order for an immediate withdrawal of all battalions except for the 2/13th. The chronic shortage of transport prevented a simultaneous withdrawal. Instructions were for the 2/13th to hold their positions until the following morning, at which time a withdrawal was to be made through one of the wadis—a precipitous, treacherous gully.

The other battalions began the withdrawal using Italian trucks. They lay 'in a jumbled mess of rifles, packs, haversacks, web equipment, greatcoats, tin hats, respirators, rations, tins of petrol and white water cans'.

The *khamsin* blowing that night was the worst the Australians had ever experienced.[7]

Now the 2/13th Battalion was occupying the escarpment on its own. John's senses were on full alert as he waited. On the night of 3 April, Les Clothier noticed that everything was 'as quiet as a graveyard'.[8] Tim Fearnside felt the loneliness. Would the transport arrive in time for them to fall back or would they be forced to fight?

Dawn on 4 April was bright and clear. Already the men could hear the enemy reconnaissance planes observing their prey, close enough to take note of the Aussies' single, three-company battalion responsible for an

11-kilometre (7-mile) front that extended out of sight. The prayed-for withdrawal transport had not arrived. All troops were alerted to prepare for battle.

The first contingent of German vehicles was spotted at about 2 pm, advancing on a wide front with trucks and infantry. By 3.30 pm about 2000 lorried infantry, supported by tanks and armoured cars, were rumbling towards the battalion positions. Two hours later the enemy had established numerous machine-gun posts on the right flank.

Up until 4 April all enemy attacks had been from the air. The Australians waited—jittery and on edge—and prepared as best they could. The first ground clash between the AIF and the Germans was about to begin.

John's B Company was positioned on the eastern flank, to the left of the big, old Turkish fortress at Er Regima, covering a lot of the battalion's front. Part of D Company was situated to the west, positioned in the fortress. The others were 'in bits of trenches and any other available protection', behind rocks. Waiting behind was A Company—in reserve.

Heartbeats increased in tempo with the waiting. And then, without warning, the enemy attacked, mounted in trucks and tanks. The whole area was under almost continuous cross-fire. D Company bore the brunt of the initial assault. Driven back by superior numbers and weaponry, many were captured, many killed. 'Just about a whole platoon was gone.'

Determined, the men of A and B Companies fought on. Though the battle continued for over five hours, there was little hope of victory. Just two companies with no real depth and spread across a wide front faced a vastly stronger enemy force. The enemy pushed them back, metre by metre.[9]

One of the wounded soldiers wrote from hospital about himself and a group of his mates who were cut off at Er Regima: 'We gave it to them for a while, but we had hundreds to deal with and only a handful of us. I got hit with a big shell from a Jerry tank. I had him crippled but the guns still worked—broke my arm in two places.'[10]

This was a common story; bravery in the face of uneven odds. But it was not without purpose. If the 2/13th Battalion had not resisted so strongly the Germans would have taken less time to claim victory. The Australian resistance had prevented the enemy from cutting off the three other retreating battalions while there was still daylight to successfully do so. The 2/13th had given their fellow battalions time to get away.

When the main body of Germans paused to consolidate at nightfall, John and his men hoped that they could grasp their chance for withdrawal and thus survival. Not fully knowing what the enemy was planning, they waited interminably for the trucks to arrive.

When the transport finally rattled in, after 11 pm, the men saw Italian Lancias, 'awful trucks with solid wheels with flat rubber tyres, not pneumatic tyres', driven by Cypriot drivers. They all clambered in—'a terrible jam' to get everyone aboard. 'The plan was obviously being formulated to take us back and put us in Tobruk.'

The road was tortuous. Unable to put on lights for guidance the drivers were under constant threat of attack. They disappeared into the night with their passengers, depleted and dispirited, to begin their tense retreat to Tobruk. The ride was 'as rough as guts'. There were now eighty-two fewer men in the 2/13th Battalion.

As they withdrew, the Aussies felt their frustration level rise to boiling point. Every now and then while retreating along the road in the rattly old vehicles they stopped and emptied out, never sure if the enemy would appear to strafe them. Before each dawn they 'bundled [back] into the trucks and cleared out'.[11]

On 6 April a furious dust storm was blowing. It felt as though the sand was slicing through them in the pitch black as they tentatively settled for the night, scattering out through the desert. It was cold; the soldiers exhausted. In no time those who were sleeping too heavily became immobile mounds. As John swept the sand from his men for safety's sake, he could see clouds of dust away in the distance and hear tanks rolling around. He knew it was the enemy. 'Oh—listen to the bastards.' He wondered what use a service rifle would be against the weapons of a Jerry tank.

Threats lurked everywhere as the men continued struggling towards Tobruk: strafing and bombing, armoured attack and even falling over the vertical sides of deep wadis on the cold, moonless nights.

The night of 7 April was one of the coldest they had experienced. They lay out in the open without protection.

One frustrated 2/13th Battalion digger later wrote in his diary: '... our nerves were ragged ... all the way back from Regima we'd steeled ourselves to action that never came and every soldier knows that the waiting before the attack is worst'.[12]

In general it had been a quick, but staggered getaway for the 9th Division. They all knew how fast the enemy could move. Despite the appalling conditions, the troops still had spirit enough to give various names to the withdrawal: 'The Tobruk Derby' or 'The Benghazi Handicap' were favourites. The latter was the one that stuck.

One event did manage to lift the spirits of every man. When nearing the Tobruk perimeter, they came across a sign that had been painted by the 6th Division back in January, with a picture of a foaming glass and a bottle of Australian beer: 'KEEP GOING—fill up in town. A good drink but bloody hard to get.'

With his victory at Er Regima, Rommel's chase thus far had been almost 100 per cent successful. The one possession still not in German hands was the harbour fortress of Tobruk. Immediately he ordered the port and its surrounds to be encircled and bombarded until he could mount an assault from the south-east.

The German troops were confident of another quick success. They had superior armour, supremacy in the air and a brilliant leader. It was just a matter of time.

Chapter Ten

The siege of
Tobruk begins

IN THE FIRST 18 MONTHS OF THIS WAR HITLER'S ARMOURED
COLUMNS AND AIRCRAFT CARRIED THE SWASTIKA FROM
WARSAW TO NARVIK; FROM AMSTERDAM TO ATHENS; FROM
PARIS TO BENGHAZI.

IN THIS TIME NO LAND FORCE, NO FORTRESS, WITHSTOOD
THEIR ASSAULTS ...

THEN CAME TOBRUK.

—From *Chester Wilmot Reports: Broadcasts that Shaped World War II*[1]

THOUGH JOHN MURRAY was not to know it, 6 April 1941 was to be a
defining date in his military life. As he was struggling through treacherous
countryside in the race to withdraw from Er Regima to Tobruk, a cable
from the British Prime Minister had been placed in front of the High
Command in Cairo. Churchill's orders were precise: 'Hold Tobruk to
the death.'

Major General Morshead had been told that the security of Egypt
depended on the Australians of the 9th Division defending Tobruk.
Under no circumstances should the Germans be allowed to seize this
strategic port for their supplies. Having lost everything in Libya,
Churchill was desperate to hold onto Egypt and the Suez Canal.
This 193-kilometre (120-mile) stretch of water was vital for British

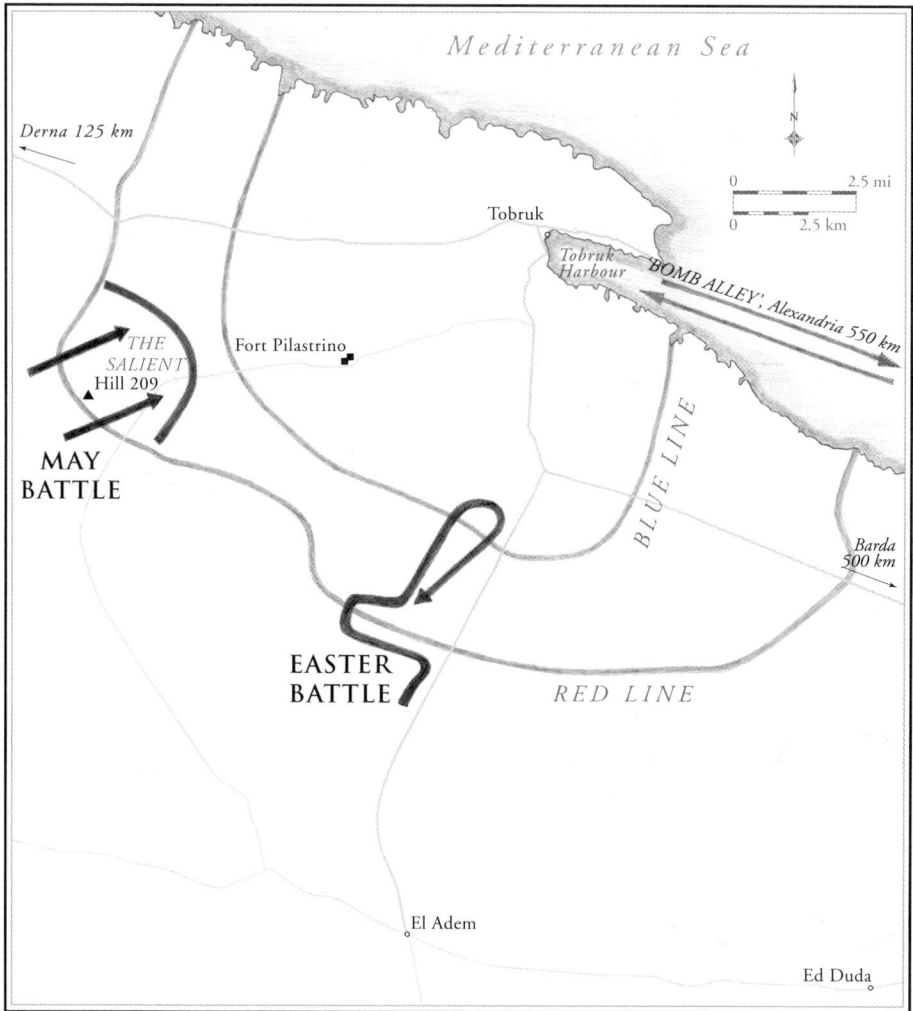

The Easter Battle—the first time the German army had been defeated; the May Battle—
the Germans won 15 square kilometres (6 square miles) of land around Hill 209.

international trade; it cut off thousands of sea miles to the British
dominions of India and beyond.

Morshead quickly became aware of a fact that would be vital in the defence
of this town and harbour. While there were few buildings left standing in the
town itself, thanks to the Italians there was a line of man-made defences
around the perimeter. The outer perimeter was known as the Red Line. Other
defensive lines were built later by the Allies—notably the inner Blue Line.

For military purposes, the defence perimeter of Tobruk could be described as a rough semi-circle, a curve of approximately 45 kilometres (28 miles), with an average distance between the town and the Red Line of about 15 kilometres (9 miles). On the outer edge, right around the perimeter, the Italians had built a deep trench containing concrete-sided weapons pits every 730 metres (800 yards), with zigzagging barbed wire between each one. The pits were capable of holding approximately fourteen men each and were flush to the ground so they could not be detected from the air.[2]

Though most of the area was flat plateau and desert, its eastern and western extremities were marked by sheer cliff walls. Through these ran passes or wadis—deep gorges eroded out of solid rock.

Rising 30 metres (100 feet) out of the desert and located south-west from Tobruk, just inside the perimeter was one of the few hills in the entire area. Ras el Madauuar was an important vantage point that provided a view for miles around. It became known simply as Hill 209.

Tobruk boasted a mix of Allied troops who found themselves together. There were about 24,000 combatants in total to defend the fortress—14,000 of whom were Australian and about 10,000 British.

Australians and the British were in the base area too, which also included Indian troops. The Poles and Czechs—mainly replacement troops—were to arrive later.

While the British supplied limited aircraft, artillery and armoured forces, the Australians provided the bulk of the infantry—foot soldiers with their support teams.

For the Aussies, work to make the perimeter impregnable started immediately. Firstly, after removing tons of sand, they had to reinforce the existing trenches. Then more ditches were dug out of the rocky earth and barbed wire was restored where it was broken.

Booby traps were placed around the pits. Between these and the perimeter two rows of anti-personnel mines were laid. Gunners had to dig in their 25-pounders and camouflage them; signallers ran wires over several hundred kilometres, to link the scattered units; more roadblocks were built. Transport drivers delivered ammunition, food and water to the front line.

As well as new posts for the men on the front line, intermediate posts were dug further back. One of the infantrymen remarked that 'if all the bloody holes' he had dug were placed end to end, he could 'bloody well get back to Australia under cover'.[3]

When work began, the battalion sweated under the sun, with dynamite and pick and shovel, knowing they had limited time. But it was not difficult to get the men to do this job. They were 'fighting mad' after being forced to retreat, when the 6th Division had so recently sealed such a victory: 'All over Tobruk, Australians, stripped to the waist, were digging, scraping holes out of the reluctant earth of Tobruk, holes from which to fight.'[4]

On the same day that the Australians made a start on their work, the Germans began to move in small numbers down El Adem Road with their tanks. The *khamsin* was still blowing. Tension was always at its highest if the enemy approached with the dust as camouflage—as indeed they did as the sun rose on the morning of 10 April. One unit diarist called it 'the filthiest day ever'.[5] Private Les Clothier aptly described the scene: 'What a cow of a country … it's blowing like hell, cold and dusty.'[6]

Unbelievably, Rommel had no knowledge of the perimeter defences the Italians had abandoned. It took some time before he was able to get a map of them. However, he pressed on, eager to begin the attack. Was Rommel following his own advice when he gave instructions for that first assault? 'When an attack is ordered, the men must never get the feeling that their casualties have been calculated in advance according to the laws of probability, for that is the end of all enthusiasm. The soldier must continually receive fresh justification for his confidence, otherwise it is soon lost. He must go into battle easy in mind and with no doubt about the command …'[7]

With his usual energy, Morshead rallied his troops in Tobruk. By now he had won the respect of his men and was confident of receiving their total support. Despite his nickname 'Ming the Merciless', the men looked upon Morshead's organising talents with awe. His instructions to the men were clear: 'There'll be no Dunkirk here … If we should have to get out, we shall fight our way out. There is to be no surrender, no retreat.'[8]

The severity of the situation became obvious when all the nurses were evacuated. They left Tobruk on a moonless night, sailing at full speed through 'Bomb Alley' on their way to Alexandria, on the Egyptian coast.[9]

General Morshead began to concentrate his men. The 45 kilometres (28 miles) of perimeter were taken over by four brigades (three from the 9th Division; one from the 7th). In total, six battalions were assigned to man the front.

The 2/13th Battalion's instructions were to move with the 2/17th to the perimeter section along the El Adem Road, to prepare for an immediate attack by the enemy. This directive was received only a little more than twenty-four hours after the men had completed their retreat from Er Regima.

Without a doubt the German soldiers assumed that they would take their enemy by surprise, with little effort, as they had countless times before, not only in North Africa but also in Europe. As they confidently advanced, they were unaware of an imaginative battle tactic being formulated by the Allies. A sense of exhilaration along with apprehension overtook the Aussies as the intricate planning progressed. Nothing like this had been tried before.

The assault would fall on one of the most sacred days to them all. Good Friday was dawning—though nothing was good about it. The battle that began in a subdued way on that day and continued for four days was reputed to be one of the most memorable battles of the entire Tobruk campaign. It became known as the Easter Battle.

On Easter Friday, 11 April, most of the sporadic tank attacks on the 2/17th Battalion were dealt with. The raging *khamsin* with its swirling dust was slowing down movement. That night a 2/13th patrol successfully repelled German engineers attempting to penetrate the defence line.

Throughout Easter Saturday tension mounted. The enemy infantry were now advancing in large numbers on the approach from El Adem.

Early the following morning, Easter Sunday, enemy vehicles began to shell the forward posts, despite the blinding sand from yet another *khamsin*. Their tanks attacked the perimeter again and again. As evening fell, the 2/13th reported a large force of enemy infantry gathering close to the 2/17th Battalion.

Before attempting the main breakthrough with their tanks, a group of thirty Germans decided to neutralise one of the 2/17th strongholds. A team of just five Aussies answered the enemy attack with a bayonet charge, around 11 pm. Despite receiving horrendous machine-gun wounds, Corporal J.H. Edmondson kept up his bayonet attack, charging and killing at least five Germans. Edmondson died in the early hours of the next morning. For his bravery he posthumously received the first Victoria Cross of World War II.[10]

Midnight was approaching. The sound of 300 enemy vehicles pierced the Easter Sunday night air. The enemy continued their push along El Adem Road into the early hours of Easter Monday.

General Wavell, British Commander-in-Chief of the Middle East, sent a message to Morshead: 'Enemy advance means your isolation by land for time being. Defence of Egypt depends largely on your holding enemy on your front … Am glad that I have at this crisis such stout-hearted and magnificent troops in Tobruk. Am very heartened by what I have heard of their fighting spirit and conduct during these operations. I know I can count on you to hold Tobruk to the end. My best wishes to you all.'[11]

Up until now, all over Europe, when the German tanks approached en masse, the opposing forces would attempt to knock the tanks out with anti-tank guns. But in the total darkness of the early morning, traditional tactics were not followed.

It was 2 am on Easter Monday, 14 April, dark and blowing a gale. Over the next three hours the roar of the German tanks became more and more thunderous. Half an hour before dawn, at 5.20 am, the first armoured vehicles moved through the gaps of the perimeter, successfully made available by the German engineers.

British gunners continued to shell the area while the Aussies put their plan into action—methodically. They had talked about it and practised. The instructions to the Australian infantry, now hidden well in their trenches, were simple: under no circumstances were they to attract the attention of the enemy tanks. *Do not fire.*

And then the tanks were upon them. It took courage. The men had to lie perfectly still and low in their anti-tank trenches as the rumbling enemy machines approached. They lay like dummies in the ditches, being run right over by the deafening monster tanks, praying that the grinding tracks would not pulverize them. Inevitably some of the men were crushed to death.

By 5.45 am, thirty-eight German tanks had run over the crouching Aussies and were three-quarters of a mile inside the perimeter, preparing for the attack on Tobruk itself. They expected the supporting German infantry battalion outside the perimeter to be right behind them.

However, the enemy did not realise that this time there were major differences. The Australian infantry were still hiding in their trenches, ready to rise up and attack the German infantry coming up the rear; and the Allied defences, now waiting on the inner Blue Line, were ready to wipe out the advancing enemy tanks. Having passed the perimeter the tanks would have no infantry support from behind. They had been left 'like shags on a rock'.

The brave action of the Australians in the trenches meant that all members of the 2/13th infantry were now able to deal severely with the hapless Germans approaching as back-up for their tanks.

John Murray joined his mates to carry out the second part of the plan, firing with great precision into the astounded enemy infantry coming up the rear.[12]

There was much talk about it after the event. One artilleryman noted that without infantry support, the enemy were sitting in tanks he could 'bloody well spit through'.[13] They had been mercilessly shot up, knocked out by 25-pounders, attacked 'at point-blank range by indomitable gunners'. Others were left blazing on the field. Some managed to turn around and lurch back to their camp.

It was quite obvious to the dumbfounded Germans that they had been attacked in an unorthodox manner. A captured document written by the commander of a German tank regiment recorded that his unit had gone in with great determination, with one aim: to charge through the enemy and take Tobruk. Facing an exceptionally superior enemy, their plans were torn asunder. The regiment failed in its task, with a total loss of 50 per cent.[14]

The Aussies happily relived the moment many a time in post-activity debriefings. No force had ever matched the Nazi assaults before this rout. Up until now the German blitzkrieg tactics had never failed. One captured German doctor commented to Chester Wilmot, the Australian war correspondent: 'I cannot understand the Australians. In France, Belgium and Poland once the tanks had gone through the soldiers took it for granted that they were beaten. But you Australians are like demons. The tanks go by and your infantry keeps fighting.'[15]

The men were euphoric. At last the enemy 'had to take a step back; they'd got their noses bloodied'. From that day on the Germans were forced to change their tactics.

Some historians have blamed the German defeat on Rommel's personality. A man in a hurry, he stressed to his troops that the Suez Canal was imperative to their success; encirclement of Tobruk was consequently to be completed with utmost speed.[16] Rommel was, at this stage, contravening orders of both the Italian and German High Commands. Moreover, he had launched the attack without proper Intelligence, before his troops were in the correct positions or ready for action.[17] Had the enemy troops possessed more-detailed information about accessibility, they could have caused much more damage. Some parts of the anti-tank ditches were only half a metre (18 inches) deep, much easier to pass.[18] As it was, the attack failed and 254 Germans were taken prisoner.

Rommel's basic error was to underestimate the determination and spunk of his enemy.[19] The Germans were not expecting a well-practised, orderly force who resisted to the end with undeniable morale. They were staggered that these enemy troops would crouch under their tanks and then reappear to attack their infantry.[20] German confidence took a blow.

An enemy commander of a troop of tanks wrote in his diary: 'We cannot understand how we ever managed to get out. It is the general opinion that this was the most severely fought battle of the war ... No German troops have ever had such a bad drubbing as we ... The survivors call this day "Hell of Tobruk" ... thirty-eight tanks went into the third action ... seventeen were shot up, many more were temporarily put out of action.'[21]

The 1941 Easter victory, followed by Churchill's congratulations, gave the Allied troops the boost they so badly needed after their withdrawal from Er Regima. The endorsement was timely. It was needed to get the men through their next challenge—another major battle within a month.

Desperate to capture Tobruk, Rommel was already planning his next assault so that he could complete his dream of a victorious takeover in Egypt.

Even Churchill eventually had to acknowledge his capabilities: 'We have a very daring and skillful opponent against us, and, may I say across the havoc of war, a great General.'[22]

Chapter Eleven

The Rats dig deeper

To my mind, the 9th Division's achievement at Tobruk was not that it held its ground for so long but that it did succeed in repelling two German armoured assaults. I believe the Easter Battle and the May Battle were the first instances in the Second World War of German tank assaults being withstood.

That achievement had incalculable benefits of the future Allied conduct of the whole war, by ... dispelling the dangerous myth of German invincibility.

—Maughan, 1979[1]

The Australians were fired up. The Easter Battle had given them an invaluable gift—renewed confidence. They were less likely to complain now, even though 'Bloody Tobruk' was a constant refrain. However, there was not much time for the Easter victory celebration; little time to recover or relax. While Rommel attended to his troop deployments around the Egyptian frontier and plotted his return, he left it to the Italians to keep up the pressure at Tobruk.

In preparation, Morshead instructed a continual build-up of minefields, day and night, on the Red and Blue Lines. Behind these two lines would be the field guns—anti-tank 25-pounders—deadly at close range. Back further again was to be the mobile reserve. Being in reserve no longer meant 'a spell'. Normal activities such as letter writing were deferred as work was continually carried out on the inner defence line. It meant digging and sleeping during the day and digging and patrolling at night.

Almost immediately Morshead changed wartime definitions: 'defence' became 'offence'. He instructed all men, whatever their responsibilities, to play a part. No one, whatever his role, was to give in. If the enemy happened to get through both the Red and Blue lines, then anyone who could handle a weapon was to tackle them. Morshead's policy became known simply as the 'Offensive Defensive'.

As early as 15 April 1941, the day after the Easter Battle ended, there were renewed attacks on the perimeter. The most sought after vantage point, Hill 209, was the main target. Mostly the enemy's advances were repelled but, convinced that Rommel could turn up unannounced at any moment with more reinforcements, Morshead warned against complacency.

He was right. By late April 1941 Rommel was back with his fortified troops, his main aim being to weaken the entire fortress of Tobruk—on water, on ground and in the sky.

First on Rommel's list was the port. There, enemy air raids were continuous. Increasingly the Allied air defence looked pathetic; the Germans by this time had complete supremacy. Most Allied aircraft had been sent to Greece to assist in the evacuation of the unfortunate troops. As of mid-April the total strength for Tobruk was thirteen Hurricanes, each in action up to three times a day. 'Pilots were shot down, bailed out and went up to fight again next day.'[2]

Something had to be done to counter the devastating enemy assaults now taking place. High-level German bombers were drawing out the Allied anti-aircraft guns situated around the harbour; dive-bombers, sometimes fifty at a time, were then swooping down to machine-gun those defence sites. Diving out of the sun, the enemy planes could sometimes not even be identified.

Urgent plans were immediately drawn up to protect the existing gun sites on the ground. It was decided the enemy had to be confused—by concealment, deception, changes of layout. A camouflage officer masterminded the construction of fake gun positions near the real ones. This ploy worked well; fewer gunners died and less site damage was inflicted.[3]

The ships of the Royal Navy were also increasingly on the alert. The only effective protection was to stay in the harbour for as short a time as possible. At Morshead's urging, they always carried out their missions in the dark: slide into a berth, unload supplies on one side, take in wounded troops on the other, and slip out again, in less than half an hour. The garrison padre often acknowledged the navy crews: 'For what we are about to eat, thank God and the British Fleet.'[4]

Meanwhile, back on the perimeter tension mounted as enemy infantry and guns were concentrated around Hill 209. Morshead gave instructions on 20 April for the Brigade engineers to lay anti-personnel mines over a distance of 3 kilometres (2 miles), especially around the threatened Hill. Work began immediately.

Breaking the stress six days later, a welcome allocation of 'comforts' arrived on 26 April from the 2/13th Ladies' Auxiliary in Australia, to celebrate Anzac Day. 'Better late than never,' the men smiled as they devoured beer, chocolate and tinned fruit.[5] They barely had time to appreciate the luxuries.

Within days, an enemy plane was found to contain alarming Intelligence documents. A single red arrow on a map ran from a village outside the perimeter, through Hill 209, and directly on to Tobruk. There was now no doubt that the German plan was to take the Hill and, from that point, overwhelm the garrison.

From month's end, enemy activity escalated wildly. The campaign of carnage over the following four-day period became known as the May Battle.

The first day of the May Battle, 30 April 1941, saw a successful German assault. Les Clothier wrote about dive-bombers coming over twice, 'thirty at a time'.[6] The enemy artillery attacked the entire 4-kilometre (2.5-mile) length of wire.

One of the members of the 2/24th Battalion commented that a sighting of Jesus Christ would not have surprised any of them at that moment when the thunder of the cannons pierced their ears. 'It was like a bloody fanfare to herald the end of the world.'[7] By 9 o'clock that night the Germans were well inside the perimeter.

From sunrise the next day, 1 May, heavy assaults on the area continued. From his position to the north-east, John could hear the force of the attacks on the 26th Brigade, situated on the high ground. Enemy tanks supported by a large infantry force bombarded the area. The Brigade's 2/24th Battalion was decimated—A, C and D Company posts were overrun and three company commanders captured. All the units Morshead employed in a counter-attack were beaten back.

During the second night there were more heavy air attacks. Twenty-two Stukas dived over Hill 209 with a chilling high-pitched whine until all their bombs had been dropped. 'The dive-bombers are a bloody nuisance,' wrote Les Clothier, with his usual restraint.[8]

From their positions back from the perimeter, John and his mates were being shelled by heavy enemy fire. Action in the Hill area reverberated against a backdrop of dust, noise and machine-gun flashes. John could not get out of his mind the horrific vision of a flamethrower used against the troops of the 18th Brigade. The 'searing flare' was deadly.[9]

By 4 May, Hill 209 was lost. All troops, including the 2/13th, were ordered to withdraw. A victorious Rommel held approximately 10 square kilometres (6 square miles) in the shape of a box, including the highest point of the fortress.

This area became known as the Salient—a 'hot spot' from where the enemy artillery could deliver the Australian infantrymen 'a taste of Hell'.

When the Battalion was withdrawn for a few days and put in reserve, John was able to renew communication with his mother. He mentioned neither the Easter nor the May battles:

> It's weeks since I wrote to you and I know you must have been starting to wonder where I'd got to ... We have been out for a few days' spell from the thick of things so I'll try and catch up with a bit of answering letters.
>
> First of all, darling, thanks so much for the parcels you have sent me. Also, all of the magazines you and Marg have sent have been great and appreciated very much. They manage to get our parcels and mail up to us in the line and you've got no idea just what it means to receive one. If one of us receives a parcel it seems too [letter censored] ... Of course you must know by this just where we are, and in fact have been for some months ...
>
> Morale is really good, and considering we are all at it for weeks at a time, and then out for only a few days' spell before we go in again to relieve someone else, it's really remarkable how the

lads can keep in a good frame of mind. The German is a very different proposition from the Italian and they fight with all the low cunning of a cur. Man to man we are better men; of that I am convinced, as we do not rely so much on the power of our weapons as he does. Strip him of his superiority in armaments and he won't be in the race ...

Today I went down with a few others to the coast and had a swim, which freshened and cleaned me up. While there, I washed my shirt by the good old Indian method of bashing it on the rocks to get the dirt out ...
5 May 1941

In his letters John referred only fleetingly to physical discomforts—the eternal dust and the fleas. Occasionally there was a hint of irritation, presumably in reply to his mother's requests for more information. His humour, evident in earlier letters, appeared less and less frequently:

Yes dear, I realise that I don't give you very much news of value. But there is really very little I can write about, which the censor would allow to go through. You know just where I am and have been for the last three months, as you mentioned Burrows' photo in the papers ... We don't see a great deal of him ... but occasionally he comes around at night to have a look at our positions, and a few words from him do the boys a lot of good.

When in the line we do all our work at night and by day we just lie down in our little bits of dugouts and get what sleep we can. So one thing you must keep in mind which may be some comfort to you is that the only time we may be exposing ourselves is by night, and that is of course your day time at home. So when your night time comes you can feel content that at the most all I'll be doing will be swatting a few flies and trying to get some sleep ...

Shortage of news of what is happening in the outside world is worse here than outback in Australia, and then there are the 'rumour-mongers' who do so much harm with their false stories of relief coming and all that sort of thing that now I won't believe, because if you do you are just bolstered up with hope and left as flat as a pancake.

Ruth's was a very nice letter, lots of news, and she seems very sorry that you have gone so far away to Dee Why as she loved to pop in for a chat. She said Sue-Anne is the sweetest thing, made me quite homesick …Your news of Peter is nice to have and especially about him applying for Mossgiel country. Hope he gets some, it is pretty good country.

A few weeks ago, I got two reinforcements in my section and one of them has been working on Mossgiel for many years, so we have some good talks about the country and the people out there. Quite a lucky break for me, wasn't it? … Of course, these silly old wars just can't go on without losing a few and naturally we are losing our share, but this unit had a very rough spin for a while. However, the spirit is just as good as ever so that's half the battle. One thing I am pleased about; we don't use any low tricks that the Huns do, and eventually they are going to suffer for it.
[Undated] 1941

With Hill 209 now his, Rommel prepared to launch a full-scale final attack. A German diarist had confidently declared at the beginning of the May Battle: 'We intend to take Tobruk.'[10] There was probably not one enemy soldier who did not believe that their success was only a few hours away.

However, the confidence of the Germans was misplaced. Rommel had not counted on the Allies' tenacity and their diabolically clever manoeuvres. A German diarist confirmed that it was a very different war from that in Europe. There were not masses of men and materials; nobody and nothing could be concealed.[11]

With their artillery blazing, the British gunners continually interrupted Rommel's advance. Again and again the men heard of German tanks and the combined Axis infantry turning tail when the British shells landed amongst them.[12]

Not only did the Germans find it impossible to move forward to take the township of Tobruk, they were also hard put just defending Hill 209. During the first two weeks of May, the German gains were gradually taken back by the aggressive Australian counter-attacking. Though many lives were lost, valuable terrain was regained.

Morshead continued to concentrate his efforts in the Hill area, adding even greater capacity with the addition of the 2/1st Pioneers, a combination of infantrymen and engineers. He was always convinced that if Rommel were forced to keep some of his best troops around the Hill, this would weaken the enemy's efforts in Egypt. Of the eight battalions Rommel could use for infantry, more than a third were needed to hold the Salient.

Less than a fortnight after the German victory at Hill 209, the 2/13th Battalion relieved the 2/1st Pioneers—on 13 May. John recalled the whispered warning of the Pioneers as they left. 'Be careful when daylight comes.' At dawn the Germans would get up and shake out their blankets. The casual-looking enemy soldiers were decoys for the Spandau gunners who would fire as soon as the Aussies revealed their positions.

On the morning of 14 May, in utter contempt of the Pioneers, the Germans began their same old trick. They got up and shook out their blankets. But this time the Aussies from the 2/13th were ready. At that instant 'we gave them everything', and according to Les Clothier, it was now 'Fritz' who couldn't move about.[13] 'The next use for many of the blankets was as shrouds.'[14] On the following day, Colonel Burrows was able to report that he had advanced his forward companies another 320 metres (350 yards).

The Germans were furious that they had been taken by surprise like that. That one action started 'the war of all wars'. From then on, John knew the Salient would be 'a rotten tough spot'.

It was clear that the Germans also looked on this area as a rotten tough spot. This ground war was different. The enemy could not use their tanks in the heavily mined territory; nor was their air power much use. During the day the Allied soldiers hid in their trenches, camouflaged from the world; daytime sleeping increased. Attack and defence was carried out at night. All normal activities in a twenty-four-hour stretch were reversed.

The Germans found the Australians different from other enemy forces, especially with regard to their ingenious solutions to problems. While the enemy always used tracer—one in every eight was a phosphorus-tipped bullet—the Aussies quickly worked out a novel way to hide the muzzle flash of their Bren guns at night, cleverly saving their limited supply of water at the same time. They would put two bayonets in the ground, sling a bit of hessian between them, urinate on the rough fabric and then shoot through the wet hessian. In contrast, the Germans revealed their positions:

'It was a bad mistake for the German. He showed his enemy where his light guns were the whole time. You could get right to the muzzle of his gun. The moment he pulled his trigger you could get a bearing on him. He never changed; he always used it.'

The Diggers gained an enviable reputation. Using superior and unorthodox tactics they continued to rebuff their enemy. They obeyed Morshead's words to 'exert and maintain a superiority of morale over him [the enemy]'.[15] Lawson Glassop wrote: 'Australians were funny blokes. If we were told to go out two thousand yards we always stepped out another fifty as a point of honour ... Strange we never called the stretch between our lines and his "no-man's land". It was not no-man's land! It was ours! We regarded it as our property. We knew every inch of it; we had his minefields taped and knew where the gaps in them were.'[16]

Rommel could hardly claim victory. So far, his two large-scale assaults—the Easter and May battles—had failed to capture Tobruk.

Life in the Salient continued. 'Brave and confident always', General Morshead regularly issued statements to the men that never altered in theme. They would never be taken; they would never surrender. They had the example of history behind them—surrounded, as at Gallipoli. They had their backs to the sea, the same as the World War I Diggers had. The only way out was the sea. They were just as good as, or better than, the men at Gallipoli. No-man's land, the area between the two opposing lines, must be theirs. Not an inch should be taken by the enemy.

Much of John's life was now consumed by patrolling to ensure that this was so. No-man's land became a vital factor in the battle of the minds. Patrolling was one strategy that had the enemy puzzled. While the Australian was a good cat and mouse soldier-burglar, the Germans were a bit like the Americans—that is, mechanised. 'Firepower was their thing.' While they patrolled occasionally, they were not accustomed to the tactic and did not practise it like the Aussies.

The Australians regularly carried out three kinds of patrols: reconnaissance, fighting and standing patrols.

The reconnaissance patrol would go out searching for information. 'You would look, lie down, listen, hear something, creep over towards it in the dark.' The important thing was 'sneaking out amongst the enemy lines, getting information, owning no-man's land'. The Germans also had this type of patrol, but with their large numbers of up to twenty-five men 'stamping about', they were easily detected.[17]

The modus operandi of a fighting patrol was digging in at a certain spot, getting as close to the enemy as possible, then attacking with bayonets or guns blazing, 'for anything from 15 minutes to half an hour'.[18] Catching prisoners this way was 'a very good way of getting information'.

The standing patrol was one that went out, dug into a spot and observed from there the next day. The Aussies had little places in no-man's land 'with funny names', like 'Jack' and 'Jill'. Their vantage point could be a cairn of stones or some other highlight, 'maybe a mile out': 'There was someone with a telephone—they ran a wire out to them—and there was an artillery man who had his telephone linked back to his guns. Then they could bring fire down on someone way in the distance … It caused a hell of a lot of trouble.'

Not only was patrolling useful for locating minefields, it was also a valuable psychological weapon, especially when the Aussies crept into German territory and left audacious signs of their silent presence. Churchill's 'V for Victory' campaign inspired some daring manoeuvres. On several occasions John and his men set off into the dark with some Vs cut out of kerosene tins. Crawling right into an enemy camp, 'to let them know that we'd been there', they silently placed the Vs near the enemy latrines, ensuring that the enemy was constantly on edge. 'We controlled the night,' said John Searle of C Company.[19]

It has been claimed that the Germans did not take into account the stubborn and gambling nature of the Australian Diggers. According to a German commander the Australians were superior to the Germans in the use of individual weapons, ground camouflage, observation and every means of taking their enemy by surprise.[20]

Several reasons have been offered for the strong teamwork, including the simple fact that everyone was at risk of being shelled or bombed, be they in the town, the port or at the front. The British, Indians, Poles and Australians all felt the same.[21]

The Aussies did not bow to efforts designed to weaken their spirit. Probably the best known attempt at enemy intimidation involved the fascist radio broadcaster, William Joyce, who moved from the United States to Ireland at the age of three, then to England where he founded the fascist British National Socialist Party. Just before the outbreak of the war, he moved to Berlin, where he conducted his propaganda radio programs. Nicknamed Lord Haw Haw because of his aristocratic nasal drawl, he regularly referred to the men of Tobruk as 'rats' who would scurry around in their underground trenches—the scum of the earth.

The men laughed at the reference, the jibes and the goading producing a still more dogged persistence. 'Rats' took on such cachet that future books would be written, films made, memorials constructed and even a medal forged in their name. Though not an official medal, many veterans from Tobruk still wear the decoration on Anzac Day.

Generous in giving credit where it was due, even Rommel praised the Australians in action. He described them as fighting with 'remarkable tenacity ... even their wounded ... defending themselves with small arms fire and staying in the fight to their last breath'.[22]

More immediately, telegraph messages, from Wavell and Churchill respectively, commended their efforts: 'Personal: Gen Morshead from C-in-C. Your magnificent defence is upsetting the enemy's plans for attack on Egypt and giving us time to build up force for counter-offensive. You could not repeat NOT be doing better service. Well done.'

'To General Morshead from Prime Minister, England. The whole Empire is watching your steadfast and spirited defence of this important outpost of Egypt with gratitude and admiration.'[23]

John continued his regular correspondence to the family, sticking mainly to personal matters. Back in Australia, Peter continued his hard work managing properties, saving for the day when he could purchase his own piece of land to provide for his growing family. John offered his help:

Mother has given me odd bits of news of what you have been doing and by this [time] I hope you are looking after a place somewhere. You really should have Albemarle*: you could do it easily with McKellar keeping an eye on the business side of things. I often imagine how great it would be to be able to go up there after this show is over and put in a few months with you at* Albemarle*. No doubt we would still find a few cartridge clips about the paddocks and a few empty shells to remind us of the good old times. Perhaps you may be able to draw a good block there somewhere in '43. If you do, I could give you a hand to put things in order.*

Conditions are very different now to when we were in Palestine. We were well off there. Here we have to live underground, or at least keep your body below ground level. You get to love the protection of your little bits of holes after a very short time and it doesn't take too many air raids to teach you to go to ground quickly …

Well kids, I do hope you are well and happy, and that young John is as perfect as I want him to be. I think a lot about the new 'littlie', and I'm dying to get back to see him.
June 1941

It was fortunate that John could not see into the future. The men were not even one-quarter of their way through the long, drawn-out siege at Tobruk and much more overseas service was to follow before their return to Australia. John would not be seeing his baby nephew until the child was four years old.

Chapter Twelve

…And deeper

In many ways the German couldn't understand the Australian approach. Like the Italians, they were stupefied that every Australian against them was there as a—can you believe it?—a volunteer. And for the Australians' part, they just didn't get the German approach, which thought dying for their … 'Fatherland' a high calling …Yet, even amidst all the killing, there was equally the bare beginning of a faintly fraternal relationship …

For sometimes a weird kind of thing would happen at around ten o'clock at night, when the Australians' 'tucker truck' would arrive … delivered to the front-line positions … The thing was, just before dinner was served, you'd quickly bang your 'Dixie' dish with your metal mug … to indicate you were about to eat. If the timing was right, you'd hear the ding-ding coming back from the Germans, to indicate they were about to eat … and both sides would knock off the war for half an hour or so …

And then, at least slightly refreshed, and with something in their bellies, they'd get back into the business of killing each other.

—Peter FitzSimons, *Tobruk*, 2006[1]

THE PERIOD BETWEEN 5 and 25 June 1941 was probably the most demanding of all for the 2/13th Battalion. In the eastern sector of the Salient, the enemy shelling was more intense and far more accurate. Vigorous patrolling uncovered hundreds of anti-personnel mines, for the most part the infamous 'jumping jacks' and booby traps.

Ironically, it was just before this period, away from the front line, but 'not out of the way of the odd piece of metal', that John received his only war wound. He was together with some of his men when a shell plunged into the soft sand nearby. Hearing the wail, he threw himself to the ground and waited for the explosion. 'I was completely deafened for a moment.' Two privates sharing the same dugout were killed. Though his hearing never properly recovered, John was soon back patrolling on the front line with his men.

Les Clothier, working closely with him during this time, recorded their excursions: '9 June 1941: There was a lot of shelling going on around us yesterday …Cpl Murray, George and I went out to reconnoitre the ground in front. Found a lot of booby traps, such as Eyetie grenades with pins pulled out, trip wires attached to detonators etc. We went right up to Fritz's main line (his outposts weren't occupied) and coming back I set off a booby trap and was blown off my feet. At first I thought I was hurt, but suffered only shock. Lost a bit of skin though.'

The main job for the battalion in the month of June had been to move forward and shorten the front line, an object they achieved within a week. Though a victory for the battalion, it had come at a great cost. Despite regular and assiduous 'delousing' activities, hardly a night had gone by without casualties from the German mines.

Fear was something each man had to deal with in his own way. Some men showed 'a reluctance'. So afraid were they of patrolling that they were physically unable to perform. There was good reason. Horrific sights of 'stiff severed forearms protruding from the sand, grey brains oozing from skulls and shattered limbs' were presumably seen by most soldiers.[2]

Almost worse were the identification procedures. The men had to observe a directive to search any dead body for sources of information, including personal letters or photographs that might provide useful details. Sometimes rigor mortis had already set in; bodies became swollen and blackened in the hot sun, emitting an unbearable stench.[3]

An attitude of unswerving toughness was expected and generally maintained. After a successful attack on a German truck, one Aussie soldier recalled his experience: '… the truck started to explode and I went out to this first bloke—he was screaming his head off and I went up to go through his papers and things like that … he's dying and Blinko yelled out to me, "Finish him off".

'And when he was walking about it was okay but when he was on the ground for me it was murder. And the bloody truck started to explode and I laid there for two hours waiting for the bloody thing to explode over our heads … this poor bugger eventually kicked his life out …

'I've got his ribbons there somewhere and a photo of his wife and two twin girls and … I lived with that bloke, I've lived with him ever since … I've always had the feeling that I should have had enough courage to put the poor bugger out of his misery, but … I didn't have enough guts to do it … and I just had to lie there and listen to the poor bastard and I lived with him for so bloody long, I still do, I never, ever forget him … I don't think I've ever recovered from him …'[4]

Understandably some of the men took a long time to return to 'normal'. John became despondent about the numbers of men in his section dying when he had not even had a chance to see their faces. When a new fellow turned up as a reinforcement, John would say, 'You go down there, son', sometimes without even seeing the soldier's face. In the dim light there was no telling his age. As he gave the instruction, he silently prayed that the faceless man would not be wounded or killed by shellfire that night.

Each man also had to deal with death in his own way. Normally the soldiers were obliged to get on with the fighting, even if their best mate was dead beside them. Rarely was there time to build a proper grave. Fellows were getting knocked down and that was how they were left—buried where they were. In the hot weather, when a body started to disintegrate, the men would sometimes scrape some sand together and build a mound over it. However, 'in no time they were rotting'. The body juices gradually came through the dry protective covering, 'which gave an oily look'.

John regretted the lack of time to honour the dead, to bury them properly, to grieve. Sometimes all he could do was just give a squeeze of the arm to the wounded or to a mate standing by. The subject of death was always a grim reminder of his worst experience. Again and again John attempted to tell the full story of the death of young Alan Toose, repeating the introduction but never finishing. It was as though he could not believe the boy's final fate: 'Alan Toose—one of the best fellows on patrol with me—a youngster from Sydney. Really only a kid. He was very thoughtful, very determined ... a wonderful soldier and said his prayers every night. He'd go into action killing. He was just a perfect soldier ... always the neatest on parade. His gear was always tidy, meticulous—never swore—a lovely boy, lovely boy Alan Toose. One day finally ... '

John was not able to dwell on the details for any length of time.

For the section leaders there was always a fine balance between sympathy and encouragement. However, there was not much patience for shirkers. John had a bloke in his team who came to him one night and said that he wouldn't do it any more. Because the soldier could not pull his weight and would be a negative influence on the others, John had to get rid of him. But the toughs were not necessarily the best either. The braggart, 'the bloke who was loud', was sometimes cowardly. Often it was the quietest young men who showed tremendous bravery. Sometimes the country blokes, sometimes the city ones. You never quite knew. Alan Toose was 'a city bloke'. The half-told story was attempted again:

'My best offsider patrolling was a boy named Alan Toose, a wonderful and thoroughly decent boy. Young Alan Toose had never been in the bush. He said his prayers every night no matter what the conditions. He never swore. A lover of his fellow man. [With a] Bren gun or Owen gun from the shoulder or the hip with spare magazines sticking out of his gaiters ... he would wade into the enemy as a cold and ruthless killer. For him he had a duty to perform for which he was trained and for which he acquired extra skills. Removed from it he was at peace with the world ... He had a lovely sense of humour. Everything about him ...'

One day, after a couple of months in Tobruk, Glyn Evans, Intelligence Officer for the 2/13th Battalion, approached John to determine his interest in Intelligence. Years later, John expressed his certainty that this overture, 'to do a bit of Intelligence training', was to save his life.

The 'I' Section was 'a mysterious type of thing'. The IO blokes walked around with maps under their arm, asked lots of questions and 'moved in exalted circles, with commanders'. Normally Evans would ask each section leader for detailed information about action and movements and then report back to Headquarters. However, on this day, his purpose for communication with John was quite different, suggesting a week or two of experience for him in the 'I' Section. John agreed that it would be interesting to find out more, as did his CO. 'Colonel Burrows thought it would give me a bit of insight.'

John soon learned there was a chain of responsibility. If the front line could not relay the information to him, 'the Intelligence bloke had to go out and find it himself. Word of mouth and observation were vital.' Once the information was gathered, the company IO would compile reports, accompanied by hasty sketches on small pieces of paper. He would get them to the Battalion Intelligence Officer who would then collate the intelligence, put it all onto a large sheet of white paper as a map and hand to the Adjutant or the Battalion Commander himself. Very quickly it would then be delivered to Brigade Headquarters.

After John had spent three or four days in the Intelligence office getting an idea of how important these reports were, Evans assigned him to Captain Jim Walsoe's C Company. Headquarters was at the Garden of Eden—'a little oasis where the tops of fig trees were sticking out of the ground'. This sunken hole in the ground, a small room that 'time had burrowed underneath the surface', reached down to moisture and provided wonderful shelter for the men. The trees above had enemy skulls hanging from them 'for decorative purposes'.

During his limited time with C Company, John decided to do some investigation of his own. He thought back to that night during the May Battle near Hill 209, when he'd seen the deadly effects of a flamethrower, a machine with 'the nightmarish appearance of monsters belching out fire', caused by fluid which ignited into a great jet of flame.[5] This particular flamethrower had been 'knocked out' in a gully, but had not been examined in detail by the troops.

John told the company commander he was 'going out on his own to have a bit of a look'. He would report back. Instead of taking his own rifle he took the Italian weapon he had picked up earlier on his journey across Libya. He could crawl around more easily with a .45 revolver than with a rifle; he could be 'a real cat burglar'. There were five remaining bullets—his only guarantee if there were any trouble—so he oiled the weapon, cleaned it and inserted the ammunition into the chamber.

Setting off in the pale moonlight John saw the familiar shadows playing on each other, shade upon shade. With senses on high alert as the view narrowed, he began stealing up the rocky gully. Everything was deathly quiet; the further away from C Company he got, the edgier he became.

There was no sound apart from distant animal howls. 'The smell of burnt cordite and metal and death hung in the air.'

Then, within 18 metres (20 yards) of it, he saw the outline of the flamethrower; it was about 3 metres (10 feet) long. He began slowly crawling towards it, silently listening and feeling with every sense to compensate for his weakened hearing—watching all the while. And then he froze. At the back of the small tank he saw two feet. The toes of the boots were on the ground and the heels were in the air—so still, not moving. Obviously this German soldier was hiding, lying in wait.

I must get the edge on him. After a couple of minutes, with heart beating fast John started crawling again, inch by inch. He pulled out his revolver, grasping it tightly at the ready. He knew he was covered, with five rounds of ammunition. If there were to be any surprise it would be from him. His heart was thumping with fear; it blotted out every sound. He continued creeping towards the tank. One of them was going to die.

There was a faint breeze blowing and on it, wafting towards him, was a dreadful stench. It was only then that he understood. *This is a dead body.* The soldier must have been shot while getting out of his vehicle. John was shaking so much that he could not have fired a decent shot at him anyway. He lay still for several minutes, trying to recover.

Keeping low, he then began the journey back to home base. On arrival he told the company commander he had located the flamethrower and offered to take some men there on patrol. He did not mention any peripheral details.

Soon John's 'I' duties were over. He rejoined his own section—back to his 'own bit of gear and slit trench'. It was only then, about a week later, that he had the opportunity to try out the Italian weapon. 'And I was flabbergasted. It wouldn't fire! It was completely defective.' He had been defenceless that night when approaching the flamethrower and had not known it: 'Extraordinary! I rehashed it again and again—and thought what an idiot I was.'

John had little time to chastise himself for his mistake. He was launched straight back into patrolling, creeping out most nights with his own section. He only took two or three with him. 'The fewer the better.' He did not want 'a clumsy clot who'd fall all over everything'. They all knew what to wear and what to do for maximum security—muffled boots, slouch hats, keeping the right distance from each other, flinging themselves down as soon as they heard the sound of a gun. While there were several magnificent city blokes, John preferred to take out country men because they were used to working at night, over rough terrain. Back home they had worked by the stars.

The North Star, 'just fixed there', helped tremendously when there were no compasses in the early days at Tobruk. 'It was usual to move by the stars, as did the ancient mariners ...'[6] With a little finger on the North Star, an arm outstretched and an open hand, the men could ascertain 17 to 19 degrees. It was a 'dodgy', primitive calculation, but better than nothing.

Choosing the correct amount of light was tricky. With a paler landscape the moon glinted on things. 'If one of the enemy walked towards them to have a leak', his men needed to be indistinct enough to disappear into the night. Though the dark made hiding from the enemy easier, it made success more difficult. Where were the mines? What sort of mines were they? Were they booby-trapped?

They would go into dangerous territory, 'the most dreadful places', but John always knew that his men were thoroughly reliable—they made 'not a sound, just a sign, a tap on the leg'—they understood each other. Once they reached their destination, they observed the Germans relentlessly laying their mines. The patrollers paused, looked, listened. Not only was their night vision intensified, but also their hearing. Sign language was vital: 'You froze if someone wanted you to stop. They sidled up to you. You might be 20 feet apart. You could actually go long distances. That's also why we had bits of "spots" which told us where we were—the cairn of stones or a small mound. When you went out there you also had to get back again. You had to reverse the procedure. The trick was not to bite off too much.'

Sometimes John would need to give detailed training to the newer recruits. One of these was George Lochran who arrived one night in the dark with a bunch of reinforcements. The first time they went out on patrol George asked John what he wanted him to do. John told him to follow and watch exactly where he put his feet—to place them exactly where his footprints were. 'And if you do that, George, you'll be safe.' George knew that while John lived, he lived.

The search for German mines went on almost every night. With light fingers they brushed the desert sand for the three little triggers of the powerful German 'jumping jack' mines. 'You found the fresh dirt and it showed even in the darkness, the faint pattern of change in colour.' If the triggers were set off, a primary charge exploded, which would then blow a nine-pound mine, packed with shrapnel, some 60 centimetres (2 feet) in the air before it burst.[7] One wrong move meant instant death: 'When you got to the minefield you had to run your fingers around to see if there were any trip wires coming out of it. If there were, you'd stop. If the wire was tight and you touched it with any force, it would detonate the mines—perhaps a whole line of mines.'

Patrolling was one way of literally unearthing information. By chance, John came across the first Teller mine found in Tobruk. 'Cpl Murray went out last night and brought back a Fritz anti-tank mine,' reported Les Clothier on 15 June 1941.[8] Introduced by the Germans after they had been in Tobruk a few months, this deadly mine, 'a bit bigger than a large dinner plate', had a large explosive charge, almost twice as powerful as any mine encountered up to then. It could be packed with almost 6 kilograms (13 pounds) of TNT.

On the night of the discovery John and his mates waited until the enemy had moved on and then crawled over to investigate, gingerly scraping the newly turned earth and sand as they went. Once John's fingers touched the detonator, he gently dug around and then pulled the mine out. It was not wired to others, so he did not have to unhook it: 'The trick was to get them before the enemy had wired them together and not to trip on the connecting wires. If he'd wired them together then one would detonate the others. If you tripped on those little wires then ...

While reliving those moments more than sixty years later, John paused and looked into the distance. Almost certainly he was recalling a time when connected mines had detonated. There was more than one instance when he could barely bring himself to complete the story: 'I've got to confess that when I was out on patrol I wasn't big brave Johnnie at all. My heart beat so loudly at times that it deafened me. I'd have to pause and wait until this thump, thump, thump—that noise, it was deafening to me. I couldn't hear.

'Patrols were very difficult for me—very, very upsetting. One of the hardest things I had to do was take out on patrol with me the married men with children ... I had censored so many letters from fellows with wives and children—pouring out their hearts sometimes. Dreadful. And I had to send them out sometimes to get killed. Awful.

'So, what could you do? You couldn't just send the single men ... but you tried to work it so that the danger was minimal for a married man and his children. It was a cruel business, it really was.'

Each man had to face the threat of sudden death. There was no doubt that trapped grenades and mines delivered particularly awful fatalities:

'And I crawled over to him … [and then] to the next bloke who was Harry, and Harry was gone, his head and shoulders blown off. Keith had stood on a booby trap, a jumping jack, and it had jumped up and exploded on Harry's chest …'[9]

Tim Fearnside, 11 Platoon sergeant, had seen the unexpected devastation of a trip-wire early on. His group of four had split into pairs to cover more ground in the time available, agreeing to meet up at a given time. Alan Walker, a young farmer from the northern rivers district of New South Wales, was Fearnside's companion: 'Within minutes of setting off on our reconnaissance, there was a sharp metallic click underfoot. I jumped clear, calling Alan to go to ground. There was a blinding red flash and he was down on his knees moaning … [My other two mates came back] the bayonets on their rifles gleaming in the moonlight. We got Alan to his feet and half carried, half propelled him towards our own lines. Alan was groaning as we took him in and then he was silent. A sliver of shrapnel had entered his left eye and no doubt pierced his brain, because he was dead when we reached our lines.'[10]

Despite the danger of this tactic, patrolling was the Allies' deadly weapon. It denied the enemy ground reconnaissance of the Australian positions, preventing them from discovering weak spots in the physical defences. This result in itself was invaluable.

In subsequent descriptions of Australian patrolling, the words 'magnificent' and 'unsurpassed' were frequently written.

Life began to settle into a routine at Tobruk. As the men became acclimatised, they perversely accepted their fate.

One day in August 1941, four months after their arrival in Tobruk, the NCOs from one of the battalions learned of a job being offered back home. It offered some distinct advantages: a bunk on the first ship back to Australia, away from all the terrible dust and death, fleas and disease; even the guarantee of a commission.

Astoundingly, there was not one volunteer for the job.[11]

Chapter Thirteen

Relief gone wrong

EVERY SPARE MOMENT OF DARKNESS WAS USED TO STRENGTHEN
DEFENCES, BUT NIGHT PATROLLING HAD TO GO ON AS WELL
IN A CONSTANT ENDEAVOUR TO EDGE FORWARD AND RE-
TAKE EVEN A FEW METRES OF GROUND LEFT CARELESSLY
UNPROTECTED BY THE ENEMY.

—Hall, 1984[1]

As THE MONTHS dragged on, there was a pattern to life in the Salient that was rarely broken. Rommel brought in large numbers of troops, determined to protect his initial gains around the Hill; the Aussies were equally intent on recovering lost ground.

Patrolling at night turned into an exhausting psychological game. The men had to dig new trenches continually, all the while facing unrelenting enemy artillery and dive-bombing attacks. The sound of steel against rock inevitably invited 'a few rounds' from the German Spandaus.

John was responsible for overseeing the trenches for 6 Section. 'You, you, you—dig in.' Each of them had only a shovel and, in no time, the men would scoop the sand off and if possible dig down further for a little more protection. However, where the rock base was shallow, they could raise their heads from the trenches only a fraction; their bodies were level with the ground. A couple of filled sandbags were the only barrier. 'We were facing towards the enemy, always. We could see their little bits of diggings and they could see ours.'

When John buried himself during the day into his 'appalling scratch in the ground', he had two options: to sleep in the scorching heat or do anything he was able to while lying flat. He wrote letters when he had any suitable materials, and smoked if he had cigarettes. But for most of the time, John barely moved. He quietly endured the interminable swarms of flies, the hopping fleas and the awful boredom.

Each day he faced the same food—monotonous fare that provided only just enough energy to continue the hard physical work each night. Hot bully stew was delivered in boxes, in the dark at night. Lighting a fire in the forward trenches was out of the question—the smoke would attract unwanted attention. John graphically described the meagre provisions to Margie:

> *We are on 'iron rations' now, but as Charlie will tell you, it's surprising just how well one manages. For instance, there are three very elementary ways of having 'Bully Beef'—half tin, whole tin (never) or none at all. Then you can have it cold, warm or hot, with biscuits, or without biscuits (quite often); then there is that yellow dressing for all our meals, which the army is unstinting with in its ration—sand!*
> *30 April 1941*

The bully beef cans were not thrown away. They were essential for use in the toilet routine. If the need arose during the day, it was not possible to get up out of the trench. The men developed all sorts of angles to relieve themselves, with the least mess possible. They also learned the discipline of timing.

In these conditions, illnesses were common. Dysentery was a curse. John Dickson, in a mortar team, recalled the weakness as he dragged himself to the toilet pits. 'You couldn't empty your bowels in the trench. If dysentery wasn't bad enough, you risked your life getting to the sanitation unit's toilets in the daytime, because a Jerry with a big sniper rifle was waiting to shoot you. You'd duck and weave to make it behind the toilet sandbags—then the sniper was watching for you to come out, to run back.'[2]

John did not escape the curse. With flies excreting on his body and fleas and lice all over him, even in the seams of his clothes, the affliction was impossible to avoid: '… my dysentery in Tobruk … I never mentioned in the letters. Awful, dreadful … it's just the most humiliating thing. You get it from flies … You're passing blood finally. Then you went back to the poor old medicos at the RAP—the regimental aid post. You just lay around in the sand … no huts, no tents … Finally you started to get a bit of strength and you had to get back. I can recall almost crawling from the RAP, probably a mile back to my unit.'

Dysentery was not the only discomfort. The men patrolling during the day had to face the storm dust and blasts of sand with nothing more than goggles and handkerchiefs over their noses and mouths. For those who remained, conditions were not much better. 'We'd breathe and eat sand and dust, cough up little pellets of sand and pus.'[3] Their trenches filled with grit, their hair was matted, their food rations were covered with the sandy dressing, their guns seized up and their eyes became bloodshot.

Water was in such short supply that the dust remained on the men's bodies. Their daily supply of 2.25 litres (half a gallon) of sun-heated water (or eight cupfuls) barely relieved their thirst.[4] Even the compulsory shaving, so torturous to perform, required a few drops of water. The army issued one razor blade to each section per week—one blade for ten men. John became expert with bits of glass, kept in his haversack; the men passed them round every morning and with concentration 'got good at sharpening'. Sometimes they would get a welcome extra blade in an envelope from home and hoard it. John never missed a shave.

Every soldier in North Africa would have agreed with the sentiments expressed in the verses written by Lieutenant Hugh Barton Paterson, son of famous Australian poet, A.B 'Banjo' Paterson:

THIS PLACE THEY CALL TOBRUK

There's places that I've been in
I didn't like too well,
New England's far too blooming cold
And Winton's hot as hell;
The Walgett beer is always warm,
In each there's something crook,
But each and all are perfect to
This place they call Tobruk.

I've seen some dust storms back at home
That made the housewives work,

Here there's enough inside our shirts
To smother all of Bourke.
Two Diggers cleaned their dugouts,
And their blankets out they shook—
Two colonels perished in the dust in
This place they call Tobruk.

There's centipedes like pythons,
And countless hordes of fleas—
As big as poodle dogs they come
A-snapping round your knees.
And scorpions large as AFV's
Come out to have a look;
There's surely lots of livestock in
This place they call Tobruk.

The shelling's nice and frequent
And they whistle overhead.
You go into your dugout
And find shrapnel in your bed.
And when the Stukas dive on us
We never pause to look,
We're down our holes like rabbits in
This place they call Tobruk.

I really do not think this place
Was meant for me and you,
Let's return it to the Arab
And he knows what he can do;
We'll leave the God-forsaken place
Without one backward look:
We've called it lots of other names—
This place they call Tobruk.[5]

But leaving was just a dream. At night, the patrolling that went on with weary regularity was starting to show results for the Allies. Rommel called on his men to counter these 'incredible excursions'.

As usual, rumours filtered through regularly. Two attempts by the British to break the siege had foundered. Code-named Brevity in May and Battleaxe in June, both had failed. The news was sobering for the men. How long would they be stuck in Tobruk?

In the early hours of 22 June 1941, an incident in the 2/13th Battalion added to the gloom. Three men were blown up, dreadfully wounded while attempting to dig new positions in ground littered with booby traps and mines. Three more were killed in separate incidents on the same morning. The following night another four were killed.

The one tactic Morshead always used against defeatism was to put the men to work, 'until they were too tired to think of anything else'.[6] Despite the constant repetition of their leader's mantra—that they were the most valuable men in this theatre of war, that they must keep going—it was becoming increasingly difficult to be convinced.

Along with the others, John was close to the edge. They were all 'very, very tired'. They had been under constant attack for almost three months—victims of bombs, mines, mortars, machine guns and flamethrowers.

After an extended period at the front, it was time for 'a spell'. On 26 June the 2/13th Battalion was moved into reserve—closer to the sea, away from the main action. The men revelled in the unrestricted freedom of movement, and even better, the swimming parties.

Then, on 30 June, they moved to the 'dust bowl' of Pilastrino, supposedly a place for relaxation. Though they had to continue digging on the Blue Line, it was a holiday compared to duties around Hill 209. Sometimes there were church parades where the men paid homage to their dead mates. On such occasions John disciplined himself to think of other things; he rarely shared his misery. There was little opportunity for the men to vent their feelings. 'Do not write harrowing letters home,' was a constant instruction:

We came out about five days ago for a spell and already it's easy to see the difference the last few days of comparative quiet and rest have made to all the lads.

It's wonderful to be able to get up and walk about in the daytime and to be able to have a sleep like normal people … About the only things to disturb us now are an occasional shell landing round about, which worries no one, and an air raid by the Germans three or four times a day. Our anti-aircraft fire is generally pretty hot for them; we watch and barrack for our gunners just as if we were at a football match.

The coast is only about three miles away so all my section went over for a swim the day before yesterday ... We were lucky in finding ... an old well of beautiful fresh water ... where we found a few shady trees with cactus and grape vines also. We had our day's rations with us and also some tea so you can imagine what a picnic we had. We just lolled around swimming, sunbaking and making tea with complete freedom from all thoughts of reality.

It's surprising how action changes many men; my worst and most troublesome man in camp life and the only man I've ever put under arrest is now one of the best and will do anything for me at all. Others we thought were good men, crack up quickly; but fortunately very few.
30 June 1941

When writing a second letter to his mother, twenty-four hours later, John concentrated on the simple, homely progress of life in Australia:

It's good to hear of young John growing well and also I simply love hearing of Sue-Anne. She must be a darling kid, and I can just imagine her following Charlie around the garden ... You've no idea how much I'm looking forward to seeing young John and Sue-Anne ... Surely it's not necessary for Marg to do war work, unless it's something light and easy. But of course she knows just what she is doing so I won't worry ...

Don't worry about not sending parcels, Mother dear, you have really been very good with so many papers and other things. Instead of other parcels, I'd be pleased if you would put the same money into a fairly good pipe and some tobacco. I'm getting sick of cigarettes and would love to get back into a pipe again ...
1 July 1941

While in reserve the men discussed one aspect of the struggle that gave them some kind of perverse hope—the fact that the opposing sides generally showed each other respect. A ruthless tactician, Rommel was also a gentleman who encouraged a chivalrous war. John confirmed this slightly bizarre notion. 'The German leader was a great soldier; it was a noble war.'

There were many stories about his principled nature. When Hitler issued an order that all Allied commanders be slaughtered, Rommel chose to ignore it, immediately burning the instructions. He treated prisoners with respect, and the wounded with dignity, even on the battlefield.

This decency from the top manifested itself in quite unusual behaviour. The troops from each side talked to each other by radio and left cigarettes for each other, swapping them during patrol. Negotiations on radio that determined smoking preferences: 'Right—good—thanks—I'd prefer so and so [cigarettes or tobacco] but that will do.'

One day John called a truce, in order to remove his friend, Ken Forrester, from the trenches for medical assistance. After John stood up, it seemed to be an eternity before one of the Germans stood up in acknowledgment. Once the truce was under way, two fellows assisted Ken, slowly trudging until they were out of sight. Within seconds, the German got down, John got down—and they proceeded to fire at each other again. 'A strange business.'

Even stranger, the 2/13th occasionally shared singing with the enemy. When Peter Robinson, a big, tall sergeant with a beautiful bass voice, began to sing one quiet night, the Germans, in their trenches a couple of hundred metres away, responded. 'They joined in. It was a rare, inspiring moment.'

On 4 August 1941 after a furious battle, John saw both sides crossing their lines to help in the removal of the dead. The Germans 'defused their minefield' to accommodate the process. Each side exchanged wounded prisoners and the Germans gave the Australian stretcher-bearers cool water as they worked together, lifting each other's wounded onto stretchers until the last casualty had been removed. Opposing sides spoke to each other in faltering English or German. 'It wasn't matey conversation, but they were looking at each other and continuing the business of getting their men out.'

Rommel's *Krieg ohne Hass* meant a war without hatred; they fought each other 'in a gentlemanly way'.[7] The courtesies demonstrated by each side on the front did not puzzle John at all. Since a lot of the German officers had been at school in England and vice versa, there was a common background. Both sides had travelled the continent making and keeping friends. A former commander of a Panzer troop noticed that if veterans of the African campaign happened to meet after the war, whatever their nationality, they 'greeted each other like old comrades'.[8]

The myth around Rommel grew on both sides. Such was his popularity that in an attempt to discourage an increase in his hero status, General Wavell, the British Commander-in-Chief in the Middle East, instructed his officers to refer to the other side as 'the Germans' or 'the enemy' … and 'not to always keep harping on about Rommel'.[9]

In July 1941, General Blamey, Australia's commander in Cairo, pressed for the relief of the trapped Australian 9th Division, citing their exhaustion. In response to this request Churchill claimed there was insufficient air protection for such a mammoth military task and that furthermore, the British were planning a third major offensive to push the Germans back, past Tobruk. All hands were needed. The mooted evacuation would have to wait until the moonless periods of August/September.

Churchill's case was strengthened coincidentally by the political confusion in Australia during this period. Because of absences, resignations and a general election, Australia saw three prime ministers, with a major change in government, over the eight weeks from the end of August 1941.[10]

Despite the fact that the Australian Government had necessarily become more and more focused on their own region as the Japanese continued their alarming push south, the Australians stayed put in Tobruk. Churchill was able to have his way.

An earlier evacuation would have saved hundreds of Australian lives. From July, activity became more ferocious in the Salient, with disastrous results. In the forty-two days up to 6 August 'a daily average of 650 shells fell [on the front] … the normal minimum on a "quiet" day was 200.'[11] On 3 August it was noted that an entire platoon from the 28th Battalion no longer existed. Almost all its members had been captured or killed.[12]

It was not until September that John's severely depleted battalion was allowed a well-earned rest. John referred only fleetingly to casualties in correspondence to his mother:

> *The time simply flies past, and it's hard to realise that we have been here [in Tobruk] for nearly six months and about seven months in Libya.*
>
> *Conditions are ever so much better now than they were some months back.*

In my last letter I told you that I was in the Intelligence section on the BN HQ. It's very interesting, Mother, and I've learnt such a lot—things that I'm learning now will always be of great help to me later on. Also it's a great chance to learn quite a lot about the administration of the Army, which can never be picked up in a rifle company.

I still have my two stripes and later on hope to get further ahead. There have been some quite rapid promotions from the ranks. But nearly all to fill vacancies caused by the usual casualties in the field ... Luckily my health remains good except for the ever-present desert sores, which are common to nearly all here. There isn't much one can do about them I don't think, only a complete change of atmosphere and food.

We are all still looking forward longingly for bright lights and civilisation. Probably we won't get any when we do get out, but quite naturally we are hoping so. A hot bath would be decent.

25 September 1941

Little by little the 2/13th realised that the bright lights were not far off.

By 17 September 1941, moonless nights made the long-awaited withdrawal of the remaining Australians possible. However, the prolonged waiting, stretching into the following month, created increasing tension.

On 17 October Les Clothier wrote: 'It must be close now. Our advance guard went down to B Echelon last night. I hope we follow shortly. We have been 7½ months in the Desert and six months in Tobruk and 12 months overseas since Monday.'[13]

There were bets about which Australian battalion would be the last to leave. By 24 October, all Australian battalions had departed, apart from two companies from the 2/15th and the entire 2/13th. John's battalion was a clear winner. Once more the men were to celebrate the dubious honour of being the last full battalion to be withdrawn. Some of them were beginning to believe that thirteen was an unlucky number.

In the dead of night, on 25 October, the men finally prepared for departure. There were now 400 left out of a full complement of around 800. They went down to the harbour in good spirits to wait for their relief ship, the *Latona*, which was carrying a detachment of Polish soldiers, some rations and water in drums for the garrison.

After their past disappointments, it was hard for the men to believe that this wasn't 'a furphy', that the 2/13th was really leaving. Like the other men, John only gradually realised late that night that things were not right. They had been 'sitting out there for hours' waiting for their relief boat when finally some small barges picked them up 'in dribs and drabs' to take them back to land.

Soon they heard the full story. Their rescue ship, the *Latona*, had been torpedoed, bombed and finally sunk at about 2 am that morning. As a result, there would be no chance for another evacuation until the next moonless period in November. Churchill had confirmed as much in an abrupt telegram to Prime Minister Curtin in Australia.

George Hill, 'a rough diamond', said to John, 'Christ, have you heard the news? There ain't no f...ing God.' Joe Madeley recalled the aftermath: 'We had no rations, we were bloody hungry, and they plonked us in a camp next to the British rations dump.'[14]

The British fed and comforted the downcast members of the unit. 'What are you fookers doing back again? ... Charlie, will I put another bucket of water in the stew then for these ruddy Aussies?' the cook's offsider asked.[15]

As was always the case in extreme disappointment, a poem was written:

> And when the word was passed around
> That we were not to leave the place:
> The phrases coarse and words profane
> Were really a most sad disgrace;
> One word the very buildings shook
> (The Tommies rhyme it with Tobruk!)[16]

A song written by Private Matt Kirby became a kind of mascot in later years—sung on battlefields, road convoys, troopships and in camp concerts. Its refrain? 'So don't get the notion we sailed on the ocean: *We're Bull Burrows' Bomb-Happy Boys.*' And the last verse:

> Some day when this war is well won,
> And Anzacs have all returned home,

Doing the things we all love so much
Back in the land that no other can touch:
Some bright Brigadier will wake up:
'The Thirteenth aren't sharing our joys!
Why Gawd strike me blind we've left them behind!'
Who? Bull Burrows' Bomb-Happy Boys.[17]

Hugh Paterson's interpretation of the failed evacuation repeated some of the droll comments the men had made and were still making. They could do nothing but shake their heads in disbelief:

'The last of all to leave Tobruk'—
We felt like heroes—donned our packs,
We gave away our primus stoves
And strapped equipment on our backs;
We said: 'It's something to achieve
To be the very last to leave.'

We waited gaily on the wharf
The inky darkness peering through,
Some thought they saw the ships arrive
Before they'd even passed Matruh;
But soon we learned the game was crook—
It seemed we wouldn't leave Tobruk.

Sometimes we even start to think,
When in depression's deepest throes,
That we are doomed to stay in here
Till Angel Gabriel's trumpet blows,
And Peter, taking one quick look,
Says: 'Enter! Last to leave Tobruk!'[18]

Following the transfer of General Morshead's command to Major General Scobie, 70th English Division, the lone Australian 2/13th Battalion now found themselves under the overall British command.

Colonel Burrows understood how shattered the men were; the best thing would be to get them to work immediately. They were thus quickly assigned to relieve Polish troops in the Derna Road sector of the Red Line. They knew they were back. The most vicious *khamsin* they had ever experienced was raging. It blew ferociously all day.

The 'last to leave Tobruk' were now camped near a pumping station that even supplied them with a shower. But in other ways they were more disadvantaged than before. They had no weapons except rifles, no food, no cooking utensils and were without any of 'the little luxuries' they had handed over to the British on their planned departure a few days before. Even worse, the men were soon to learn that the hard-won positions in no-man's land, outposts such as 'Plonk', 'Jill' and 'Butch', had been lost. 'God,' John said, 'we'll all be gone soon if this is what's going to happen.'

When he wrote to his mother, John was not able to tell her about the evacuation that had gone so horribly wrong and that he would not leave Tobruk until the next dark moon:

> *We are still here in the same old spot, although you have probably heard to the contrary ... You know, of course, that we have been in action for longer than any other Australian Division in this war and as far as defence is concerned, we feel we know a bit about it.*
>
> *We have been close to and under shellfire for six weeks constantly; we've had more air raids in the area than any other place in the world and we've also done a dickens of a lot of active patrolling, making contact with the enemy lines. That might all sound terrible, but it really has not been so bad and we've had very few casualties for that period of action ...*
>
> *Since last writing, I've been transferred back to my old section again in the 'B' company ... I was very fortunate to get the few months training in Intelligence and it has given me a far greater knowledge of army work than I had before. I'm still a Corporal, darling, but don't worry. I won't give up trying to get ahead and I know I'll get my opportunity later on.*
> *29 October 1941*

And so life went on. Moon-watching suddenly gained in popularity. Most of all the 2/13th men wanted to see 'the dark of the moon' which would herald their departure. Though they understood they were keeping the Germans at bay, and gained some satisfaction from it, they were keener still to get going. There was a job to be done closer to home.

Chapter Fourteen

Last stand at Ed Duda

The 2/13th was part of a force from the Tobruk garrison that made a crucial contribution by recapturing Ed Duda in a night attack ...

Under the heading 'This was Pure Hell' Private A. Armstrong recalled it thus: 'After we took position, we were shelled continuously for two days. Had we not been relieved after the second night I think half the coy [company] would have gone shell happy. It was terrible. I can't describe it.'

—Johnston, 2005[1]

It was 11 November 1941 and celebrations were in motion. All World War I veterans were offered a drink of rum by Colonel Burrows. However, the irony of celebrating Armistice Day, observing the end of one war at the height of another, did not escape the men.

Six days before, the news of impending departure from Tobruk, with an exact date and time, had really shaken the members of the 2/13th. They had heard that they would be shipped out on 11 November 'in the dark of the moon' and would be relieved by the Polish Officers' Legion.

All too soon their high spirits sank. When one of their mates, Bill Walmsley, was killed by a mine the day before they were due to leave, tensions soared. Then they received word on departure day that the expected Polish regiment would not be replacing them. Expectations and emotions were see-sawing with the continuing orders and counter-orders.

It seemed that deferment of all withdrawal plans for the 2/13th Battalion was top priority for the British. In September 1941 Churchill had warned the Australian Government not to deprive Australia of the glory of a victory in Tobruk. He was now pushing even harder for their continued presence, giving assurances that the British in Singapore would protect Australian shores from the Japanese. While additional naval support at the first sign of any direct threat was offered, Churchill simultaneously pushed his view that the Japanese would issue threats but would not act.

One reason Churchill continually prevaricated about the departure of the Australians was Operation Crusader—an all-out effort to break the Tobruk siege, planned for late November 1941.

The aim of this relief mission, which the 8th Army had been plotting since June 1941, was to push the Germans west out of Egypt and through Libya, way beyond Tobruk. There was an intricate plan for each stage.

British forces in Tobruk were to link up with the 8th Army just outside the perimeter. The success of this link-up hinged largely on securing three key points of elevation that dominated the road between Ed Duda and Tobruk. Once this vital route, the Tobruk Corridor, was theirs, they would press on westwards and expel the Germans from the entire area (see map, Chapter Ten, page 106).

It was unthinkable to the British that there should be any disruption to this plan. Churchill considered the rising Japanese threat to Australia secondary to his agenda. In fact, any arguments to move the Australian troops from Tobruk at that time were met with intense disapproval by the British. 'Everybody [in the British political and military leadership] was furious.'[2] Even the King of England remarked that Australia was different from the others in the Dominions, in its criticism of the British Government.[3]

And so the 2/13th Battalion waited—and waited. The deadline for their departure passed.

On 16 November 1941 the heavens opened and drenched the desert. Some thought it was an ominous omen of the future. The following night was one of the worst John had ever spent in his trench—now soaked and muddy. In five minutes there were 10 centimetres (4 inches) of rainwater and within ten minutes there were 46 centimetres (18 inches). A cold wind was blowing; the dry desolate wadis became raging torrents.

Unforeseen events were multiplying. There were extraordinary breaches of ground rules all around the Salient. Both sides were being washed out of their holes in the ground, but the men were moving about with little concern.

Les Clothier observed they were all in the same boat. 'His blankets are out drying too,' he wrote.[4]

Next, the men were told that Operation Crusader was due to get under way in a week's time. Rommel was apparently so intent on taking Tobruk that he had not fully appreciated the external threat posed by the British. When Headquarters heard that the German leader planned a major attack on Tobruk around 22 November, the Crusader plans were put forward—rain or no rain.

Despite the soaked, glue-like soil, the British forces pounced on 19 November, launching a full-scale attack. The element of surprise gave the Allies a momentous head start. 'It has come in a way we did not expect,' wrote a German officer of the Afrika Korps, 'and there's hell let loose.'[5]

For those inside the Tobruk garrison, information about the battle was scarce. Even before it started they were dubious about its final success. Knowing of the two unsuccessful siege-breaking actions by the British earlier in the year—Brevity and Battleaxe—the men's general reaction was that they would believe it when they saw it. However, on 22 November, three days after the launch, Les Clothier was reporting that the operation from Egypt was 'going great guns'. It seemed that in no time Tobruk would be relieved.[6]

Following repeated representations from the Australian Government, the British Command in the Middle East had agreed that the 2/13th would only be used in the Crusader campaign if absolutely necessary—'not to be employed except in an emergency'.[7]

However the action did not go smoothly; rumours warned that the 8th Army offensive seemed to have become 'bogged down'.[8] In less than a week, the Germans had used their superior tanks, though fewer in number, to almost completely turn around their fortunes. Rommel's tanks were massed—and deadly.[9]

Soon it became clear that there were insufficient British troops to guard the link-up corridor from the invading Germans. One of the three points of elevation, Ed Duda, was now central to Allied success. It had been captured, lost, recaptured and lost again.

By the afternoon of 28 November it was decided by the British that the presence of the Australians was essential. The British had no choice but to call on their last reserve—the half-strength Australian 2/13th Battalion. Tim Fearnside described the British call for help as being 'dumped in the middle of it'.[10]

Though he may have suffered qualms privately, Colonel Burrows issued the order for his men to move across the Tobruk perimeter and out to Ed Duda.He knew his men were second to none. They were to join up with the British and New Zealand units already there. A message from Churchill had been circulated to all troops. They were expected to do their duty with 'exemplary devotion' and would indeed be adding 'a page to history'. At the perimeter the British General, Major General Scobie, told the boys, 'Ed Duda must be held at all costs'.

And then the Aussies set off in the dark—a convoy crawling in the freezing cold, 13 kilometres (8 miles) across the desert. This was the first time the men had been outside the wire for longer than a night-time patrolling expedition. Many felt strangely 'free' as they traversed enemy territory.[11]

Fortunately the 2/13th had no knowledge of the odds that would face them. It was only later that they saw the official recorded figures for the Ed Duda battle: 450 Germans against 160 Australians.

The first contact—with immense loss of life—occurred early the next morning, on 29 November. The men had settled into position when it happened. It was dark, just before daylight, and the territory was unfamiliar. They had gone in trucks, de-trucked and carried their gear, ammunition and weapons to the foot of a long rise. They were directed to what was believed to be a reverse slope, settled down supposedly out of the view of the enemy and waited for morning's instructions.

At dawn 'the German observation bloke was amazed to see a battalion scattered around', over 100 men on the forward slope some 5 metres (5.5 yards) away from each other, fully exposed. He immediately issued instructions to his gunners. The 210-mm guns were brought into action minutes later, firing huge shells weighing over 90 kilograms (200 pounds), at point-blank range. Some of the shells detonated, causing a hole 'the size of a bowling green'; some did not. An un-detonated shell generally kept rolling and whoever it hit was dead, because 'it was a great lump of lead, heavy and hot. The weight of those shells could kill two or three men'.

The devastation was appalling. Colonel Burrows gave immediate orders to the uninjured men to pick up their gear and walk over the top of the hill, down to the reverse slope. Keep their distance man to man. Every man was to walk; no one was to run. The men gathered up their swags and doggedly marched—hearts beating fast—over the crest and down the other side.

Constant enemy shelling through the day led to further casualties. More bad luck occurred that night, when a counter-attack was planned. Unbelievably morale was high; the Australians' freedom depended on this action. With great determination they began to arrange themselves into formation, ready to march to the start line. It was shortly after 10 pm. In the pale moonlight, shivering from the cold, they waited for the order to move forward.

No one was prepared for what followed. A massive missile descended on 10 Platoon. Of its twenty-six members, only eight were able to struggle to their feet. Most were killed, including the poet, Sergeant Hugh Paterson. Colonel Burrows immediately took command of B and C Companies, giving the order to file past the wounded.

As John marched forward, he could see a heap of severed limbs; he could smell the blood. The shell had daisy-cut right through the middle of the platoon, 'killing practically the whole lot of them—a lot of legs blown off'. Poor old Private Clancy Sirl pleaded with his mates. 'For Christ's sake, put me out of my misery.' He had lost both legs below the knee. 'Would somebody shoot me for Christ's sake and put me out of my bloody misery?'

They had to march on, past where Tim Fearnside's brother Fred lay dying in a mass of writhing bodies. They continued to move, doggedly, until they no longer heard the cries, knowing that up ahead they themselves would face more of the same. John began to shiver. 'It was shattering for the blokes.'

The whole action was meant to be coordinated with the artillery. The tanks should have been firing up ahead of them, giving them a creeping barrage, which they could follow. But on this occasion they went up with just rifles and bayonets, 'without any support at all'. On each side of John, fellows only 5 metres (5.5 yards) from him were knocked down. George Hill and Roy Luck both went down with a burst of fire. George was the mate who only weeks before had said, 'There's no f… God'.

But John continued on. A sense of fatalism kept him moving. As he got close to the top of the rise he heard 'the staccato, foreign jabber of

Platoon Sergeant Tim Fearnside (left), author of several books about the war and a good mate of John's, and John Murray in Tobruk.

the enemy'. He heard Burrows shout, 'Go for them boys, go for them and let out one great bloody yahoo when you get near them'.

With his rifle and bayonet at the ready John charged, closing in minute by minute. Adrenalin raced through his body. His confidence came from the knowledge that the Australians had a name for always being prepared to use the bayonet. 'Cold steel—a wonderful psychological weapon.' They had all received detailed instruction in its use at home—on hanging models of men, made from straw.

Now was the time for their practice to deliver. The entire battalion of men let out 'such a wild Australian yell that I'm sure they must have known who we were'. In chorus they were 'shouting, yelling and cooeeing like madmen'.[12]

The stupefied enemy heard the bellowing and saw the shimmer of moonlight shining on the bayonets. They dropped everything and ran.

Tim Fearnside was relieved when he heard that his brother Fred had been removed on a stretcher from the 10 Platoon melee and taken back to the base hospital in Tobruk. 'At least he's out of it.' But sadly the next day his sense of relief was turned on its head: 'John Murray, who had led our No 5 Section in the attack, came up and indicated he had something to say.

By the set look on his face and the way the others kept clear, it could only have been bad news. He said that Fred had died of wounds—in Tobruk. He put his hand on my shoulder and went on his way. I thanked him and wandered off along the ridge and sat down on the ground and wept.'[13]

Later that afternoon, with morbid anger overwhelming him, Fearnside decided to wreak revenge. He had heard there was an injured German soldier some 75 metres (80 yards) to the rear of their position: 'I went back to kill him. An eye for an eye, a tooth for a tooth. He was wounded and alone and he would die in a strange and unfamiliar place … He moved before I did, raising his hand in a half salute. 'Wasser, bitte, Kamerad!' I hesitated, impulsively looking around to see if there were any to witness my guilt. Then I gave him a drink of water and went back up to the ridge, angry and confused, the unused [Beretta] cold in my hand.'[14]

After delivering the news of Fred's death and seeing his friend's mind 'in a hell of a state', John felt an urgent need to leave his section and follow Tim back to the wounded German soldier. He had noticed the glint in Fearnside's eye. 'Come on Tim. Break it up. Leave him to me,' he'd said when he caught up. Looking down from the ridge, he noticed that the young red-headed soldier was, at most, eighteen years old.

The enemy guns were still firing their huge shells that night— 30 November 1941. John carefully dragged the injured German's limp body 18 metres (20 yards) to a hole which he built up with a few rocks to protect against the bombardment. His legs were 'in a hell of a mess'—heavily bandaged and soaked in blood, as red as his hair. The boy was in great pain, softly moaning, so John pulled the blanket even closer over the top of him, and through the night kept rolling cigarettes to offer him. When the boy muttered, he replied 'with a comforting pat'. The night was long and they were both exhausted. 'We weathered it out together.'

At dawn, a British officer arrived to inspect the ground. He immediately agreed to get the young boy back to base for medical attention. With one of his own soldiers helping, he dragged the injured soldier down the slope to a gully 'where they were able to get him on a vehicle and take him away'. The boy asked the lieutenant to thank John 'from the bottom of his heart'.

Unusual mementos from Ed Duda still survive: John Searle came across a prayer book in near perfect condition in an abandoned British staff car, dated 1928 and belonging to a bishop from New Zealand; John Murray found a superb pair of binoculars with gradations for artillery work, dangling round the neck of a dead German tank driver. On his discovery, conscious of the golden rule that all booty was to be handed in, John looked at Bull Burrows who had just arrived on the scene. 'What about these?' he asked. John appreciated the reply. 'Will you promise to look after them?'[15]

At 3 am on the morning of 3 December 1941, the men left in convoy for the long trek back to Tobruk. They had to cross over the ground where 10 Platoon had been decimated. Not one man from the battalion would have said several days earlier that he would be pleased to return to the perimeter. They celebrated that night with a ration that had been issued to each man: two tins of beer and 100 cigarettes. A sure indication that the siege had been broken.

Further east, Rommel had kept attacking with fierce shelling, but to no avail. The screaming shells were met with equally fierce defence from the British troops. Facing the might of the well-equipped 8th Army the Germans had lost ground. On 7 December, Rommel began to withdraw and 10 December saw the Germans and Italians relinquish their hold on Hill 209.

By the end of December Rommel was forced to withdraw west, back to El Agheila, where he had first begun his offensive in March that year.

Tobruk had been under siege for more than eight months.

The diversionary role played by the 2/13th Battalion at Ed Duda had not come without immense cost. A splinter of shrapnel from the explosion of a 210-mm shell had pierced Colonel Burrows' brain while he was plotting the next move for his men.

John remembered the words spoken about Burrows while enlisting in Martin Place as though it were yesterday: 'If you want a good war he's the man to join.' Following the Ed Duda action, their Commanding Officer was out of action for the rest of the war, made a Brigadier in Australia and given a training command. Almost immediately Lieutenant Colonel Turner was appointed to replace him as CO of the 2/13th Battalion. Burrows would be missed. He had always been in the middle of the action; his greatest concern was always for the welfare and safety of his men.

A tribute was soon penned:

> Goodbye, old Boss, though you're leaving
> We will always remember your name;
> You're the man who formed this Battalion
> And brought all its glory and fame.
>
> Though we're fighting again with another,
> And sharing war's sorrows and joys,
> Way deep in our hearts we will always be called:
> 'Bull Burrows' Bomb Happy Boys!'
>
> We remember the time at Ed Duda,
> When you joined us way up in the line,
> And put all your weight in behind us—
> As you've done with us time after time.
>
> You weren't a little tin soldier,
> Just carrying pips and a crown;
> And there's none of us boys whoever could think
> Of letting the 'old Bull' down.
>
> When there was a job to be done,
> We knew you'd be doing your share;
> And whenever you had to judge one,
> We knew that your judgement was fair.
>
> So the 13th is saying good-bye, Sir,
> And wishing you all of the best;
> For we all know a man when we see one,
> And we know that you've well earned your rest.[16]

Ed Duda had resulted in scores of casualties. When the 2/13th arrived back they heard that the Tobruk hospital was impossibly overcrowded, accommodating more wounded than the base could cope with.

The grotesqueness of what they had seen left each man with his own reflections on the unfairness, haphazardness and fate of war. The *Latona* might have taken them all to Egypt a month before, if only its phosphorous trail had not attracted that deadly bomb. John was convinced it was all a numbers game.

Counselling was not available and some men did not recover. John remembered at Ed Duda where 'one fellow almost went mad, wandered off ... you could see him just going into the flashes of shellfire ... he couldn't take it any more'. Most of the men, however, were astoundingly resilient. If only now they could hear how Lieutenant General Rommel would later describe them—these 'extraordinarily tough fighters' from Australia: '... immensely big and powerful men—an elite formation of the British Empire'.[17]

A few days before he left Tobruk, General Morshead unveiled a memorial in a simple ceremony to honour the dead at the war cemetery: 'At the setting of the sun we are met to honour those whose sun has set ... the smooth brown sand of the desert is broken by 800 crosses and the mounds of 800 graves. Silhouetted against the sky is their memorial—a plain grey concrete obelisk—bearing the inscription:

> 'This is hallowed ground, for here lie those who
> died for their country.
> At the going down of the sun and in the morning
> we will remember them.'

It was difficult for the 2/13th to accept that they were now 'free'; that the war had 'moved overnight'. John found the experience disconcerting: 'Tim Fearnside was still the platoon sergeant. He used to call me "Jack" by the way. He said, "Jack, the war's gone past us now. We can just sleep tonight. We're not wanted."

'But we couldn't sleep. We couldn't relax. We couldn't possibly occupy one of those fortified positions and relax. We had to have sentries on for anyone to sleep. Strange.'

There was time for plenty of talk on that first night back—and plenty to talk about. The Poles had captured Hill 209; Japan had bombed Pearl Harbor; America had joined the war. Almost too much to take in. At least their talk helped them accept the rotten fact that they were the only ones left in Tobruk.

Now awaiting their evacuation, those who had not been injured at Ed Duda thanked their lucky stars. Their wounded mates had been bombed on their getaway ship, about 55 kilometres (35 miles) out of Tobruk Harbour. Only about a third of the victims had been saved.

On 15 December, the British paid tribute to the 2/13th in a short ceremony during which Major General Scobie praised them for the vital part they had played, making particular reference to the misfortune of Colonel Burrows. One of the many farewell messages the men received after the ceremony included a note from 3 Squadron, RAAF. 'Best of luck. Will keep an eye on you over the desert.'[18] Yes—they were leaving by land.

At long last 16 December 1941 dawned. It was time to depart and the men piled into trucks. Staring steadfastly towards the perimeter, they were convinced it would be impossible to erase from their memories the small outcrops of rock in the desert; the narrow slit trenches forced into parched ground; the wind-blown wadis.

At 7 am they reached El Adem Road. They could barely believe they were leaving the place. 'We hoped to hell that nothing would stop our departure.'

Chapter Fifteen

Leave at last

AFTER FAR TOO MANY DISAPPOINTMENTS, WARNING ORDERS
AND THEN SUBSEQUENT CANCELLATIONS, THE BATTALION
MOVED OUT OF TOBRUK, BOUND FOR EGYPT. IT WAS OBVIOUS
THAT ... THEY WERE ALL TOO READY TO BELIEVE THAT
SOMETHING COULD EASILY PREVENT THEM FROM GETTING
AWAY AT LONG LAST.

—Fearnside, 1993[1]

JOHN WAS ELATED. The 2/13th were now travelling across the Egyptian desert, in a long line of trucks. A lot of the men were dressed in the German or Italian uniforms they had found dumped along the way, because their own were in tatters—they could barely remember the last time they had received an issue. Being mid-December it was cold, so they were glad of the extra warmth.

Many things had changed during their eight months of isolation in Tobruk. While travelling through Egypt, John saw large numbers of 'little fleabites of vehicles' which turned out to be American jeeps going through their paces. They were all out in open formation, approximately 90 metres (100 yards) apart. It was the first time he had seen such a spread of vehicles.

After crossing the Suez Canal, they crowded into an old train headed for Gaza, 'an engine with some open carriages', which would take them on the rest of their journey. They could hear the bleating of sheep from some of the other creaky train carriages. 'It was a shambles, but who cared?' An understanding command ignored the exploding fireworks 'gathered from somewhere along the line'—and the accompanying loud yahoos. A myriad of colours, a cacophony of sound, but not bombs for a change.

After almost a week of travel they finally arrived. It was 21 December 1941. EPIP tents (English pattern, Indian patent) had all been laid out, with eight men allocated to a tent in the old British manner. Parcels from home were piled up waiting to be opened. They had their first meal of fresh meat in ten months; beer came out in a steady stream from the canteen.

John could not remember being happier or more relieved, especially as he knew that the celebration would be followed by a good period of leave. Another battalion was appointed to look after them, to make sure they 'didn't fall into a slit trench or drown' while over a whole week about 300 of them 'kicked up an awful row and overdid it completely'. Knowing what they had been through, their wise commanders turned a blind eye.

When John and the others of the 2/13th Battalion set off from Tobruk, they were unaware of the continuing dispute over maintaining the Australian troops abroad. Political communications between the British and Australians had become increasingly tense.

The men had heard little about the disastrous events unfolding in the Pacific and initially did not appreciate the need for extra military protection at home. At first the Japanese threat was not obvious. Europe was the main event; Asia just a side-show.

With Germany fighting on several fronts there seemed no reason for Japan not to continue expanding its influence from Manchuria and parts of China further south into Thailand, Malaya and the Dutch East Indies. To an extent these Asian countries saw Japan as a liberator, welcoming the idea of being freed from French, British and Dutch colonial rule. But soon it was obvious that the Japanese came as conquerors.

Even before the men left Tobruk, the Japanese had launched an air attack on Pearl Harbor, the American base in Hawaii. By the next day, on 8 December 1941, they were landing on the Malay Peninsula. Churchill claimed to have suffered nightmares from the shock of hearing about the loss on 10 December of HMS *Repulse* and HMS *Prince of Wales*, two British battleships off the Malay coast.[2]

Written ten days after his arrival in Palestine, John's letter was filled with Christmas greetings and news of Palestine, referring only obliquely to the Japanese aggression:

... Well, darling one, it's too late to wish you Merry Xmas, but you were so much in my thoughts that you must have felt it. However, may you enjoy all that happiness can bring you for 1942 and I hope to goodness we are all back home again for next Xmas.

We're here in Palestine at last ... I am writing away in a nice big tent, which I live in with some others, warm and comfortable. No dust, no trenches, no flies, and above all away from all evidence of war except our uniforms, rifles and equipment. We arrived here a day or so before Xmas to find a good camp already set up for us with our parcels and mail which had been piling up for months. Opening all those parcels was just like opening a Xmas stocking.

We were the last Australians to leave [Tobruk] ... all the others left about two months before us ... So we stayed on and took part in that swift and decisive blow against the Axis forces in the desert ... So that's it: it's over and finished ... thank God successful; and no doubt that little spot has made history. Certainly Australians will always remember it.

After a slow journey by various means of transport, we arrived here just in time to wash the filth from our bodies, get a complete new issue of clothing and start celebrating ...

It's hard to settle down, very hard indeed; I have lost so much and gained so much that it is hard to get to an even keel. Tonight I leave for Cairo for eight days ... my first decent leave since I left you. While there, I'm going to be very civilised; dine and wine well and get myself cleaned up properly.

Today I am twenty-six; still very young, darling, but I suppose I will have to call myself a man now, although I'm afraid that I'm still very much a boy in most ways. I find that I can look back over quite a number of years; it's amazing isn't it how they slip by. Ironically enough my oldest and first memory is of Armistice Day when we were holidaying in Cronulla.[3] 'What will we do with the Kaiser?' That will soon be changed to 'Hitler'. Amazing, this mad world of ours, really.

Now you have the threat of things closer to you, quite close indeed. Lots of us feel we would like to be a lot closer to home than we are at present. Who knows? Before long you may hear of us being closer. If we stay here, there should be a very fair chance of us not seeing action again. I think most of us who were right through this last show desire it that way. I think nearly nine months of continuous action is just about enough for a while …

It's great to have news of you again and to know what you are all doing … I'll write again from Cairo, darling, and tell you all about it. There's nothing I need now, Mother dear, I have everything. The little watch is still faithfully ticking away and the pipe my best friend. Thanks terribly darling.
31 December 1941

Leave at last! Eight days of clean beds, hot baths, tasty meals and normal sleep in Cairo weakened John's intentions to write home:

In my last letter I said I was going to write to you from Cairo, but I was too busy there seeing and doing things so please forgive me. Had eight days there altogether, my first leave for twelve months, so you can well believe just how I felt about it. I really did have a good time, and most of all I enjoyed hot baths and clean beds and the complete lack of all regimentation …

Except for paying respects to officers in the street, one felt completely free from the army … I really did have an enjoyable time. Cairo in peace should be quite fun.
[Date indecipherable]

Leave was over too soon and then it was on to Syria, where the battalion's main purpose was to protect the rich oil fields in the Middle East from any German advance through Turkey. On 13 January 1942, the men arrived in Latakia on the coast where they were to stay in a camp on the outskirts for the next two months.

This was not only a city of scholars, museums and antiquities—there were also brothels. For the first time in Australia's military history, senior regimental officers approached a brothel, Maison Dorée, run by a madam called Henrietta, for the exclusive use of a battalion. Tim Fearnside noted that the girls were a 'cheerful lot', known to the troops by names such as Angel, Baby, Big Tits Betty, Vera the Turk and Rosie.[4]

John limited his letters to other matters:

On arriving back at camp again we once more received our moving orders, so here we are now in Syria ... The country is very pretty ...green valleys and high snow-covered mountains. First time I've seen snow, but we know all about it when the wind blows directly off it ... We have five blankets and plenty of woollens, thank goodness. Most of the boys received scarves and balaclavas etc in their parcels just the same as I have.

You have been wonderful at home, darling, sending all those parcels. I received another last night with a lovely knitted sweater. Very good of you, darling, to send me things like that. It does make a difference. Thanks for your cable too. Mrs Gill also sent me a Xmas cable; very sweet of her. Margie has been very good too. John Oldham came up to our camp in Palestine to see me but I had just left as one of the advance party to come here. I was very sorry to have missed him ...

There's still plenty of fighting to be done in Europe yet and I'd like to be in it, but somehow I think we will be put against the Japs. It will be very much the same I suppose wherever they put us.

You know it's very strange how nearly all of us hate it but will be in it again whenever they say the word. Those of us who came right through those nine months have had good experience I suppose, which will be useful in whatever type of war we have to fight. Anyway, when it's finished, the foundation stone will surely have been laid for a secure and lasting peace, even [though] the reconstruction period is going to be tough for everybody.
21 January 1942

The new camp offered comparative relaxation where the men could eat calmly and sometimes manage a full night's sleep without waking up in a sweat. Everyone was now able to catch up with their correspondence:

A few more lines, darling, to let you know I'm well and happy ... We've got to know each other so well, and lots of us have been through some tough spots together, so we know just what and what not to say to each other. Charlie could explain what I mean—he had more of it than I've had.

We're feeling much better now. We needed a good long rest with good conditions and so far we're having it. Our camp is in very pretty country and we get plenty of leave to a little town close by. The people are quite friendly and we can get quite decent meals at various little cafés for a few piasters. They are really quite an unfortunate people, they've had to bow to so many conquering nations through the ages that they must find it very hard to form anything individual of their own ... most of them are very poor.

I've said the country is very pretty—and it really is ... The sheep are the same old kind, coarse-woolled and black-faced, but they are sheep for all that; and sometimes when I hear a lamb calling its mother or catch the faint sheep smell in the wind, I am not in Syria at all. But those are rare and precious moments and one can't help being caught unawares just once in a while. It is very sweet while it lasts, but too much is a bad tonic and makes one unfit for the job in hand.

My closest friend is Tim Fearnside, my platoon sergeant. You don't know him yet but, God willing, you shall ... We were closely together right through Tobruk except for a couple of months, which he spent in hospital from a wound. His brother was killed in our last action [Ed Duda] but he carried on and did a splendid job with lots of responsibility, in a manner in which only real men can. Tim spends his spare time and lots of the Army's time writing, and one day I think he will make a name for himself ...

We play football here on a hard and stony ground ... no one seems to get hurt very much. There is an orphanage close by, run by the priests ... it's nice to get amongst kids for a while who are not everlastingly holding out their hand for 'baksheesh'. French is their tongue, but most speak Arabic fluently and some a little English. Some of our lads have polished up their French pretty well, but every time I try to make myself understood, searching for a few words, and making wild signs with my arms amongst a gathering crowd, some little kid generally turns up and helps me out in simple English. So, I'm giving up.

If I want a meal it's much easier to point to my mouth and start chewing air with relish. Paying for it is, of course, life's next big problem. I pull out a handful of notes and coins of all shapes and sizes and start sorting them out knowingly, and trying to look unconcerned. But it's no good—I'm mixed up—some are Egyptian, some Palestinian and, of course, some 'must' be Syrian ... I can never get rid of the feeling that I've paid about ten times too much. A soldier should always be an ambassador for his country should he not? I mightn't be a Casey or an Eden, but I bet after dealing with me they either think Australia must be a pretty good place or else I'm just another damned fool. Probably the latter.

Well darling, we hear news of the war out your way and it doesn't sound so good. The Japs have certainly collared the first round, and made things look awkward but there are plenty of rounds to come, and there's absolutely no doubt now about the final issue. It's just a matter of time and a full effort by everyone.

We all want to be home now; there is quite a lot of talk amongst the boys of how they would like to be 'doing the Japs over'. Some of us don't say much and notice that most of the talk of fight comes from reinforcements who have seen 'nothing yet'. They are mostly good kids and keen, but nevertheless I like to get away on my own sometimes.
1 February 1942

It was no wonder that there was talk of 'doing the Japs over'. The men heard more and more of the extraordinary Japanese push south. Conquest by conquest. In January 1942, the Malay capital, Kuala Lumpur, had been captured. Manila in the Philippines was taken, Dutch (east) Borneo was invaded, the Wake Islands fell, Rabaul in New Britain and the Celebes were attacked. After the Japanese bombing of New Guinea on 22 January 1942, Australia became mesmerised.

Far greater shocks regarding the Japanese invasions in the Pacific were to follow in February. The 2/13th could do little but listen with worry and wonder as news came through.

On 8 February 1942, 23,000 Japanese soldiers surged through the Malayan jungle and mangrove swamps, attacking Singapore across the Johor Straits. Churchill had not paid due attention to his military advisors who, according to military historian Dr Ong Chit Chung, had warned of the imminent threat and had even put in place a plan, code-named Matador, to prevent the land invasion. Requests for additional back-up had been ignored as the British leader concentrated on his 'priority areas', Russia and the Middle East.[5] Churchill instructed that the battle for Singapore 'must be fought to the bitter end at all costs' and the 'commanders and senior officers should die with their troops'.[6]

And die they did. By 15 February 1942 Singapore had fallen. So much for Churchill's 'impregnable fortress' in the Pacific. One hundred and thirty thousand British were taken prisoner along with 32,000 Indians and 15,000 Australians. Churchill privately admitted that the fall of Singapore was 'the most shameful day of my life'.[7] Curtin's predictions about the danger to Australia had been correct. On 19 February 1942, four days after the fall of Singapore, Darwin was bombed.

Murray Fletcher, a postal worker in Darwin, survived a direct hit on the local post office. He lived to tell the tale because he was fleet enough to reach a prepared trench. The fellow he was with waited a second or two longer and ironically was blown into the trench by the blast. He was severely injured and died shortly afterwards. The next raid, on the postmaster's residence, adjacent to the post office, immediately killed the nine people sheltering there.[8] The announcement of eleven fatalities in Darwin by the Australian Government was a gross understatement: 238 were killed.[9]

In March and April 1942, Australia's Christmas Island was occupied, Bougainville in the Solomons was taken, Ceylon (Sri Lanka) was raided and Burma was abandoned by the British. More and more territory was falling to the Japanese. An 'air of panic ... hung over some quarters of the Australian population'.[10]

While he could see the facts plainly before him—Japan had crippled the US fleet in the Pacific, overwhelmed the British and seized much of South-East Asia—John remained deliberately low-key. Having mollified his mother about his improving health—his bolstered blood from green vegetables and the clearing up of 'Barcoo rot' [scurvy]—he went on to refer to the situation in the Pacific. Concern in the form of some quiet advice was buried deep in his letter:

Have been wondering lately if you have had to move from Dee Why owing to [the] present situation. If you have to move go outback, darling, you'll like it there, and I'd feel a lot happier. It's hard to know if they will send us home or not. It's possible they may leave some of us over here ...

Naturally we feel we should be closer to home ... Strange how us youngsters can't be told anything when we imagine we're grown up and know everything. I can remember before I left talking to Charlie once and can realise now that he was thinking, 'I hope to Christ you don't have to go through what I did.' Charlie knew what I'd have to go through but he was wise enough to know that a man must be true to himself first. I would not have had it any other way. So Amen to that.
23 March 1942

On the day that John wrote this letter, code-breakers in Canberra deciphered a Japanese plan to seize Port Moresby and from there threaten north-eastern Australia.

The American General Douglas MacArthur had been appointed Commander-in-Chief of the South-West Pacific Area five days before. With total support from Prime Minister John Curtin for this and all subsequent orders, the general immediately ordered Allied land forces to 'prevent any landing on the north-east coast of Australia or on the south-western coast of New Guinea'.[11]

Readers of the weekly *Bulletin* magazine would have shakily reflected on the prescient editorial comment a fortnight before: 'War has ceased merely to be on Australia's doorstep. It is on the mat reaching for the knocker.'[12]

Meanwhile John continued his war duties in the northern hemisphere. April 1942 saw the 2/13th Battalion redirected to Tripoli in Lebanon, to guard oil installations and to defend against any possible German advancement. The 150-kilometre (93-mile) march from Latakia progressed through a mostly inhospitable area with big, round granite rocks and oil tanks scattered around. Along the way John caught glimpses of olive groves and green mulberry trees, a surprising and refreshing change from the hard desert sand.

And there were other differences. The girls from the Maison Dorée, with their madam, Henrietta, turned out to say goodbye to the men on the march to their next destination. The men were 'tickled pink' to see them.

Fearnside thought that not even a general reviewing his troops would have got such an efficient 'eyes left' from the soldiers as Henrietta and her girls received that afternoon.[13]

Each night on the journey John was asked to entertain the men with his accordion, accompanying Frank Graves, a talented cornet player who had been a member of the J.C. Williamson orchestra in Sydney. When the CO approached him in the officers' mess one night, John said that he would prefer to be playing in the battalion band. A memorable childhood experience in 1918 had fostered his love of martial music:

'Mother took us on a holiday to Cronulla and on a dirt road, on Armistice Day, a brass band came marching by ... I was not quite three. That was my first clear memory ... those glittering brass instruments and the noise ... it always affected me.'

Much to John's delight, his suggestion was taken up; he was accepted immediately as one of the battalion band members. Bull Burrows and the whole contingent had earlier declared it was the best band in the AIF. Always winning competitions proved it.

Settled in the camp at Tripoli from 20 April for two months, where they were doing mobile training daily, John and the men gradually came to the conclusion that they would have further military responsibilities in the desert. The Allies' situation was looking precarious in Russia, Britain and in Western Europe. Even worse, they were now on the defensive, west of Tobruk. Losing in North Africa would have catastrophic consequences. When the men heard that the New Zealanders of the 6th Brigade had been mobilised and were heading towards El Alamein, their suspicions strengthened.

Until then their thoughts had been focused on returning home. John had written to Margie:

> *Things are getting beyond a joke. A fair thing's a fair thing, but this is certainly no good. What's the use of having a lovely niece if I'm not going to get to know her? ... Life is not so bad over here, but we'd like to be a bit closer to home the way things are moving. It's not so hot twiddling one's thumbs ... when big things are going on all around.*[14]
> *[Undated]*

Big things were going on all around, but still the Australian Government stalled. Time was needed to debate the proposal regarding their overseas troops. On 10 March 1942, President Roosevelt had promised Prime Minister Curtin two additional divisions in the Pacific for support against further Japanese attack. However, in return, it was expected that the 9th Division would stay put.

Would the 2/13th Battalion be able to return to defend their homeland, or would they again be used on the other side of the world to assist in the defence of the Mother Country? John's destiny and that of his entire division was now in the hands of the Australian Government.

Chapter Sixteen

Shattering news

A DEATHLIKE HUSH, FOREBODING GREAT EVENTS, LAY
HEAVILY ON THE BATTALION, BEARING DOWN ON THE
OPTIMISM OF THE 'HOME AT ANY PRICE' PROPHETS AND
KINDLING SPECULATION AMONG THOSE KEENER TO KNOW
'HOW SOON?' AND 'JUST WHERE?' THE UNIT WOULD BE SENT ...

—Fearnside, 1993[1]

WHEN THE 2/13TH Battalion was moved to Aleppo in Syria for more
training, the men suspected that their redeployment in the desert was just
a matter of time. But it was a single news flash in June 1942 that sealed
their fate. Sounds of any flippant fun quickly dwindled in their camp as
the grim bulletin spread: Tobruk had fallen into German hands.

Seven months before, in November 1941, when they had left Tobruk,
brimming with confidence in the aftermath of the Crusader success, the
men did not know that Rommel had withdrawn in such order that he had
'left the British forces far behind' in North Africa and within months was
rebuilding his own forces with supplies from across the Mediterranean—
preparing for another advance on the garrison.[2]

Rommel's attack on Tobruk on 20 June was swift and successful.
Just before the attack, Allied Intelligence reporting to London had
claimed that 'the garrison was adequate, the defences in good order, and
90 days' supplies were available for the troops'.[3] How wrong the advice
had been.

This time the enemy had far greater knowledge of the terrain and the defenders. After a day and night of heavy dive-bombing attacks and artillery assaults from the Germans, the fortress was forced to surrender at dawn. Rommel had his jewel in the crown.

Churchill was visiting President Roosevelt in Washington when he heard the news. For him the fall of Tobruk was one of the worst blows of his career; an unbearable humiliation.[4] He now needed all the support he could get. 'Another British failure would be the end of Winston,' claimed the Minister of Information, Brendan Bracken, a close confidant of Churchill's.[5]

These developments were indeed disastrous for Britain. Rommel was hailed a hero in Berlin and promoted to Field Marshal. He now drove his troops eastwards in a relentless advance along the coastline, further and further into Egypt. Mersa Matruh fell to the Germans on 29 June. When they reached El Alamein—a small coastal town in Egypt that stretched from the Mediterranean inland to rocky ridges—they stopped. After resupply and regrouping, they would continue on to Cairo and from there to the prize—the Suez Canal. Their quest was almost over.

Now more than ever, the Australians were needed in the Middle East. Morshead reported the British observation to Australian Prime Minister Curtin—that the 9th Division was 'the main pin of the operations', the formation the British 'could least afford to lose. Without it the battle would collapse.'[6]

Under intense pressure the Australian Government was forced to make a decision. The chiefs of staff reasoned that the two promised American divisions would require the same amount of time to reach Australia as would the 9th Division. Moreover, massive Australian shipping movements could be avoided by choosing the American protection offered. In the end, placated by the promise of alternative support, Curtin reluctantly agreed to the negotiated proposal. The 9th Division would remain in the Middle East.

Once again, rumours that travelled through the ranks throughout their engagement pre-empted information and changed the mood of the troops.

There was a certain bitterness amongst the men in the 2/13th. Soon they would see leaflets scattered all over the countryside by the Germans asking them, 'What about Port Darwin?' Stories emerged that some men had been dumped by their girls in Australia for being 'too yellow' to

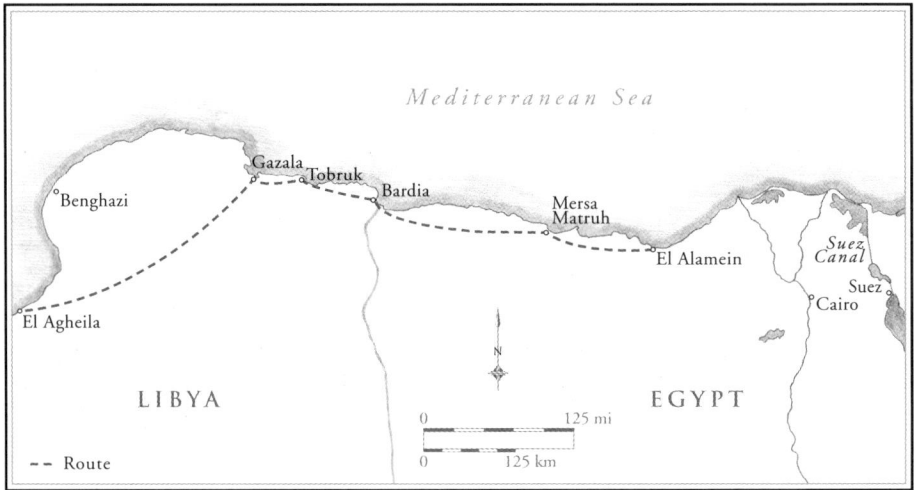

Movement of German and Italian forces towards El Alamein, 1942.
Tobruk was taken in June.

come home and face the Japanese; some had received white feathers, symbolising cowardice, in letters.

However, it was as though the 2/13th men knew what was expected of them. Les Clothier wrote on 28 June that it looked as though they would move to Egypt 'to meet Rommel's boys'. The enemy had taken Mersa Matruh and the position was now 'critical'.[7]

On 30 June 1942 the 2/13th Battalion was heading towards El Alamein. 'The quiet, peaceful-looking hills of Palestine with their green fields of crops and orange groves were passing to the rear in the gathering dusk as the train puffed, rocked and jolted over the uneven rails conveying it south.'[8] They would spend that night on hard ground, near a tiny village on the outskirts of Alexandria.

On this occasion John did not travel in the normal crowded truck or rickety train. Now a member of the battalion band, he was invited to accompany the ambulance officers and stretcher-bearers who formed a large part of the musical company. Travelling through Cairo and Alexandria in the ambulance vehicle was relatively comfortable, especially as the boys had a primus stove which was adequate enough for cooking and capable of producing 'luxurious' cups of tea.

In a letter John wrote to his mother there was no mention of their new destination—El Alamein:

We have left Syria and you probably realise where we are though I'm not allowed to tell you. But you will know definitely before this reaches you.

I received two letters from you a few days ago, one had the letter from Jane [Peter's wife] to you enclosed; thanks so much it was lovely to have all that news. Also received a small parcel of barley sugar, thanks again, darling.

Expect that for some months you would not have been very surprised had I rung up from somewhere in Australia ... Well, darling, it looks as though there is still plenty to do over here and perhaps it's a good policy leaving some New Zealanders and Australians over this way ... Lots of chaps moan all the time about us not being home, but strangely enough the worst of them are reinforcements who have only recently arrived here and have not seen action yet ...

I consider the army has more than done its share. For my part I have been well clothed and at most times well fed. My leave has been quite liberal and I've nearly always been treated as a human being and not as I expected as just another animal with a number. I have seen some wonderful countries and have made some good friends, and I am convinced I am a wiser man than before.

The time spent in actual warfare is short compared to the periods of inaction, so if one can ease all thoughts of war and its rottenness from the mind and hold only the nobler examples and profitable experiences in the memory, then a lot has been gained.

The various contacts made in the army change men much, mainly narrow-minded men broaden and expand; braggarts and bullies come down to a better level; cowards become brave. There are of course the few who turn the other way and become wasters of various types, mostly caused by a degree of inferiority complex. Unfortunately, the army allows men to have that complex because psychology has not yet found its place in the army vocabulary. A great pity, because its wholesale use would solve many an individual problem, and put many a man on the right track. However, I won't bore you with any more of that, because it's all rather obvious.

Summer has been on us with its usual vengeance and we found parts of Syria very hot; certainly a land of extremes. But with the hot weather come the fruit and the grain harvesting and we watch and wonder at the prevailing primitive methods still used by the tillers of the soil. The inland country of Syria contains large belts of wheat country and very little machinery is used to take in the grain. Quite easy to let the imagination go back several thousand years.

Well darling one, I do hope you are well and happy and have everything you want. Rest assured that I have wonderful health and am fit in every way …
7 July 1942

And then, around mid-July 1942, something quite remarkable happened in John's military career. He was invited by the CO, Lieutenant Colonel Robert Turner, to attend the Officer Cadet Training Unit (OCTU) in

At the Officer Cadet Training Unit in Cairo, July 1942.
John (third row, third from right) said this appointment was to save his life.

Cairo—a four-month 'condensed Sandhurst course' which produced officers for the Commonwealth forces.[9]

Visiting senior officers would come from various parts of the world and lecture battle-hardened students, usually a couple of hundred at a time. John thought the two-month general course, concentrated and demanding, was brilliantly conceived, as was its follow-up—another two months of specialist instruction in infantry, signals, engineering or the artillery corps. Simultaneously, he was amazed it was being held at all: 'Quite extraordinary, with Rommel knocking at the gates. There was the general, 40 miles from us, while we were learning how to deal with him.'

This was the chance John had been waiting for, to get his commission. Lieutenant Colonel Turner's letter to John's mother, a month or so later, confirmed the selection:

BN 2/13 AUST INF
12 AUG 42

Mrs C.G. MURRAY
Culworth Ave,
KILLARA

Dear Mrs Murray,
No doubt your son has advised you that he has been selected to attend an Officer Cadet Training Unit [OCTU] in the Middle East. On completion of his course at this school, I have no doubt that he will pass out with a commission.

John Murray has always been an example to the men under his command and has shown those qualities of leadership and devotion to duty, which will qualify him for the promotion for which he is now training.

I hope that when Cpl Murray obtains his commission he will be posted to my command, when I have every confidence he will continue to display those qualities which bring credit both to himself and to the unit.
Yours sincerely,
Robert Turner Lt-Col
Comd 2/13 AUST INF BN

Once John had settled into the routines of the school, he was able to catch up on his letter writing. His next three letters, written in quick succession, would have more than satisfied his mother's desire for her son to take advantage of the opportunities offered by the Army. She had regretted the sudden interruption to his education and had done everything in her power to compensate for the shortfall. In return, John was determined to repay his mother for the sacrifices she had made. A career advance in the Army was high on his list of priorities:

Nearly all mental work, which you know I needed badly. The standard of training has been raised here considerably, and compares with anything in the world. A commission is earned here now, not given away.
October 1942

These months have changed me quite a bit I know, and I'm sure not for the worse. Things I have learnt will stick to me through life and be really valuable assets.

We make wonderful friendships here with the chaps from all over the place, and learn to understand the outlook of people from other countries.
11 October 1942

Places I've been to and things I've done in the army really amaze me when I think back. If I'd set out with lots of money to travel these countries, I could never have experienced so much.

We Australians on the whole are very lazy when it comes to learning about other countries. For instance, I have been over here now for two years and can hardly speak a word of Arabic, except of course the very few essentials, whereas every day I contact British troops, who only after a comparatively short time, can speak the language very well. And I'm afraid that goes for nearly all of us.

Well, darling, in three short weeks from now I hope to have my commission and be an officer of His Majesty's Forces.

It seems hard to realise now that time is approaching, and I often wonder just how much difference it will make to me. I have already changed considerably after nearly four months here; it's hard to explain just how ...
19 October 1942.

While John was keen to outline the advantages of the course in Cairo, no one knew, least of all he, that the time ordained for his training would coincide with one of the most brutal battles his battalion had ever seen. Three days after John wrote the last letter, terrific explosions 64 kilometres (40 miles) east of Cairo heralded the beginning of the main offensive at El Alamein.

Between July and November 1942, the Australian 9th Division suffered in total almost 6000 casualties. From John's own battalion sixty-seven men were killed in action and another twenty-seven later died of wounds. Almost half of them were officers and most of them were killed in October, days before his return from Cairo.

On several occasions John claimed that this one event—the invitation in the middle of 1942 to attend OCTU—had saved his life. 'I'm alive today because I missed it. I know that I would have never survived Alamein.'

Chapter Seventeen

El Alamein

THE MEN OF THE 9TH DIVISION FACED THE MAIN GERMAN
DEFENSIVE POSITION IN THE NORTH ... WHAT FOLLOWED
WAS A BLOODY SLOGGING MATCH WHICH LASTED FOR 11 DAYS
... [GIVING] MONTGOMERY THE OPPORTUNITY TO PUSH
ALLIED ARMOUR AGAINST ENEMY POSITIONS FURTHER SOUTH
... THE 9TH DIVISION HAD DRAWN UPON ITSELF SUCH ENEMY
STRENGTH AS TO WEAKEN ROMMEL IN THE SOUTH WHERE
THE DECISIVE BREAKTHROUGH TOOK PLACE.

BY 2 NOVEMBER, AGAINST HITLER'S ORDERS, ROMMEL
WITHDREW HIS FORCES TO SAVE WHAT WAS LEFT OF THEM
FROM ANNIHILATION.

—Cochrane, 2001[1]

WHILE JOHN TRAINED in cloistered OCTU rooms from July to November 1942, the men at El Alamein led a significantly more frenzied existence.

Les Clothier's diary entries stated a simple progression of facts: on 2 August after a massacre on Ruin Ridge the 28th Battalion no longer existed, all 'captured or killed ... with quite a lot of unburied about'; 3 September saw Hell 'a-popping down south' with big tank battles; on 7 October two men were run over by tanks at night, one dying with a crushed chest; 10 October saw heavy bombing from planes and 14 October recorded the biggest operation of the Middle East air-force, '1000 planes taking part'. And this was all before the main offensive.[2]

Meanwhile, desperate for added protection against the Japanese, the Australian Government continued insisting on the promised reinforcements. Prime Minister Curtin had warned about a 'direct attack on the [Australian] mainland' in a cable to Churchill on 29 September 1942. His 'missive' was passed on to Churchill's chiefs of staff, to 'consider at leisure'.[3] The following month, on 17 October, Curtin again called for support.

Churchill had other matters on his mind.

Colonel Turner gave the boys a pep talk on 22 October, telling the men it would be 'the biggest show ever put on in Africa'.[4] The main offensive at El Alamein was to begin the next day.

The role of the 2/13th Battalion was to attack the gun lines in the north after the 2/15th and 2/17th had cracked the first two German lines. But they need not worry, Turner assured them. They had forty-eight tanks in support.

It was exactly 9.40 pm on 23 October—the first night of the great offensive. The moon was almost full and there was a cool southerly breeze blowing.

John was more than three months into his course, in Cairo. While he prepared himself for lectures the following day, the men in his battalion prepared themselves for action. They all knew the routine.

Les Clothier gave the details: 'Well, tonight is the night for the big show ... there'll be several sea landings, paratroops and another attack down south ... the day after we go in there'll be 90 Sherman tanks and others out in front of us, plus a motorised group watching for a counterattack. I'm carrying 250 Tommy-gun rounds, six pencil and one drum magazine, pick, 6 sandbags and battle dress. Well, diary, here's hoping I come through okay ... '[5]

In the beginning it was a textbook attack. The 20th Brigade led the assault in the northern sector, where the heaviest number of enemy mines was planted. The initial charge was made on cue by the 2/15th and the 2/17th—a shock to the enemy who did not expect their strongest defences to be attacked first. The desert erupted in flames: '... the artillery was behind us ... 30 miles of guns wheel to wheel and when they let go ... the whole horizon was lit up and these bloody shells going over the top and I thought to myself, "Thank Christ they're going the other way".'[6]

However, it soon became obvious that the meticulous planning of the British General Montgomery, had neglected one thing. So thick were the German minefields that his 8th Army tanks were unable to get through. Without the support of the tanks, the Allied infantry began to struggle.

The next day, a successful enemy attack in the late afternoon devastated the leadership of the 2/13th Battalion. Intelligence Officer Barton Maughan was wounded and hospitalised after a shell blew him out of the battalion quarters dugout.[7] When a piece of shrapnel from the same shell killed Colonel Turner, Major George Colvin found himself as the replacement, immediately promoted in the field to Lieutenant Colonel.

The Australian battalions continued fighting, still with no back-up from British tanks. As the 2/13th officers in A, B, C and D Companies attempted to deal with the confusion, they were slaughtered. By 4.30 am, on the third day of the offensive, the remnants of the four companies were reorganised into one small bedraggled company. There was still no sign of the tanks.

A temporary pause allowed the reorganisation. The hostilities see-sawed, with severe losses on each side. Machine-gunning, shelling, exploding mines and hand-to-hand combat created a fog of smoke and dust.

Not until the night of 29 October did the men of the 2/13th manage to snatch some sleep. For Joe Madeley it was the last straw. 'After five nights of fighting amid unrelenting shelling, my nerves were wearing down. For the first time since I joined up, I remember finally saying to the mate beside me: "Gawd, I'm scared stiff."'[8] Les Clothier wrote with typical understatement: 'We had some bother.'[9]

Churchill became increasingly alarmed by the stalemate. This campaign, after all, was to be an event that would restore his reputation after the fall of Tobruk.

And then, as if by magic, over the next few days the situation changed for the Australians. Morshead had brought in a new brigade, the 24th, to assist the beleaguered troops. Dwindling German fuel supplies were causing growing concern to Rommel. He admitted to his wife in a letter that almost all hope had gone. He was sleeping with his eyes 'wide open', such was the responsibility he had to bear.[10]

Montgomery began his surge ahead from the south, having correctly predicted that the 'crumbling might take ten or twelve days'.[11] He had kept the men informed of all military plans, ensuring that there was plenty of realistic rehearsal for every unit and convincing them that they would 'hit Rommel for six out of Africa'—an apt prediction since those fighting under his command, the British, Australians, New Zealanders, South Africans and Indians, were all from cricket-loving nations.

While John was suitably impressed by General Montgomery's prescience, he had reservations about the man: 'Montgomery was very good you know ... strange fellow ... but so intense and so sure of himself ... a brilliant bloke, but not the bloke you'd want to know socially I assure you ... a mean miserable little man ... would never have a drink in the officers' mess ... But the right person for the right time ... the man of the hour.'

On the night of 2 November 1942 'the man of the hour' came charging through with his 'Operation Supercharge', the 9th Division maintaining intense pressure on the Germans further north. The German front was forced to retreat to the west. At 5.30 pm Rommel had ordered a general withdrawal to avoid complete encirclement.

From then on the Allies were in command. By nightfall, the sound of heavy vehicles confirmed what all wanted to hear. The enemy had begun their retreat. The Australian sector 'quietened down' as Montgomery directed enemy attention elsewhere.

On 6 November 1942 the men moved to a rest area on the coast. There was still work to be done. It was a tradition that not one of its dead had ever been left in an unmarked grave, 'except in two or three instances when recovery was impossible'.[12] There was to be no move and no rest until this grisly task on the El Alamein battlefield had been completed.

Once this traumatic responsibility was faced, gradually the men responded to the well-deserved congratulations that came their way. The generals were lavish in their praise of the early Australian effort which 'renewed the morale of the battle-weary troops, most of whom had lost several dear comrades':[13] General Montgomery described Morshead's men as 'magnificent'; General Leese of the 8th Army praised their 'magnificent fighting', the 'immense part they played in the battle' without which 'the final breakthrough could not have been achieved'.[14]

In Britain, by 8 November, 'everybody from Prime Minister [Churchill] to charlady was overjoyed. The church-bells were rung'.[15]

Around this time, mid-November 1942, just days after the final showdown, John returned from OCTU. He had missed gaining first prize in the course by one point.

The carnage of El Alamein was over. On his return, Commanding Officer Colvin immediately approached him, promoting him to the job of

Intelligence Officer for the 2/13th Battalion. The offer would be made official with a gathering of senior battalion officers in the tent.

John felt immensely proud. During the friendly, entertaining ceremony of a small band of officers, 'old and treasured pips' were put on his shoulders and a couple of welcoming speeches confirmed his appointment. John's old friend, Bill Ash, joined in the celebrations. They had smoked Grandfather Ash's cigars under his house in Turramurra and had many common memories from childhood.

After the party the CO approached John:

'Come and see me tomorrow morning at 8.00. Show me where things stand. We'll take a look at the whole situation together. Bring all relevant materials to the meeting.'

'Yes, Sir.'

The next morning John reported to his superior. On presenting the papers he had frantically managed to collect overnight, he felt Lieutenant Colonel Colvin stare at him with disdain: 'What's this? Bloody rubbish! I want to tell you something now. Never, ever bring a shoddy piece of work like this to me again. I will not accept it. Go off now and bring back something worth looking at.'

John learned from that moment that Colvin would 'accept nothing but the pristine best'. With sharp words, the new CO had given him a lesson he would never forget. John wrote to his mother about the promotion, but not about his dressing down:

> *I wrote quite a long letter to you yesterday but have not posted it, as certain changes have come about since then, so have decided to write again and tell you all about it.*
>
> *Firstly, I have received my commission ... Secondly, I am now the 13th BN Intelligence Officer and that to me is quite an important event in my life.*
>
> *Finished the four months' school at OCTU about ten days ago, and none of the Australians leaving at the same time as I were commissioned from the school. We all returned immediately to our units holding our previous rank. That was rather a blow, but it was an AIF order, so that was that.*
>
> *However, as soon as I joined the BN, the CO made instant application to have my commission put through. Last night I was*

summoned to the CO's tent where there was quite a nice little gathering of our officers. As soon as I walked in they pounced on me with very hearty congratulations and then they proceeded to punch the necessary holes in my shirt and placed my pips in position ... Today I have taken over my new job and have been receiving congratulations from everyone about the place, and also getting used to being saluted.

Well, darling, I'm particularly glad for your sake, because I know you have been dying to see me get on ... It means that I have lots more work and responsibility, but a definitely nicer position while in the army ...

There have been lots of changes in the BN lately, and as you have no doubt read in the papers, the fighting was very hard and bitter and once again the infantry had to carry the heavy burden. The BN did a magnificent job, never failing to capture its objective in the many attacks. You will read the full story of it some day.

Well, darling one, do keep well and happy, and have no worries concerning your little son. Won't be long before we are all home again ... Much love darling.
18th November 1942

Too soon John had to get on with his dismal responsibility of writing up detailed reports of the El Alamein offensive, a period of about four months altogether, including the preparation and final battle. Barton Maughan had left copious notes for the job.

It was an awkward assignment for him, this 'gruesome task' of piecing together the long campaign which had resulted in so many 9th Division casualties.[16] Not only had he missed the intense last ten days, but because there were so many deaths amongst the senior officers he was hard-pressed to get the right story.[17]

Nevertheless, despite immense Australian losses, John was able to record the main El Alamein battle as a victory, which ultimately led to the German retreat from North Africa.

After playing such an integral part in the victory, many of the 9th Division regretted not being able to accompany the 8th Army further west into Tunisia, to be part of the final annihilation of Rommel's Afrika Korps.

Six months later, back in Australia, John was to write to his mother:

What wonderful news from Tunisia. Every one of us has been
following it very closely, and I'm afraid our spirit is still with the
Eighth Army. How we would have loved to have been there to
share in the final fruits of that victory. We can picture those
wonderful men who were our brothers in arms over there in the
desert. Men of all colours, and from all parts of the Empire.
     It has been truly said that the Eighth Army has fulfilled the
role of the Crusaders. The messages we have just received from
Generals Alexander and Montgomery, expressing their regret
that the 9th Division was not with them at the kill after having
played the most important part in making the whole operation
possible, has made us very sorry indeed that we were recalled ...
We have some wonderful memories to cherish forever.
12 May 1943

Churchill now had his victory in North Africa, thanks in no small part to the
efforts of Australia's 9th Division. Towards the end of the El Alamein
campaign, he had advised that the Australians were to be used 'freely'; that
'no further reference to Australia [was] needed'. Once the battle was completely
over, he wrote that they should 'make the best arrangements possible to send
the Australians home, if their return was still demanded'.[18] Taking this attitude
into account and considering his own repeated instructions for the return of
the division well before this time, Australian Prime Minister Curtin found it
difficult to celebrate the El Alamein triumph.

On 22 December 1942, the long trip across Egypt towards the Holy
Land culminated in a victory parade at Gaza Airport. Hot, tired, irritated
and resentful Australian soldiers practised for the parade, cursing those
who had organised it. There was a long, drawn-out presentation of arms.
Then triumphant, thankful words from General Alexander, Commander-
in-Chief Middle East Forces were spoken—a moving acknowledgement
of effort and sacrifice for all remaining men of the 2/13th Battalion, and
indeed of the whole division: 'When great deeds have been done there is
no harm in speaking of them ... Your reputation as fighters has always
been famous, but I do not believe you have ever fought with greater

bravery or distinction than you did during that battle, when you broke the German and Italian armies in the Western Desert.'

'The listening ranks stirred … shoulders went back and heads lifted. The memories of Tobruk were sharper then …' The moving address was followed by the 'inexpressible sadness' of the 'Last Post'.[19]

It was to be John's third Christmas in the Holy Land; cards, letters and parcels were piling in from Australia. Families in the Antipodes could hardly believe that they were to be deprived yet again of the full complement around their Christmas tables. The Army had at least attempted to replicate the festive celebrations:

> *Since last writing we have left the desert once more for our sunny home of Palestine, and are very happy to be here indeed … Xmas has gone by once again, darling, and I'm afraid I was rather homesick at times, even though every effort was made to make everyone happy.*
>
> *This is our third Xmas over here, seems hard to believe doesn't it, but nevertheless hard, cold fact. We have been very fortunate in spending each of them in a decent camp in Palestine. This year we went to a lot of trouble for the men to ensure them having a good Xmas. Our Xmas dinner was held on the parade ground with the officers waiting on the men. Turkey and plum pudding, fruit and nuts, and a bottle of Australian beer per man. The remnants of our band supplied music … From somewhere or other we got big gum tree limbs and stood them in the ground in amongst the tables. On a little mound of earth at one end of the gathering, the Australian Flag floated out in the breeze. Just as the meal was ending, General Morshead and our Brigadier arrived informally and walked all round and through the tables shaking hands and talking with the boys …*
>
> *So far I am very happy as an officer, darling, my work is very interesting and I have ten very nice lads in the 'I' Section. I don't know how long I will be lucky enough to be left in this job. It is rather unusual for the junior officer in the BN to be made IO. However, I'll just hope for the best … My job is mainly to keep the CO supplied with all information and maps, etc and also to keep an eye on security within the unit.*

Amongst the officers in the BN, there are many GPS boys, most of them in fact. From Kings, Mal Vincent, Barton Maughan, Paul Martin, Keith Wilson, Doug Greene and myself were all at school together. Kings have the majority amongst the officers. Freddie Treweeke was killed in the last battle, he was doing a wonderful job and everyone was sorry to see him go. We lost a lot of good men of all ranks, including many good friends of mine. But that is the price we pay.

I often wonder just how it is one becomes so casual to losses and how little affected one is when men go down each side of you. I suppose it passes quickly through the surface and becomes rather a deep wound, which, if one is strong mentally, only gives trouble when allowed to. Certainly a man's makeup is very strange. If I go to the pictures I shed a quiet tear in most sad spots, a picture that is only fake and make-believe, and yet the terrible and ghastly sides of war have very little effect, except perhaps on my nerves.

How well I can now understand Charlie's thoughts when he used to allow himself to remember on such days as he marched or gathered with the all too few of the old hands. A few days ago we had a tremendous parade of Australians in honour of our fallen comrades. General Alexander took our salute, and when we presented arms and the massed buglers played the 'Last Post', it is something few of us will forget.

Perhaps I should not write the sort of stuff I write to you; other people, if they knew, would possibly not think well of a son writing to his mother and talking about war, but darling, you are my mother, and when I write I feel that I am talking to you, not writing. And who should share my thoughts but you? To you only I owe all I have and all I am, and believe me darling, whatever I have been, I have always been proud of it and will continue to be so. I don't think I have ever been able to pretend to you and I don't see how it is very fair to either of us if I were to make my letter a pretence. I know I don't write many letters, not half enough, but when I do write, I try to write just how I think at the time and not force myself into writing just a sequence of necessity. Sometimes I have plenty of opportunity with a writing pad in front of me to write lots

of letters, but I just can't write them, then suddenly, like tonight,
I feel there's only one thing I can do and that is write to you.
Rather weak perhaps, but nevertheless a fact.

Thanks darling for all your parcels, pipe, etc. And all the
letters. I've had letters from all the family lately and parcels from
Margie. What a darling niece I must have, and how I long to just
catch her up in my arms and talk to her and play with her.
Also my little man John outback, I think he and I will get along
rather well together …

Recently I spent a few days in Alexandria and had a
marvellous time fitting myself out with clothes. I walked into
a big shop in ragged old desert clothes and in about an hour came
out looking a different person. It reminded me very much of other
days when I used to come down from the bush and either you
or Lorraine used to take me in hand and off we'd go into DJs or
somewhere and buy lovely things …
December 1942

The time was fast approaching for the 2/13th Battalion to depart. They would not easily forget the experience. One encounter stood out as an indicator of how different and even endearing this place could be.

Shortly before his return to Australia, John was on reconnaissance in Syria with Arthur Warner from 6 Section, son of a British engineer. Fluent in Arabic and many of its dialects, he was 'a dream of a fellow' to have in the 'I' Section. John used to take him everywhere he went.

One day they were out examining an area near the coast for road access. The chief of 'a sleepy little village surrounded by olive groves' pulled Arthur aside for an earnest conversation. Arthur told John it was embarrassing but necessary for him to repeat their conversation, because the chief 'wanted an answer'. If John would sire some children for the village, the elder would organise some of the girls of the village for him to impregnate.

John saw it as 'rather interesting'. An old man was looking at the rundown genetic strength of his village and was savvy enough to think an 'outcross' would revitalise it. 'What an extraordinary thing!' John took it as an enormous compliment. He told Arthur to tell the old man that it was unlikely they would be back, but that he was honoured to be selected for such an important role.

Soon the 2/13th Battalion, along with the entire 9th Division, would be leaving forever the land of orange groves, olive trees and desert sands. Rumours were rife about the need for them to be back on home territory.

The last day in the Middle East arrived. Cleaning camp, parading with gear, marching to their final point of departure—the men called it 'D' day. Their sea kits were more cumbersome than usual, bulging with souvenirs. However, when the *Aquitania* set sail from the Red Sea on 27 January 1943, they were still not aware of their destination or where they would be next deployed. This was always an aspect of military life that caused great frustration.

At first they anchored at a port city on the Red Sea. Then, on 3 February 1943, the convoy lifted anchor and headed south. Unbeknownst to them 'the troops had to face the hazard of crossing the Indian Ocean … with the lightest of naval escorts'. Initially the British chiefs of staff had considered sending them home completely unescorted. And this was for an army 'who had played such a leading role in the British victory at El Alamein'.[20]

Along the way their ultimate destination became clear. They attended lectures on the topography, climate, vegetation and indigenous peoples of New Guinea.[21] The men reasoned that at least they might see home for a bit. Surely fighting in the jungle would mean extra training—probably in their own country.

They began to point to the Southern Cross at night. Images of Sydney Heads flashed through their minds.

Chapter Eighteen

So near and yet so far

WE TURNED OUR THOUGHTS TOWARDS HOME. THERE WAS
A NOTICEABLE—WHAT SHALL I SAY—SORT OF ISOLATION
MOVEMENT AMONGST US. I STARTED TO THINK ABOUT MYSELF.
WHAT WAS I GOING TO DO? WHAT WOULD IT BE LIKE GETTING
OFF IN SYDNEY? ABSOLUTELY MARVELLOUS ... I THOUGHT
WHAT A WONDERFUL EXPERIENCE IT WOULD BE FOR US TO
DO THIS—TO COMPLETE THE CIRCUIT ... SO AWAY WE WENT
ACROSS THE OCEAN ON THE AQUITANIA.

—John Murray, 2003[1]

ON 18 FEBRUARY 1943, John caught sight of his homeland, albeit the
coast of Western Australia. When the ship docked at Fremantle, he had
never felt so happy to be an Australian, despite a bit of cheek from the
wharfies who ribbed the men about not being there to save Australia when
they were needed.

Long-awaited mail was brought on board and each man tried to find
a corner where he could pore over the words. Many of the men
communicated with their families to give notice of their imminent arrival:
hundreds of telegrams were sent from Fremantle. John decided to
surprise his mother and family.

As the *Aquitania,* in a convoy of super liners, made good pace across the
Great Australian Bight, John marvelled at how the bow of the ship 'cut
into the great mountains of water'. He watched huge areas of the ship

disappear, only to reappear magically some time later. This was a ship they all unashamedly loved with 'its antiquated engines and four tall funnels superimposed over a framework of greyhound sleekness'.[2] The 'good old *Aqua*' was taking them home.

On 25 February, officers of the 2/13th Battalion celebrated their association with the *Aquitania* by inviting the ship's captain and his officers to dine with them. It did not escape their notice that on the front of the red printed invitation, which was emblazoned with a large 'V', only fifty names of the original 125 officers appeared.

As the men got closer to home they were fighting conflicting emotions; Australia was not to be their final destination. Lieutenant Colonel Colvin had warned the men in the battalion that their role in the future would be even more exacting than that in the Middle East. 'Good luck and good leave,' he concluded, making it all too clear there was more to be done.

'We're due in Sydney tomorrow. Well, diary, here's hoping I have a good homecoming and may I be able to continue this and look back on my ME [Middle East] war memories through this book in years to come,' wrote Les Clothier.[3]

On 27 February 1943, it seemed like the *Aquitania* was tipping. Everyone crowded on deck, wanting to get their first glimpse of the Heads. As they steamed into the harbour a lot of small boats, tooting and whistling, came out to meet the giant ships. While the *Aqua* slowly drew close to No. 7 Woolloomooloo Wharf, John's eyes were glued to the old landmarks, sparkling in the morning sun.

An eerie quiet fell over the packed decks. Having 'completed a great circle' and seen 'unbelievable sights', here were men staring at their homeland, silent, like children. Feelings were too fraught for them to do anything much more than just stand, still and quiet. John glanced around. There would be none unmoved by the scene, few whose stomachs weren't 'churning with happiness and longing', like his.

As they finally docked, who should be amongst the first to greet his men on the deck but Brigadier 'Bull' Burrows. The noise level exploded as a rowdy welcome from the band on the wharf played the refrain of 'Bull Burrows' Bomb Happy Boys'. As John recalled the first lines of another verse written after the Ed Duda action, 'Good-bye, old Boss, though you're leaving, We will always remember your name', he thought about the number of his mates who had not lived to hear either of the songs. It was the combination of a homecoming, familiar sights and the sounds of this musical tribute that brought lumps to their throats. Tears were streaming down many faces.

Everything went according to a tight schedule. The wharf gates opened and at 5.45 pm the men disembarked. After boarding 'the good old double-decker buses', they travelled along the Sydney streets out to Parramatta Road. Along with all his mates in the battalion, John just wanted rest. Few had slept well the night before. After the long return journey through 14,500 kilometres (9000 miles) of dangerous waters followed by the emotional arrival in Sydney they were all exhausted.

John was soon drifting off. Not even images of his mother's astounded expression, the buzzing questions from his family and anticipation of Margie's reverberating laugh could keep him awake.

John had always been close to Margie. Seventeen months younger, she was an 'ideal little sister'. During the drawn-out months in the Libyan desert he would sometimes recall their early childhood days together—two of them climbing massive pine trees, playing tennis for hours and tending their horses 'with all the paraphernalia'. Having to keep up at times, Margie never complained. 'She was calm and cool. A truly wonderful little sister—affectionate, loyal and always reliable.'[4]

John's opinion of his sister never changed. Reflecting on marriage in a letter to his mother, Margie's image dominated. He hoped his own wife would be just like her—'competent, amusing and adaptable'—claiming there were 'not many girls around like our Margaret'.

But first it was his mother he was going to surprise.

As John set off early the next day on 28 February 1943, with his 'valise, a great big swag and a kit bag', his light step reflected a buoyant mood. He was eager to reach his destination as quickly as possible—'to see my lovely mother'.

It was a warm morning. The sky displayed increasing swathes of blue through the clouds as he headed towards Circular Quay. He could not help but quietly stare at the immense stretches of water—he'd been surrounded by sand for too long.

When he boarded the ferry for Manly, the first of the northern beach suburbs, John began to feel like a school child again—in uniform, fidgety, rubbing his hands together with suppressed excitement. He looked down at the water, clear and deep. Still early in the morning, there were very few people on board. However, one family quietly observed him from a distance; the husband, wife and children were fascinated by his movements.

John was unaware of his antics—walking up to the bow, looking out this side, looking out that side, over to his left to the zoo, over to his right to the parks and gardens in the residential area. Pacing backwards and forwards.

Finally the gentleman came across, smiled and said, 'May we ask, is this a homecoming for you?' John was overcome. Holding back the tears, he took off his cap. 'Yes, it is.' Here he was, back home at last in early 1943, having left this harbour in October 1940. That was a long stretch. He wasn't sure what else to say. The man nodded and said, 'Please enjoy your leave!'

At last John arrived at Manly and with subdued excitement hailed a taxi.

'Where do you want to go to?'

'Dee Why,' he replied. The sound of the suburb was strange to him.

The cabbie was curious. 'Are you just back?'

'Yes, I am.'

John did not trust himself with a longer answer. He settled into the back seat, trying to compose himself. Once in Dee Why he had to find his mother's home; he'd never been there. She had moved to the suburb while he was in Tobruk, and with Charlie serving in the Army in faraway Queensland, she was living there entirely alone. The cabbie found the street and the house—No. 6, The Crescent.

'Do they know you're coming?' he asked.

'No, they don't.' John now wondered if he'd done the right thing. 'I've got no idea what I'm going to find.'

The driver was quick to reply. 'Well, I'm going to wait to make sure there's somebody there.'

John unloaded his gear, went up to the front door, breathed in deeply and knocked. 'You can imagine—it's hard to imagine—it fills me with tears. Mother opened the door. My darling, lovely mother. She stood almost in shock staring at me. "My little John." "My little John." That's all she said. And then, 'You've come home.' It was lovely. It was beautiful … She hung onto the door … She just hung onto the edge of the door. I came in a little bit and put my arm around her—hugging her.

'Then I waved to the taxi and went and got my swag from beside the letterbox … And then she said, "Let's go out to the kitchen and have a cup of tea."

'That was always Mother—to have a cup of tea. I sat down with her at her favourite spot and me alongside, holding her hand—holding her and looking at her.'

The next few weeks were a blur—partying, theatres, restaurants, pubs, family gatherings, meetings with friends. Margie had responded to his hopes for female company. She had invited his good friend, Mary Williamson, to stay for a couple of days.

All too soon John's leave was over. He had not even managed to get to the country to see Peter. That pleasure would have to wait. With little enthusiasm he made plans to return to his unit. Not one of the men could have pronounced that they were happy to return to Walgrove. 'Back in camp after a month's glorious leave,' wrote Les Clothier. 'Everyone is going crook about the so-called 'war effort' in Sydney and wishing the blasted war was over and done with.'[5] Though dispirited, the men exchanged many exaggerated stories through the night, with much roaring laughter.

However, one member of the battalion did not join his mates. Perhaps the Australian postal system was partly to blame; his wife had not received the homecoming telegram he had sent from Fremantle. Eagerly arriving home, he discovered her in the arms of a US serviceman. He killed the American soldier and was subsequently incarcerated for manslaughter.[6]

There was one more official duty to be performed in Sydney. On 2 April 1943, with boots polished and rifles buffed, the men marched from their camp to Rooty Hill Station and then took a train to the centre of the city. Hundreds of khaki-clad men with gleaming bayonets were soon marching up Elizabeth Street towards Hyde Park.

Despite the overcast skies and dull, wet streets, the city pulsated with the music of military bands, cheering voices, waving arms from windows, towering buildings, tiny pieces of floating confetti and smiling faces. As they approached the Cenotaph in Martin Place the shouting rose in a crescendo to a roar. Then, as if by magic, all was hushed as each unit switched their gaze and paid tribute to the dead. But the crowds were hard-pressed to stay silent. Again there was a deafening roar as they turned into George Street, and moved down past the Town Hall, where the Governor-General stood ready to take the Salute.

And then within two weeks came the orders that would take the men away. On 14 April 1943, they boarded trains for the long trip—this time to the Atherton Tablelands of tropical North Queensland for jungle training. Spirits were high until, after days of travel, they pulled up at the little siding of Kairi. Their campsite was a disaster, without decent facilities and with no materials to build a proper camp. Les Clothier described it as 'very primitive'.[7]

According to Tim Fearnside, this time was the unhappiest period of all for the 2/13th Battalion. The troops had been dumped in an isolated camp, expected to willingly devote themselves to more training. But now, in place of the desert fleas, the men were dealing with the painful Gympie or Stinging Tree and little red insects that spread the dreaded scrub typhus. When the boys did a bivouac each week, they ended up 'covered in red ticks and a good dose of scrub itch'.[8]

For most of the men, homesickness was always near the surface. John felt they were 'too close to our family ties'. At times he was frustrated and impatient with their circumstances. Trivial incidents got on his nerves and interrupted his concentration.

After so many months of high-adrenalin action in North Africa, it was difficult to settle into the new army routine. But in compensation, away from the front line, John appreciated the luxury of time to think, to assess his life. More and more his mind wandered to personal plans for the future. Most letters to his mother mentioned correspondence received from females. Towards the end of November 1943 he told her, 'I write to two girls, Mary and Pamela, and get fairly regular letters from them too and stacks of papers from Pam.'

John had experienced his mother's concern and anxious control even before his departure for the Middle East: 'What happened was that Mother was worried that I was having a little fling with Pam Weston at Katoomba or Leura [before I went away]. Pam and I liked each other all right but we didn't get silly about it. I think her parents thought that something was developing. Just how Mum got to know, I don't know. She warned me that it would be a very good plan if I was very careful not to leave a trail that I couldn't keep well swept—going away as we would be ...'

Constance's quiet control continued on John's return: '... When I came back [from the Middle East] Pam did put in first claim ... she was in Sydney staying very close to where Margie was at Wollstonecraft, with relations. But ... Mary Williamson was round the ridges too, staying at Margie's place.'

Constance would have none of it. When John sensed his mother 'coming in quietly, occasionally warning me about the lengths to which girls would go to catch me', he was convinced that he would have to take a stand, to fight against being 'managed':

Darling, you worry so much about the girls I go out with, don't you? As a matter of fact, your being worried rather worried me a lot on leave too ... it just made me wonder whether I was at fault in my sense of values. I have thought a lot about it and find a solution difficult. One thing I know, and believe me, I have had enough experience to know, and that is Pamela is a very good girl, as good as any I know. Perhaps to you she seems too easy and perhaps very broad-minded. Maybe she is, but she has a very firm grip of herself and she doesn't beat around the bush. She knows exactly what she wants and is quite outspoken about it ...

All these things I like very much in a girl because there's never any doubt as to where you stand. You can talk so straight to a girl like that ... I like people to be open. It's because I am myself, I suppose. The younger people of today are becoming more and more like that.

Perhaps I shouldn't write to you like this, but truly, Mother, I don't want to ever get into the position that I have to hide things from you and more or less live a private life of my own. A certain amount is essential, of course, but I'm sure you know what I mean. Some day I suppose I will marry—and believe me, she will be a girl of my own choice ...

Still never fear, darling. It will work out somehow and all will be well. I know your main thoughts are for the happiness and success of your children. You are a wonderful mother.
4 May 1943

There were other tensions during this time. John's next letter alluded to a discussion they'd had about the worries and hurt each had suffered while he was in the Middle East. He had rarely spoken directly about the death and destruction he had witnessed, never broached the subject of his father:

Of course, you worried about me when I was away over there. It is only natural too, Mother dear, that it would have some effect on you. In many ways it has been far harder for you than for me.

We have both brushed lightly over our hurts. I am younger and, of course, it has had far less effect. I suffered my own private agonies

and if I want to I can still drag them out and count them one by
one. They are quite numerous. But I keep them well locked up.
12 May 1943

Letters now indicated that irritations on the Atherton Tablelands were emerging. Things were starting to niggle. John described amphibian instruction for example, with a degree of impatience. They had 'fooled around' and got into 'awful silly little craft, paddling around and falling in, keeping our weapons dry while coming onto shore'. He recognised the change:

Perhaps I'm a bit moody these days—starting to show signs of age
or something—and in my saner moments, regret lots that I do, say
and write. But there's really no harm done. It's probably the best
thing in the world for me to go through a stage or two like this ...
20 May 1943

When John heard stories about what had happened in the Pacific during the year before his return to Australia, he became more determined than ever to destroy the enemy.

He hoped that General MacArthur's overall command would be effective. He was not aware that the general, though one of America's most famous and decorated soldiers, was subject to critical questions about his command almost immediately. His early orders were considered to be 'ill-informed and maladroit';[9] and he had a reputation for enjoying the armchair, reluctantly going to New Guinea for the first time on 6 November 1942 and never once visiting the front line.[10]

Nevertheless, Australians, including Curtin, had breathed a sigh of relief upon the shift in reliance on Britain for protection in the Pacific. A form of tremendously welcome assistance was being offered by the presence of the United States.

With both moral and physical support from the Americans, the run of Japanese victories was finally reversed in 1942: at the Battle of the Coral Sea in May; at the Battle of Midway in mid-July; at Milne Bay in September; and along the Kokoda Trail in New Guinea in November.

Australians were still reeling from news of the Kokoda campaign. It had lasted four months, from July to November 1942—approximately the same time the 2/13th Battalion was in El Alamein. John had heard much about it from Margie, whose husband, John Oldham, had served there as a doctor for three months.

As early as June 1942, the Japanese had decided to approach Port Moresby from the north coast, marching about half way along the track to Kokoda and climbing over the treacherous Owen Stanley Ranges to reach Moresby on the south coast. It seemed to the Japanese that there was little to stand in their way.[11]

The young defending Aussies from the newly formed Australian Militia had received only basic training and were initially pushed by the Japanese from Kokoda almost back to Port Moresby. Many were killed or perished in the appalling jungle conditions. The young 'poorly trained, poorly led, under-equipped and vastly outnumbered' force was severely depleted when regular troops from the AIF 7th Division finally relieved them.[12]

John's brother-in-law was part of this Division. When on leave in Australia John Oldham told Margie gruelling stories about tending the sick. Their splints were often made out of tree branches to stop the bleeding of their shattered limbs. He would work through the night repairing wounds 'under the beam of flashlights held overhead by orderlies' or conduct amputations of gangrenous limbs with the patient under hypnosis, often the only available anaesthetic.[13] The operating theatre, frequently sinking in mud, was a hut with a canvas awning.[14]

Fortunately with the added support of the AIF, the tide eventually turned. General Horii, the commander of the overland Japanese invasion force, faced serious supply problems. Reports of cannibalism were not exaggerated; Australians found the corpses of some of their mates with flesh hacked away. At least one parcel of enemy 'meat' examined by a doctor was considered to be human.[15]

Soon the Japanese were being pushed back towards the north coast— in full retreat. January 1943 saw the enemy finally forced out of this part of New Guinea. However, the Japanese still dominated vast areas of the country, to which the 9th Division would soon be directed.

Back in the Queensland tablelands, John was restless. Disincentives to action were slowly beginning to emerge: depressing statistics of sickness in the jungle, the apparent lack of compassion on the part of the Army over genuine requests for leave and the prospect of fighting alongside raw conscripts.

Despite these drawbacks, the men accepted, sometimes grumpily, that hard work was the best solution to their problems. Men from the 6th Division had been seconded as instructors: 'clued-up fellows' such as Dick Turner and Frank Westhoven, who had been patrol officers in New Guinea. Under their tutelage, long route marches, sniping practice, bridge-building lessons and practice in carrying extra-heavy loads were all endured. Les Clothier offered some clarification: 'There were cross-country jaunts and three-day bivouacs ... with the vines either stinging or chewing at you. There were dummy Japs everywhere, worked on strings and pulleys, and they bobbed up everywhere and you had to bayonet some and shoot others.'[16]

On 2 July 1943, John was pleased to hear that they would be moving to a camp at Cairns to begin their amphibian training, alongside American sailors. John's responsibilities as Battalion Intelligence Officer expanded.[17] On 10 July he apologised to his mother for not writing sooner, giving as a reason full days of training with his men, followed by a large amount of office work at night.

In his next letter there were clues that mobilisation plans were afoot. On the day he wrote, his battalion had been warned to prepare for a move. The camp area was handed over to another battalion and the men bivouacked that night:

> *Now as regards this holiday of yours up to Cobar with Peter and Jane ... It's no good waiting for me because I can assure you there's no chance of me getting any leave for a long time to come ... Let me know what you decide on. I'm enclosing a cheque which will cover your fare with a first class sleeper both ways ... Don't say I shouldn't do it, because I can do it and love to and also want to, so leave it at that. Anyhow, is it ever possible to repay a good mother for all we owe her!! Never by money alone, I know—but it can help to make a thought of some expressive and concrete value.*
>
> *That probably doesn't make sense—but I suppose you know what I mean!*
> *20 July 1943*

With preparations for leaving Australia in full swing, John's thoughts turned towards the nature of their new assignment. In the North African desert they had all lain low during the day and become active at night. In the jungle the reverse would apply. They would need to hole up at night; it was too easy to get lost in the dark. The men would be forced to use vines to prevent disorientation, stringing them from one point to another, even to go to the latrine. They could get 'fifteen to twenty yards out of a good vine'. On more distant forays, they would need to lace them together.

As Intelligence Officer John's main tasks would involve mapping and assessing information, writing it up and then getting it back to the CO as quickly as possible. The principles always remained the same; just the ground would be different.

By 26 July 1943 all members of the battalion were aboard the *Maetsuycker*. Though John had tried to remain optimistic, in general he was feeling like the others—downhearted.

However, astoundingly, morale remained high. With embarkation procedures complete and having had their final medical inspections, early on the morning of 27 July, the men headed out to sea in convoy—'a wonderful mob, who looked on themselves as ready to fight again anywhere'. As they sailed from Cairns and gradually turned to the north, the men were still expressing willingness to pit themselves against the new enemy: 'I don't think we ever thought we couldn't beat the Japanese, you know. We were quite experienced troops, we were professionals by then and we had never been beaten and I suppose we were confident that we could do the job when it came to it … '[18]

Chapter Nineteen

The jungles of New Guinea

THERE IS A LIMIT TO ARMY LIFE BEING ENJOYABLE. THIS IS
OUR THIRD CAMPAIGN, AND WE HAVE QUITE A NUMBER OF
CHAPS WHO HAVE BEEN WOUNDED TWO OR THREE TIMES.
AND STILL RIGHT IN THE THICK OF IT.

—John Murray, 1943[1]

As THE *Maetsuycker* and other ships of the convoy headed towards New
Guinea in late July 1943, each man in the 2/13th Battalion was left with
his own thoughts. Resigned to leaving his family yet again, John was able to
garner new energy, eager to see new territory and a different culture.
However, he was concerned for the men who were to be 'in the thick of
it'—again to face the dread of charging from the front line, this time with
encumbrances of jungle vines, mud, slush and near zero vision.

Doubtless many shared this common fear. Surely it would be tempting
fate to fight again, having survived miraculously until now. Though John
had not articulated views like this before his departure, it was clear he
silently harboured them. Later he wrote to his mother:

*Even a frontline soldier, trained as he is to get into close quarters
with the enemy, realises underneath that his luck can't last forever,
and that it's only a matter of time.*
17 October 1943

It was not only the soldiers. Families suffered too. The kinds of sentiments expressed by a young woman, Nola Bridger, about her brother, were openly voiced by many: 'We felt very bitter about Steve because we felt he'd done his share in Europe. Why did he have to go to New Guinea? Especially after he was killed we thought, "Why did they have to send him when he'd done his part in those three years?" It was such a long time out of his life to be away, and he was home for such a short time.'[2]

Though John was confident the men were well trained, that they 'could jump from one situation to another without any trouble', he was acutely aware that survival did not depend on skill, training and experience alone.

In the desert the Rats were experts; in the jungle, they were mere learners. No simulation exercises in Queensland could have prepared them adequately. The men had heard that it was almost impossible to see the green-clad enemy in the thick foliage of the jungle. The Japanese were masters at concealment and sniping; since 1940 they had amassed a wealth of experience in this type of warfare. Added to this were other negative aspects of jungle warfare: the threat of disease; the difficulty in transporting and treating injured soldiers; and the reported suicide-bombing techniques of the enemy.

There were countless reasons for John's belief that the luck of the remaining original troops from the 2/13th might not hold. Besides which, it had been a long and arduous training period and the men were tired.

The 9th Division's first port of call was Milne Bay, on the extreme eastern tip of Papua, about 370 kilometres (230 miles) east of Port Moresby. Arriving on 30 July 1943, the men were given a good dose of the conditions they could expect. Downpours, sludge, humidity and fevers were to be their daily lot for the next couple of years. Almost immediately training restarted, with US troops and their amphibious units. Practising beach landings again and again suggested to the men that their first real experience was not far off.

At this stage the 2/13th still only knew that they were to fight in New Guinea. They did not know that they would soon have explicit instructions to capture Lae on the Huon Peninsula—the main enemy base on the north coast of New Guinea.

General MacArthur had a sweeping plan. After the successful end to the Papuan campaign, the aim was to clear out all invaders from the Peninsula. He could then forge ahead with a new assault that would eventually rid the Pacific entirely of the Japanese. From the north coast of

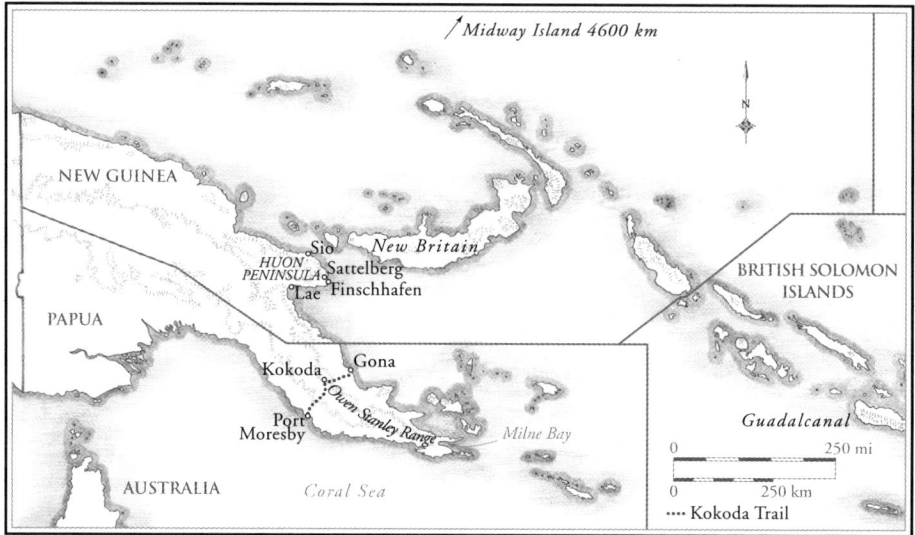

Two areas of intensive conflict for Australians in New Guinea: the Kokoda Trail (1942) and the Huon Peninsula (1943).

New Guinea the troops would pave a victorious way north, always heading to the far reaches of the Philippines.

MacArthur had already suffered one defeat in the Philippines, in April 1942, when he had lost to the Japanese. He was determined to reverse the disaster. His stated intention later became famous: 'I shall return,' he promised.[3]

As training progressed, it quickly became quite obvious to John that this situation was very different from the desert. 'You'd be surprised to see just how little we manage with—can't understand how I ever used to carry so much stuff before. It really wasn't necessary,' he wrote.

Each man had to carry all battle and personal requirements on his back, probably the most important of which were extremely small and of imperceptible weight: anti-malaria tablets, water-purifying chlorination tablets and salt and vitamin tablets. Also essential were anti-mosquito lotion and anti-mite lotion for scrub typhus. As a further precaution, the men would wear gaiters at all times and roll down their sleeves at sunset.

John was caught up in the furious preparation for the initial attack. He wrote a brief letter to his mother not long before the planned assault, explaining his failure to correspond:

Have neglected you very badly lately—forgive me! But I really have been extremely busy, day and night. Sometimes midnight when I get to bed. But it's all very interesting and good experience, so that's the main thing.

Had a long letter from Margie today and two long ones from you yesterday. Lovely to know you are all as well as can be at home. How I'd love to be with you all again. Never mind—the time will soon come round again for a nice long leave and the war should be very much closer to a finish by then.

Soon be starting the fifth year of the war—remarkable isn't it? I've been 3¼ years in uniform and spent 2½ of that overseas. The years simply slip by as I get older. Soon be 28! And nothing done yet. When this show finishes I'll get something done believe me. I've learnt a lot in the army—some very valuable experiences too. The main thing will be to turn it to good account later on ...

Afraid I've little news, except that I'm well and happy. I do hope you are too, darling.

20 August 1943

Lieutenant Colonel Colvin spoke to the battalion on 29 August about their role in the planned assaults on Lae. Since the Huon Peninsula dominated the straits that separated New Guinea from New Britain, it was considered a vital possession for control of the area. The Peninsula was estimated to be holding an enemy force of around 7000 troops.

John was privy to the details of the attack on Lae before the other men of the 2/13th. It would consist of two pincer movement advances: the 7th Division, along with US paratroopers, landing from the air; and the 9th Division making an amphibious landing on the coast, east of Lae.

Once their destination was clarified, it was John's role in Intelligence to put members of the battalion into the picture. However, gathering information was twice as difficult in the jungle. Aerial reconnaissance was severely hampered by the nature of the terrain. While it was almost impossible to get precise bearings, everyone, nevertheless, was obliged to study sand models of the landing. It was up to the 2/13th to establish two beachheads or entrance points for the 9th Division—at Red and Yellow Beaches.

It was 6.30 am on 4 September 1943. The men were crowded into the landing craft—specially designed boats known as LCIs (Landing Craft,

Infantry). The craft, each holding about 200 men, beached on the narrow strip of sand in a pre-ordained order, well apart from each other. The men rushed down ladders on each side of the bow towards the heavy fringe of thick jungle, rifles held high. John felt a surge of adrenalin. While some ran straight ahead and some to either side, to be reunited with the unit as soon as possible, their thoughts were all along the same lines: 'Where are you, you Jap bastards?' Much to their astonishment, the landing was unopposed. There was no sign of the enemy.

Their battalion had landed north of Lae. Now it was the trip south towards the town that was filled with tension. They had no knowledge of where the enemy were. 'Always we were expecting attack.'

On reaching Lae, they heard that the base had already fallen, with little resistance, to units of the 7th Division. The Japanese had used inland tracks as escape routes so, with camp set up, the 9th Division sent out probing patrols to outlying areas to find out where the enemy were strengthening their defences.

At this time a different priority emerged for John. One of the duties of Intelligence was to question captured enemy soldiers or known supporters. There were highly trained officers to do this. John knew that he had to send someone to the Lutheran 'Hopoi' Mission, located in the surrounding mountains and run by a couple thought to be German sympathisers. The missionary and his wife would need to be interrogated. A patrol was despatched immediately, 'to neutralise' the mission: 'You have to assume the worst. It was like a pre-emptive strike. It's like a snake. You've got to do what you do with the bloody thing. You don't give him a chance to get you …'

To the discredit of the battalion, the mission was looted. Beautiful possessions including lovely old silver were taken. When the two old Lutherans eventually arrived back at Headquarters in the jungle, having been carried by natives down treacherous paths over several streams, they were exhausted. John immediately arranged for them to be transported by ship to Australia: 'And that was the last the poor old fellow saw of his possessions. War is cruel, isn't it?'

It was almost immediately decided that the 9th Division would move on for another amphibious landing, this time in the Finschhafen area, on the eastern tip of the Huon Peninsula. This destination and its surroundings could provide base installations for MacArthur's future island-hopping operations towards his coveted destination of the Philippines.

Along with the two other Intelligence officers of the 20th Brigade, John was now liaising more and more at the Brigade level. Former Sydney University law lecturer Brigadier Victor Windeyer was in command of the 20th Brigade.[4] He was 'precise, unruffled and resolute … firm, fair and friendly'.[5] An extremely thorough and highly respected man, Windeyer kept his men informed at every turn. Characteristically he would deliver a set of orders concisely and calmly, without any reference to notes. John enjoyed his style.

Windeyer must have had some misgivings about the landing at Finschhafen, as he 'invoked Gallipoli to emphasise what was to happen if it was confused'. He was right. The two landings were similar: both prepared in haste; both facing enemy who were ready; both struggling with problems of navigation after transfer to the small craft; and both in the dark.[6]

The battle for Finschhafen would be unlike the one in Lae in almost every regard. MacArthur had seriously underestimated the strength of the Japanese opposition. Documents subsequently revealed that there had been 2000 Japanese troops in the area and that the plan had been to augment this number to 4000. When the 'vainglorious and self-seeking' general was confronted with his error of judgement, rather than bring in extra Australian troops he made a concerted effort, 'through highly selective censorship', to cover up the blunder.[7]

For the 2/13th Battalion, it was just another attack. On 22 September at 5.15 am they began their landing in the dark, some boats at Scarlet Beach and some at Siki Cove. Confusion dominated the landings, perhaps because of the weather conditions which the troops found 'as dark as the inside of a cow'. Instead of moonlight there was cloud and mist over the sea.[8]

Lieutenant General John Coates, at a much later date, saw faulty maps as the cause; and John's report in the *War Diary* points to the management of the craft: 'There was very considerable confusion. Much of it was caused by a reluctance on the part of the LCIs to move in quickly—thus being longer under fire with the troops exposed on the open decks.'[9]

Whatever the reason, the enemy at both landing places were ready. Hidden in the thick jungle were deadly snipers. As each wave of soldiers landed and raced 18 metres (20 yards) over the beach towards the undergrowth they were 'looking down the barrels of automatic rifles'.

Undeterred, the Australians returned the fire. No one faltered. With bayonets fixed, the fearsome mob charged in over the narrow strips of sand, 'firing point-blank and yelling their heads off as they stormed in'. The blood-curdling chorus panicked the Japanese, who turned tail and ran.

The area was secured in no time at all. When dawn broke, despite the beach being quite chaotic while commanders tried to find their companies, the sand and jungle fringe were free of everyone except the Japanese dead.

Though the enemy was defeated in this instance, the initial intensity of their defence at the Finschhafen landing was a foretaste of what was to come. The men found the surrounding area a hive of enemy activity—planes attacking day and night and reinforcements arriving in a never-ending stream.

Within days, a battle had developed for Kakakog Ridge, a vital elevation that both sides were determined to win. Dominating the whole area, it would serve as a vantage point from which the victor could take control of the surrounding territory.

This battle was 'one of the toughest battles in which the Battalion was engaged' with deadly attacks from well-concealed snipers in vines and trees.[10] When casualties skyrocketed in two platoons making a crossing over Ilebbe Creek and heading for the ridge, Lieutenant Colonel Colvin instructed his Intelligence Officer, John Murray, to find out what was causing the increased slaughter. John arranged a successful ploy: the tree tops on the other side of the watercourse were machine-gunned; the Japanese snipers killed. However, during the crossfire when he narrowly missed slaughter himself, he witnessed two officers in front of him—both from the 2/15th Battalion—being 'silenced with a grenade, shot down in a burst of explosive flame'.

Both officers were 'originals' and highly respected; they had been mentioned in Despatches in the Middle East. One of them, Lieutenant Neville Harpham, was from a property in western Queensland; the other, Lieutenant Eric McNaughton Christie, from Ingham, in tropical north Queensland, near the coast. They had both fought through Tobruk and El Alamein, 'only to die here'.[11] John sat with them as they died, on 24 September 1943.

The vision of their violent deaths never left him. Years later in Tenterfield, when he was at the stock and station agent Dalgetys, a young fellow casually walked into the office for service. John froze. The likeness was uncanny. He quickly checked the fellow's family name and got the answer he expected—Philip Harpham, a nephew of Neville's.

'Good God,' John exclaimed to him, 'I knew your uncle!' With some effort he described the death scene. After all the years since Neville's death, it gave the parents great solace to hear that John had been kneeling beside their son when he died.

Every man saw a mate die. They did what they could, in the time they had, to give comfort. Often it was just a squeeze of the hand or a promise to tell family. Replayed ad infinitum, like a stuck gramophone needle, the pictures were etched forever. It was impossible for John to get Alan Toose's death out of his mind and into words.

But then John straightened his back and finally managed, with several pauses, to complete the retelling. Repetition emphasised the number of times the vision had captured his mind: 'A lovely boy, Alan Toose, who in the desert was one of my favourites. He was in my section right from the moment we joined up at Ingleburn ... He had a lovely sense of humour ... everything about him. He was about eighteen when he joined, I suppose, a pharmacist's assistant. He had a lovely disposition ... His gear was always tidy—meticulous. Always the neatest on parade. And he developed into a ruthless soldier. He really knew his job and ... [Long pause.] Can I tell you later? It's hard for me now ...'

John breathed in deeply. He had done so many times before, but this time his determination was stronger, his breath deeper:

> Now ... I was a section leader through Tobruk and getting many casualties with patrolling ... My best offsider patrolling, without a doubt was Alan Toose. I protected him always. Blokes would say, "Ah, cut out that bullshit," but I stood by him. But really no need to. He was a strong character.
>
> I sent him back to Australia from New Guinea, you know. He needed keeping away from war for a while. He was a danger to himself. And he was someone who should have lived. I left him out of battle deliberately because he was worn out. I told the CO—"I've left him with the LOB (the left out of battle) group". Always before you went into a major action there was an LOB group chosen—an officer and a couple of NCOs and thirty or forty soldiers. The nucleus of a battalion if it got wiped out.
>
> He wore himself out, Alan. When I left him out of battle, it was one of the hardest decisions I'd made, knowing how much he loved the battle. He was very

annoyed. He couldn't come to grips with that at all. I did it in good faith. There were one or two others too. I wanted them preserved. They were too valuable.

Now Alan skipped Australia and got on to a ship—he deserted Australia. He joined us in New Guinea. Just turned up in the regiment … He got up [to New Guinea] and re-joined the battalion and I found him next day. Someone said "Toose is back", and I said, "Oh no, I don't believe it."

He looked at me, you know … so I said, "Right-oh, look after yourself." And only days later, a couple of stretcher-bearers coming down the hill, and there was this young fellow—right through the guts—a burst of Jap fire at Finschhafen. I found several boys carrying him back towards medical help.

I fell out with my medical officer, named Gates, over this, because I went back on my own and found him. I said, "Look, young Toose is coming down. I know you will, but for God's sake do everything you can to save this boy." He said, "Don't you try and tell me my business." He took it the wrong way.

You see this is where the desert won. By Alamein in the desert, as your father [John Oldham] would have known, you'd get one through the guts and you'd be back in the surgery in a forward surgical tent with one or two doctors who would crudely operate immediately and save a bloke's life. But in the jungle he had to go right down by stretcher-bearers through that treacherous country—hours—maybe the next day. It took too long. He'd be dead by then …

He only lasted half a day or so … No need for it … No need for it at all.

… I found several boys carrying him back towards medical help. He was dying. He knew he was going. We paused and I held his hand. He knew it was up. I knew it was up too when I saw him … I said goodbye to him— just gave him a squeeze of the arm. We looked directly into each other's eyes. We didn't speak … They moved on

and left me to walk into the scrub out of sight to give
several wrenching sobs—yes I wept—and I weep now as
I speak—I'm sorry.

Tears flowed from John's pale blue eyes. He could not look up. He was
still looking at the stretcher—back in time—in the depths of the jungle.
Crying for all the deaths he had witnessed. He apologised again for
weeping.

Chapter Twenty

Jungle life goes on

THE QUALITY OF THE 9TH DIVISION'S SOLDIERS WAS
EXTRAORDINARY. IF I WAS SEEKING TO UNLOCK THE MYSTERY
THAT PSYCHOLOGISTS AND THE REST OF US WRESTLE WITH
AS TO WHY MEN FIGHT WELL, AND HOW ... WE SHOULD SET
OUT TO TEACH ... LEADERSHIP, MORALE AND MOTIVATION—I
BELIEVE I COULD DO NO BETTER THAN CONCOCT A 'STALWART'
THEORY, ABOUT HIGHLY MOTIVATED PRIVATE SOLDIERS
AND NON-COMMISSIONED OFFICERS FROM THE UNITS OF
THIS DIVISION WHO EXERCISED A FORCEFUL AND POSITIVE
INFLUENCE ON THOSE AROUND THEM ...

—Coates, 1999[1]

LIFE FOR MEN in the 2/13th Battalion now required stubborn single-mindedness. Death had come to over forty of their mates—so late in the war. They had been through over two years of continuous service in the dusty Middle East and now this—the 'bloody jungle'.

John's responsibilities had evolved. His duties were to collect and share; to uncover the plans of the Japanese. In addition to being responsible for the dissemination of information, he was directly involved in journal-keeping—recording information from his own rough notes or that received from his staff in the IO section. If it was pouring with rain, 'rigged-up protection' made it possible to produce the final reports. Mostly he devoted night-time to fine-tuning his records, keeping notes 'meticulously … in longhand of each day's actions'.[2] During the day he was in the field, always having to be 'ready with the goods'— detail written in a neat, legible hand. 'John, give me the war diary please,' was a constant refrain from the Battalion Commander, Lieutenant Colonel Colvin.

The day-to-day records demanded an unusual focus, especially when the action became confused. The Starvation Hill assault, on 26 September 1943, which effectively cut Japanese communications between two key areas in the Finschhafen campaign, was one such time. John's reports, written in a curious shorthand to describe detailed action, formed the basis of the official battalion war diary, now lodged in the Australian War Memorial:[3]

'16.25 [hours]. Sounds of hy [heavy] fire from C Coy. C Coy plan was to attack with two pls [platoons] fwd [forward], 13 Pl, Lieut Thompson, on the West slope of the spur on the right of the track, 14 Pl. Lieut Webb along the track and 15 Pl Lieut Mair, in rear with Coy HQ and to reinforce success. The attack went in but 13 Pl could not keep to the side of the spur as it narrowed when nearing the enemy and became very steep; so 13 Pl was forced to merge with 15 Pl on the track. The bamboo was still the same tangled thickness. Progress was slow and noisy and the pls suddenly broke through the thick bamboo at the foot of a very steep rise and came under heavy M[achine] G[un] fire and rifle fire from posn [position] on top of the rise. The present access of advance was too steep to assault the post frontally and we had already suffered nine casualties. 13 and 14 Pls went to ground fwd of the bamboo, and any further attempt at fwd movement drew hy fire. It was then decided to attack from the left flank with 15 Pl fwd, 13 Pl in sp [support] and 14 Pl to give covering fire from the right. 15 Pl was moved to the left of 13 and 14 and astride a small track which branched across the head of the gully on the left to the next spur running NE whilst forming up to attack, 15 Pl were fired on by an LMG which the enemy brought fwd from a post NE down the next spur. The enemy fired from 20 yds, and into the rear of 15 Pl. Formation was broken up before the attack could be launched.'[4]

The comment John made to his mother about his handwriting a few months into his New Guinea service was not borne out in his war diaries, in which he wrote detailed, fastidious notes:[5]

> *I've been doing nothing else for days now but write my unit war diary. By the time this war has finished I should develop quite a good hand! I'm rather determined to improve my handwriting because it's really a bad thing.*
> *10 December 1943*

John was pleased to be recording victory after victory. Lae and Finschhafen had been taken and by 2 October 1943 the Australians were declaring triumph over the whole of the coastal area of the Huon Peninsula. 'Not a bad record,' wrote one 2/13th diarist, '... Lae and Finschhafen in four weeks! What would happen if they fed the lad[s] well on fruit, beer?'[6]

To his mother John wrote:

> *Once again, of course, we won and I'm sure we will keep on winning when given anything like an even break. These boys of ours know how to fight, there's no doubt about it, and after all our ups and downs in the desert and the valuable experience we gained there, the Jap will have to stage some very big comebacks to shake our morale.*
> *4 October 1943*

Despite the success of the Australians on the Peninsula, the Japanese still owned and controlled large areas. They continued to attack Allied positions:

He's a stubborn little chap this Jap ... However, our boys give him some awful hidings when they find him ... Their morale couldn't be higher and it will take a very awkward situation to worry them at all. They have taken to this jungle fighting like ducks to water ... They must surely be amongst the most widely experienced troops in the world.
2 November 1943

Though John occasionally referred to his duties and the fighting, much of his correspondence was designed to keep his mother's mind off the conflict. Again and again he described the jungle's finery:

In most ways I love this country. It is really full of beauty ... and there is no glare and dancing heat. All is green, beautiful shades of green. Around me at the present moment are palms and coconut trees, red and yellow hibiscus, sweet scented frangipanis and all sorts of ferns and flowers growing wild and in beautiful tangled profusion ... Glorious butterflies, brilliantly coloured, glide lazily around through the trees stopping every now and again to show themselves off. The breeze is blowing in soft puffs and is very sweet.
4 October 1943

Beauty of his surroundings aside, aged almost twenty-eight, John was still without a permanent Australian base. He could not help but wish for home:

... as I've said before, [returning home] is something wonderful to look forward to. It really will be marvellous won't it ... I am eager and keen now but realise I must bide my time and for the moment put that same energy into my present job. Still a long time to go ... Three and a half years now—soon to be four. Remarkable isn't it? Never in our wildest dreams did we consider we would have to do what we have done. Who would have thought so on that first night I went home in uniform to Killara. Remember that?
4 November 1943

There was no doubt that part of his longing to be home stemmed from the danger the jungle surroundings posed to his health. Malaria was always on John's mind. The dive-bombing of anopheles mosquitoes, the carriers of this deadly disease, was never effectively combated. Some of the Australian soldiers rejected the anti-malaria drug, Atebrin.

John, however, had always been prudent:

> *If precaution prevents sickness then you can be reasonably hopeful that all will be well with me ... Anyone who really tries to avoid sickness and disease by doing the things that are always being drummed into us stands quite a good chance of avoiding it ... I really don't think you can stop getting malaria into the blood, but you can prevent it coming out in fever with a bit of care.*
> *17 October 1943*

Statistics concerning death from this disease confirmed that his thoughtful vigilance was more than justified. Australian casualties from malaria were 9250, compared with the 2037 killed and 3533 wounded in action in New Guinea.[7]

As the war progressed John began to reveal more about the mental and physical effects of being in New Guinea. Despite all precautions, he finally succumbed to malaria. Like his homesickness it became a constant. He was more fortunate than the 'poor devils' so sick from the disease that they were transported back to Australia. One victim recalled his treatment at Goulburn Hospital. 'At that time, they were giving soldiers electric shock treatment for shell shock, and a doctor told me he wanted to give me electric shock too, to stop my sweating. I said, "No way, my sweating is from malaria". To this day, I often wonder if some of those boys given shock treatment only had malaria, like I did.'[8]

There was little protection from the hot, disease-ridden jungle— it 'rains like the devil every day'. The sodden ground presented an evil presence. Ultimately exemplified in the way death so quickly enveloped life in the jungle, the two-sidedness of beauty was never far from John's mind:

Certainly a piece of work nearly perfected by nature, but somehow nature never gives all for the contentment of us humans. Here she has created a beautiful body but at the same time planted a malignant growth—the one fighting the other. Nor can we enjoy one without suffering the other. Rather applies to life in general, don't you think?
4 October 1943

This dichotomy was never far from John's mind. Towards the end of 1943, small signs of irritation were beginning to show:

I endorse all the things that have been written about it [New Guinea] but am rather amazed that those writers left out all the worst things. It would always be much better to sprinkle a little more realism and truth into the writing and we would all be more prepared for it, and not have to find out by hard experience.

No wonder there are droughts in other parts of the world. All the rain comes here …
17 October 1943

I have a ground sheet rigged up over my head to keep the most important half of me dry and I'm sitting on some sticks to keep my bottom out of 6 inches of water and mud. I can't think of more pleasant surroundings from which to be writing!!
4 November 1943

Sometimes it was a comparatively insignificant matter that made John agitated. The loss of a silver identity tag deprived him of a nostalgic reminder of home. Worn every hour of every day, they were called meat tags—the army issue was a dull composition of a reddish raw meat colour, attached to a piece of cord. The piece of metal was stamped with each man's number, name, rank, religion and blood group—important when there were casualties. When a soldier was killed 'they took his meat tag and anything else they could grab from him—proof positive that he'd died'.

John had always treasured this silver tag sent from home, even though it had its drawbacks. One of his men had yelled at him while they were out on patrol, crawling on their stomachs over the gritty sand, 'For Christ's sake, hide that bloody thing. The moon's glinting on it.' But losing it in New Guinea hurt. He thought of it often, glistening in the moonlight or with heavy rains pouring over it. Perhaps a native had found it? It was a reminder of Tobruk, a reminder of death, a reminder of home.

Loss upon loss—large and small—they were taking their toll. It was not enough to plan for the future. Without realising it, John's level of anxiety rose. Writing constantly, as though the very act would hurry along his return, he sent his sense of desperation home. Longing and loneliness echoed through almost every letter as his emotions swung:

> *I've been a soldier for nearly three and a half years—seems incredible—and yet sometimes it seems like a lifetime … Heaven knows when we will get leave again. One of these days I will just walk in. I'd love to be home for Christmas but don't think it's possible now.*
> *4 October 1943*

> *No knowing when we will get home darling. The way I feel at present, I won't go outside the front gate once I do get home again. How I look forward to some home cooking.*
> *17 October 1943*

> *Goodbye for the present darling. God bless you and keep you for the happy years we are going to have when all this is over.*
> *2 November 1943*

> *I'm still terribly well darling and quite happy, although like everyone else my dominating private thoughts, sometimes outspoken in weaker moments, are of course of you and home and everything I love and miss so much.*
> *4 November 1943*

Strange how our letters mean much more to each other these days, or at least that is how I feel about yours. I read them three or four times now and I can't ever remember reading one more than twice before. Perhaps I'm settling down more and seeing everything more clearly than I used to …

When things settle down is the time I have to do lots of writing—all sorts of things to attend to. But it's better that way, you don't get time to brood over things.
10 November 1943

Somehow our letters … seem to me to be much richer and far more understanding. It is something I am very pleased about really because often a boy grows a little apart from his mother as he gets older. That's something we will never let happen!
November 1943

My mates of the early days have thinned out sadly I'm afraid. They were few enough when we got home, but now …
17 November 1943

A few weeks ago I wrote a very long letter to you, but thought better of it and did not send it. It was inclined to be on the morbid side … The trouble is I get all sorts of flashes of imagination based I suppose on some of the things I know and have seen, and let myself go rather wild. Then later when I read it over I can't understand even having written it. However, if you do receive letters of that nature, then don't take them too seriously, because sometimes they aren't me at all really.
Late November 1943

Back in Australia there was a feeling of weariness. Margie's husband, along with many others, had left once more for New Guinea. On that departure date, 3 November, families and friends asked themselves how much longer their men would be forced to be away: 'We didn't anticipate it would go on for such a long time. We thought that when the Americans came in that that would accentuate the end of it. Actually it dragged on for a long time and we were beginning to count the cost of it very much in the last two years of the war ... not only the cost of what was being destroyed or lost in bombing raids, but the cost of lives that were being lost. It was coming home to us how futile war can be.'[9]

In November 1943, the main aim for the 20th Brigade was to clear out remaining Japanese units from the entire northern region of the peninsula. The advance was slow but dogged. The enemy continued to retreat. While their resistance was weaker and now only spasmodic, the entire brigade was engaged in pushing them out through Sattelberg and up to Sio on the north coast of New Guinea. Though the Japanese had pulled back they had not left the area, and should not do so, according to their military instructions, without a fight.[10] It was not in their nature to withdraw.

And so the battle went on, with John each day faithfully recording its progress.

As if an antidote to the present, by the end of November John was turning his thoughts into concrete plans and looking at his future in financial terms. He discussed the purchase of property with his mother and family:

> *Your tally up of cash available was very interesting to me because within another twelve months I will have at least 500 pounds to my credit—with my deferred pay and savings ... The main thing would be to get a start and have enough up our sleeves to exist on for perhaps a year. There is a way out of our problems I know and I'm equally sure we will find it and happiness too ...*
>
> *We can't take risks. That's something I'm determined on. But I'm also determined that we do something for ourselves—and how much better it would be collectively ... Next leave we had better go into the matter thoroughly.*
> *21 November 1943*

John was more and more confident that final victory in New Guinea would not be long off and that he could return to put his plans into action:

Christmas at Finschhafen. From bottom left to right: Signals Officer Freddie North, Medical Officer Bruce Gates, Lieutenant Cyril Huggett, unnamed Salvation Army representative, Lieutenant John Murray, Colonel George Colvin, Jim Parks (Colonel Colvin's batman), Major Joe Kelly.

... we know now there are no troops in the world to beat us at jungle fighting—us—the soldiers who little more than a year ago, were advancing in wide open formation across the open desert under terrific shellfire—who at night-time owned 'no-man's land' always ... Now we are fighting the very extreme in warfare, sneaking through the jungle like cat burglars, knowing how to sleep in the mud and rain, knowing how much to carry on the back and what to leave behind. We have given the Jap the greatest thrashing that he has yet had in this war—and that is a fact. They have met a different type of soldier—men who never let ground go once they gain it ... Men who know the finest arts in improvisation and put them into effect. Men who don't know the meaning of the word defeat ...

Seems to me I've been talking a lot about our Division. But don't worry, it's the best thing in the world and the worst for the Jap, for us to be very proud of ourselves ...
10 December 1943

Margie was hoping that both her brother and husband would return on leave for Christmas. Throughout much of her second pregnancy, while her brother John Murray was pushing north to Sio, John Oldham had been bogged down further inland in the Markham/Ramu River Valley offensive. A sibling for Sue-ann was due in January 1944. John wrote to his mother, 'Don't suppose it will be long now before Marg has an addition to the family. Hope all goes well.'

Margie would see neither husband nor brother join the family Christmas celebrations. Two days before Christmas the 2/13th Battalion came across a village from which the Japanese had hastily withdrawn. Dead enemy were strewn around the place, equipment scattered. In spite of the unbearable stench, the battalion secured the area. To add to their discomfort, the Japanese rained fire on them. Eighty-three 75 mm shells came pounding down at dusk, on Christmas Eve. Miraculously there were no casualties:

> *Our first Xmas in action—all the others were very pleasant in Palestine. On Xmas Eve we had a decent taste of Jap shells instead of carols, just to remind us that there really was a war on.*
> *3 January 1944*

Major John Oldham wrote a poem on 1 January 1944. Its second verse:

> Our lads are pledged to battle
> In the Valley of Ramu:
> Where kunai crests the hilltops,
> And scars the mountainsides.
> Where rippling streams and rocky pools,
> 'Neath misty clouds and rain
> Are swung to surging torrents
> —As the thunder claps again.

He signed it with a New Year's wish: 'Written from the Valley of Ramu. May I never see it again, for all its rugged beauty.'[11]

Fifteen days later John Murray's second niece, Julian Oldham, was born. 'I'm sure our nursing sister [Margie] must be very capable if she handles babies just like you handled us,' John wrote to his mother. He was pining to be home. 'Longing for leave. It will come along soon I hope,' he wrote to Margie a few weeks later.

By then he was able to hope. The men were advancing north along the Huon Peninsula, with very few enemy encounters. It appeared that the Brigade's role was drawing to a close.

Along with John's thoughts of home was sombre reflection on his personal life. He was worried about his increasing age, still without a wife or family. References to girls in his letters became more regular. His determination to marry became a focus:

Lovely letter from you yesterday—full of news and plans. Also one from Pamela. Thanks so much for the airmail handkerchief and bottle of ink. Makes all the difference both to my nose and my letter writing! I hate writing in pencil ...

I'm so full of ambition and the desire for security for us all, coupled with the fact that I'm getting that bit older every year and so gradually realising that life does not go on forever and the start must be made around 30.

The war might last another 3 or 4 years in the Pacific, and that would mean I'd be 32, unmarried, and nothing done. If I marry now I know it would tie me down considerably, but there are other things to be thought of. I don't want to wait until I'm 40 and then start looking around.
21 November 1943

By the beginning of 1944, the idea had taken hold. John was warning his mother to prepare herself for his marriage—a timely caution given his mother's earlier intrusions into his personal life:

You never know of course—I may go off the deep end and get married. Of course it makes you terribly worried when I talk like this and I know you would hate the thought of it, but you've got to face it one of these days and I can only hope that you will all back me up no matter who she is. It's quite a big factor to all get on well together—but nevertheless not absolutely necessary. After all, it will be me that marries the girl and not my family. Hard words aren't they? But quite true all the same.

I'm rather a lonely young man you know and you must realise also that I'm an extremely physical type. We all are for that matter, and I've had quite enough of the sordidness of 'picking women up', and a mistress is not altogether my idea of things either. And I know you don't want to see me getting in and out of tangles like that. I'm not the type to get away with it anyway.

All this talk is not just because I'm a soldier and away at the war. Don't get upset, darling. I'll probably be an old bachelor yet ... There aren't many girls about like our Margaret ...
3 January 1944

Though Lorraine was not yet married, both Peter and his sister Margie had been married since 1939. By 1944 they'd produced four children in total.

John did not want to be only an uncle forever. It was therefore no surprise to his mother that on his next leave to Australia it was girls and a hectic social life that dominated his activities. He had already warned her that it would be thus, making it perfectly clear on a number of occasions that he would not be 'managed'—especially in his plans to conduct an independent social life:

We may get about three weeks or a month and my heaven I'm looking forward to it. Margie's place, if not too cluttered up with babies, will be ideal for leave, though I may keep a room at the Wentworth or some other place for convenience. I always like to do that because there's nothing like complete independence when you're on leave.
3 January 1944

Sorry darling if I was defiant in my last letter, but the fact is that I really hate people taking a hand in my affairs ... I was lonely [writing the letter] and still am. I hate the nights. Seldom do I go to sleep before 2 o'clock in the morning, so I don't go to bed till after midnight now. Sometimes I wander round on my own when everyone else has gone to bed. It's good to be alone a bit but not too much. I had far too much of it when I was younger in the bush.
4 February 1944

By the end of January 1944 the Australians in New Guinea could see that the enemy had been soundly defeated. In addition to all the different Australian units, the Papuan Infantry battalions had played an integral part, as had individual New Guinea natives. Affectionately called Fuzzy Wuzzies, the natives knew the jungle intimately and had tirelessly carried rations, ammunition and the wounded.

Although satisfied to have contributed once more to a major victory— his 'enthusiastic and untiring efforts' were praised in reference to the commendable job done by the Intelligence Section—John Murray was nevertheless desperate to get out, to return home.[12] Towards the end of February he was making definite arrangements. Leave could not come soon enough.

Letters home now overflowed with plans:

Of course what I'm really looking forward to is being out with Peter for about a week. I want to get up early one morning, just at daybreak, and ride a good horse over the country while the sun comes up. The whole bush wakes up then and it is really the best time to be with Peter again too. There's so much we can talk about. The longest Peter and I have ever been apart. We have a lot to catch up on.
4 February 1944

Mentioning his intentions so often in letters, John was now dreaming vividly at night—fleeting visions of his return. Everyone, officers and men alike, started to lay bets on which day embarkation would be announced. On 29 February 1944, they filed on board. Finally, 8 March saw them sailing through Moreton Bay and up the Brisbane River, calling out and cooeeing to the girls who lined the banks.

Dirty and smelly—'a very low grade mob'—they badly needed civilisation. They'd had no clean water on the ship. 'We could be smelled a mile off.' However, Lorraine came to the rescue. By then she was living at an army camp and working for the Americans. Her American boss, Colonel Ballantyne, invited John to a welcome home party at Lennon's Hotel in Brisbane. John extended the invitation to his commanding officer. Sizing up the situation, Ballantyne took charge. 'Colonel, would you and John like to have a shower?' Colvin replied immediately, 'That's just one thing we would love to have.'

Finally, after a boisterous party, they were taken back to their camp, where John drifted into a deep sleep. After reveille at dawn the next morning and an issue of clothes and ration coupons, he would set off to his home.

It was 9 March 1944. Most of the men were due for about forty-two days' leave. No one disputed that they needed it badly. They were sick, worn out and 'full of malaria'. They had 'run all over the Japanese', but the long months had taken a severe toll.

Chapter Twenty-One

Security and survival

I'VE GOT MY FINGERS CROSSED THAT WITH SOME LUCK I WILL
ARRIVE HOME LOOKING FIT AND HEALTHY—HOPING VERY
MUCH THAT I HAVE THE MALARIA WELL UNDER CONTROL ...
IN FACT, A VERY HEALTHY YOUNG MAN WITH A SPRIGHTLY
STEP. JUST WAIT 'TIL I GET HOME WITH MY NICE UNIFORM AND
SAM BROWN POLISHED UP! WILL YOU COME OUT WITH ME?

—John Murray[1]

'HOME LEAVE WAS always a man's affair,' according to Tim Fearnside, 'which seemed to bring a spate of men newly married or engaged to be married.'[2] This was hardly surprising when the social program of these same men was observed. Fulfilling his intentions for independence, John took a room in a hotel—this time at Usher's Hotel in Castlereagh Street, Sydney.

Girls were not allowed in their hotel rooms but the men nevertheless partied with them until dawn on their first night back. The partying called for surreptitious behaviour. It was 'an awful business getting them back before sunrise, thinking that their parents might wake up and seeing the poor things having to explain'. But not awful enough to forgo the celebrations.

After the festivities, John spent his planned week with Peter, in the west. Clearly marriage was also high on his agenda: '[Afterwards] I went to Ivanhoe and the Williamsons picked me up. *Coolaminya* was delightful and I knew the family well. It was during that leave that I was hale and hearty with Mary ...

John and Ruth, stepping into their bridal car, 13 April 1944.

'Old Jock Williamson, the father, was a lovely old fellow. During that little visit he pulled me aside and said to me "if anything should ever happen to you, you can always come and live with us ... if you get wounded or incapacitated". Nice thing to say. He thought I could be badly wounded. I deeply appreciated that.'

Back in Sydney, John often stayed up until first light, revelling in the freedoms that leave offered. One of those evening-to-dawn encounters was to change his life forever.

John had planned to dine with his mother and Margie at Wollstonecraft, one April evening in 1944. After a quick shower and shave he headed off, around 6 pm. Wanting to soak up the atmosphere he decided to walk through the city, before catching a train to the north shore. He arrived at Wynyard Station in plenty of time.

And then he saw her. A beautiful tall girl, with long, dark wavy hair, a willowy figure, high cheekbones and red lips. Despite the years away from Australia, John recognised her immediately. Ruth Stanton-Cook was a close friend of Margie's; they'd been at school together. As a young girl she had spent much of her time at *Colchester* where a close bond had developed between all the children. Her mother had abandoned her when she was three years old, leaving Ruth and her brother behind in Australia and taking her only sister to Britain. When her father remarried, paternal maiden Aunt Tess accepted responsibility for her upbringing. John's mother had instructed her children to be kind to Ruth, to treat her like a sister, as she was motherless.

While still in the Middle East, John had received letters from the family telling him that Ruth's fiancé, Max Parker, a RAAF pilot from South Australia, had been shot down over the English Channel. She was desolate but had continued working in the city, catching her usual train home each night to her aunt's home at Gordon, in the northern suburbs of Sydney.

John was overcome at this chance meeting, delighted to see her again. He quickly calculated that she would now be twenty-seven years old. Engrossed in conversation, they got onto the same train. During the train trip Ruth did something that indicated care, intimacy and confidence. Bending over close to take the handkerchief from his pocket, she wiped a small patch of shaving cream from his ear, with studied concentration. They both laughed out loud.

John was 'entranced'; thoughts raced through his head. He thought about Mary Williamson and Pam Weston, but Ruth 'came shining through'.

He could hardly believe how urgent it was for him. He was obsessed with the idea of her. He must not lose this girl. They talked and talked. So lost was he in conversation that he missed his stop and continued on to Gordon. 'I could have danced all the way down the Pacific Highway at the end of that night.' When he proposed the next day she accepted immediately and two days later, on 13 April 1944, they were married.

The war had forced swift adaptation: wedding gowns were easy to hire; church ministers made every effort to make themselves available for mid-week wedding services; and rather than wearing a suit, the groom often wore Army attire.

Deep red roses, a hired white gown and an officer's uniform and cap set the scene for a memorable day. After the ceremony a shiny black car conveyed the couple, still twirling in a whirlwind of love and desire, from St James Church of England Turramurra to Aunt Tess's home in Gordon where a small group of guests—fewer than twenty—enjoyed a feast of rationed food. Ruth revelled in the apparent exaggeration of the story to her friends: 'I was engaged and married in half a week'.

On leave from New Guinea at the same time, Margie's husband, Dr John Oldham, was able to extend his brother-in-law's leave for a short honeymoon, with a medical certificate prescribing more rest for his malarial symptoms. Since Ruth was the purest of virgins, and had said, 'John, what do I do?' on their wedding night, the extra time for tuition was desirably beneficial.

The same day that John married saw a series of recommendations in a report from General Blamey. Therein were suggestions that nine infantry divisions, one armoured brigade and one army tank brigade would be necessary to provide an Australian offensive force and maintain home security.[3] Too soon, John was back in service. He was to be tied to a military camp in Queensland from April 1944 for one entire year to fulfil those military obligations. At least the Atherton Tablelands looked better than the jungle.

John missed his wife and family terribly. Routines at Ravenshoe camp did not always sufficiently divert his attention from the separation. Almost immediately after arrival he wrote an eight-page letter to Ruth. Sixty-two years later John said of the sentiments expressed in that correspondence: 'I feel exactly the same as I did then—my feelings are the same. If I could possibly write another letter [to her] like that now, I would':

Ruth Darling

Two beautiful letters from you waiting for me when I arrived in camp this morning. Thank God for letters—they will mean so much to both of us in the months that lie ahead.

It's impossible for me, also, to put into writing just how much I love you, darling, and just how much you mean to me; how much more I will want and make of life now I have you …

And yet, we are only just beginning to love each other—it will grow and grow until it reaches the stage of perfect unity of mind, soul and body … It has been a big upset in your life darling— bigger than I at first realised. It is extremely difficult for a girl of your age, type and environment—and please let me say innocent ignorance—to plunge so quickly, and without mental preparation, into marriage. Very few, I know, could have done what you have done—and, darling, if possible I love you more for it. Your complete and faithful acceptance to meet the unknown was a sacrifice I will never forget. You married a man who, because he had as he thought 'knocked about' as men do, considered that he was capable of meeting any situation and coping with it. Smug fool that I was. How little I knew I judge from how much I have learnt and realise how much more I will yet learn. We will learn together …

You've no idea how much more contented I am to know that my days of searching are over—to know that I have the settled feeling of peace within—to know that whatever I have to do you will be beside me—to have—to confide in—an incentive to every task. Darling, I love you.

It is beautiful here in our new camp—scattered tents and huts amongst gums in the bend of a wide, slow-flowing river … Spent most of last Tuesday and Wednesday at a staging camp only a few hundred yards from where Lorraine lives and works … Tuesday night we went into Lennon's and two of her old Colonel friends gave us a nice dinner and a few spots up in their rooms. All very enjoyable, and nice to see so much of Lorraine …

Gather each and every thread, my darling, and let me help you hold them firmly and tie them all securely—it is most important. Tell me everything darling—always—be honest to each other in our letters—share our thoughts—hopes—dreams—fears— try to comply fairly with each other's wishes—be tolerant of each other's views—then there can only be one destiny, and it will be ours as sure as night must follow day.

I don't usually write long letters and those I do are as a rule very disjointed and like a grasshopper from one thing to another …There are hundreds of things I want to tell you darling … You know I've told you dozens of times how beautiful you are and you won't believe me. But I'm telling you what I think— not what you think. To me, you are my ideal of perfection— what I want, what I will always want—what I have …

Darling, I wish you were here with me. The other occupant of the tent went to hospital today so there would be just us. Outside the night is very cold, crisp and starry … We are 3000 feet above sea level. But inside the tent is warm … The hurricane lamp is standing on an upturned pannikin, flickering slowly and casting strange shadows through the tent. All is quiet except for an occasional low murmur of conversation from a tent close by … By day the army and work claim most of my thoughts, but at night?—darling—you are so close to me now that I feel I could almost touch you; that if I spoke you would answer quietly and it would not seem strange. So every night I will think of you most, until I sleep—and hope that I may even dream …

So goodnight my angel girl, keep well and beautiful, don't work too hard or worry over me, think how we will soon be together again, plan for that, it is worth planning for—please don't want for anything that is within our power for you to have. I want to see happiness radiate from you … our marriage is a licence for happiness. But above all—and I am sure of it—as I love you, then love you me.
7 May 1944

Though John was separated from his wife, he was thankful for his new status. 'God is good to me, Mother dear', he wrote in an outburst of wellbeing as he expressed gratitude for his wonderful health, his enthusiasm for life, his good position in the army, his darling mother, brother and sisters and Charlie, and above all, his beautiful wife. His wife's letters to him 'expressed her very soul' with thoughts and feelings so close to his own.[4] He ensured that his mother did not feel superseded:

> *What a wonderful holiday I had, darling. Did all the things I wanted to do and found a wife also. It's been really the best 50 days I've ever had in my life. Have seen all the family too, and now things are ever so much clearer for the future. We are all far more united now than we have ever been, although none of us are living together. I'm almost getting excited about wondering just what our future is going to be. Something good I am sure. Wonderful to realise how we are all working for that one thing too—the future. With this spirit we could not fail ...*
>
> *Your children do worry about you a bit you know—although sometimes it may not seem apparent. But heavens, there's really no closer family than ours.*
> *9 June 1944*

Ruth wrote to Constance also. Part of the long letter to *Mother Darling* shows her delight in the 'new status quo':

> *Dear old Pete—how nice of him to be so thrilled about having me for his sister-in-law. Well, I am more thrilled about it all myself, as you know, and am so fortunate to have such wonderful in-laws as I have ... Oh darling, I have always felt you more like a mother to me than anything else ...*
> *30 August 1944*

As Battalion IO John's life was comfortable. There were few complaints. Bill, his batman, 'an excellent chap', was always working on ways to make his digs more habitable. However, what was asked of the men over the twelve months at Ravenshoe required a steely resolve, an almost impossible tenacity.

Without the adrenalin of battle and particularly without the company of family, spirits began to waver. It was therefore with pleasant anticipation that John accepted another invitation for advanced training, this time to attend the Senior Wing of the Intelligence School, for six weeks from early July. This allowed him to see much more of Ruth whose immediate journey north he arranged, and Lorraine, who was still working for the Americans in a camp nearby. They all met up several times at the Officers' Club in Brisbane and at Lennon's Hotel.

Ruth wrote to her mother-in-law from Southport, where she was temporarily living in a small cottage close to John's army digs. On the card was a photo of the Pacific Hotel:

> *Mother darling,*
> *Just a card to show you where John's school is. The mark denotes where his bedroom is—or one of them! ... We are terrifically happy but it's all too short. Still we have been very fortunate. With all our love to you,*
> *Ruthie.*
> *4 July 1944*

Renewed intimacy between the couple did not seem to interfere with John's performance at the school. He received an excellent report: 'Pleasing personality, works well as an organiser or one of a team. Essentially practical outlook and good military background. Has done consistently good work. Is recommended for G111 because of his common sense outlook and ability to work well with superiors or subordinates.'[5]

John wrote that he knew his mother would be happy he was 'going ahead and not standing still or going backwards'. His most recent training could very well lead to advancement in rank—'a step up from when he had walked into the kitchen at Killara all those years ago' as a lance corporal, with one stripe on his arm.

He was now one of 101 commissioned officers—a lieutenant in a battalion through which, in all, 2605 other ranks passed.[6] He knew she would be bursting with pride if she could see a third pip on the epaulette of her son's uniform.

After spending a few days in Brisbane with Ruth, the couple were again forced to part. However, John wrote of his contentment to his mother:

I'm very glad and happy I'm married. It has made a very big difference to me and has filled that rather lonely and empty side of my life. A soldier is a happier man to know he has comfort and security anchored at home for such times as he does get leave. I feel far more settled now that I have Ruth, and she really is such a darling.
25 September 1944

Well darling one—you know of course how happy I am these days with such a beautiful wife. What a lovely girl she really is—the only thing that hurts is being so far away.
29 October 1944

John now had even stronger incentive to plan for the future. As the interminable months at Ravenshoe passed, he devoted more and more of his spare time to laying out the map in his mind:

One thing we can be sure of—we will get country somewhere and settle down and be happy together. And I do want to see you and Charlie with us somewhere—all working together.
29 October 1944

His dreams and more practical ideas made his general planning worthwhile and financial planning very real. There would even be some advantages to another overseas military posting:

You know I'm being taxed now for the first time since I've been in the army, but if we go outside Australian waters before July next year, then I will get all my tax back again ... All the same, I'll be glad when it's over and I can live a normal life with my wife in which we can both work together for our future, instead of being continually separated the way we are, and are likely to be for a few more years yet ...
25 September 1944

Each time John wrote he further developed the theme of family land ownership. Even the farms that surrounded him in the tablelands attracted his sharp eye. They were always green because of the rich volcanic soil and the rainfall of almost 180 centimetres (70 inches) per annum. He was interested in the acreages that supported dairy cows where no specific cultivation was required for feed. The ground seemed to grow anything:

> *Do you know Mother, I can't help becoming each day, more and more strong on the idea of a decent farm for us all instead of a property out west. Unless, of course, we could get a really decent place on a par with* Tiltagoona *[the property Peter managed].* *25 December 1944*

John felt that a purchase of land in the north glowed with advantages. A farmer making 100 pounds per month could double his income with 'proper, energetic farming'; houses and furnishings in the area were constructed out of glamorous-sounding timbers such as silky oak, cedar, maple and walnut. And the climate was glorious. Out west, they would be gambling with ever unreliable seasons and the inevitable dirt, dust and drought. John would look into both options 'from every cold and callous angle', always examining 'the worst side'. The idea of land in the north should be given serious consideration.

The family was not entirely convinced. John referred to their concerns in his letters, frustrated by the distance between them all. After preparing a detailed synopsis of the appealing financial aspects of buying one of the best dairy farms in the northern district, he asked his family to tell him if they knew of anything better. Anything, of course, that would be within their reach.

Just before Christmas, John was very happy to inform his mother of a change of address. Barton Maughan, the former IO, first of the 2/13th Battalion and then the 20th Brigade, had accepted a promotion to work in Intelligence with Lord Mountbatten in India. Immediately John was invited to take over his role as Brigade Intelligence Officer. He would now be responsible for three battalions. It meant he would 'have to leave the good old 2/13th' after four-and-a-half years:

I have once more followed on in Barton Maughan's footsteps and taken over his job. Strange how history repeats itself, don't you think? I will probably soon become a captain, which will be one more step up the ladder.
5 November 1944

John was now attached to Brigade Headquarters, conferring with Alec Hill the Brigade Major or Victor Windeyer the Brigade Commander, to whom he was directly responsible. 'More brain work and less running round,' was his summation of the new duties.

His mother did not have to wait long for the announcement of his promotion to come through. Within a couple of months she was addressing her letters to Captain John Murray.

Yet another Christmas loomed. John found it much more difficult to look forward to Christmas fare, this time to be presented in the blazing sun on the B Company parade ground. The Army did its best, but nothing could replace home. At least his mother would have company on 25 December:

I'm happy to know you are spending the day, not alone, but with my sweet and darling wife, who is really another daughter. She certainly considers you as mother, and that's something I'm terribly happy about.
25 December 1944

He was already imagining the next Christmas. Surely he would be home for it, at last with his family? A profusion of muscatels and almonds, glasses of sherry, gifts, papers, ribbons and tags. Warmed flaming brandy around the plum pudding; silver coins inside the dome; nieces and nephews squirming with excitement. Mother would allow almost anything on Christmas Day. How could the Army possibly replicate the spicy sensations of childhood?

Well, today is Xmas number 5 that I've spent in the army. Time flies certainly, and it's hard to imagine now that I've ever been anything other than a soldier. This is about the longest job I've had—getting quite a steady young chap, aren't I?

A very Merry Xmas to you, darling, and health and happiness and all you desire and deserve for 1945, and the many years to come. This is the first Xmas I believe that you have not had one of your family with you—one of your children ...

Only this morning I had a letter from Ruth saying what a wonderful thing it is for her and us both, for our future happiness, to have you for a mother. Some young marrieds are unfortunate, in fact, most of them—but we are the very happy exceptions and always will be.

One thing we must try very hard to do after the war, and that is to concentrate all our efforts on having a complete big family reunion for Xmas. Every one of us with our wives and children. What a happy party that would be and I know how you would love it.

You and Charlie, at each end of the table with your immensely enlarged family. With wives, husbands and children, there are now 13 of us!! Ruth and I hope to swell that up a bit too, if only the army gives us a decent fair chance.
25 December 1944

With the enforced separation from his wife, it was becoming more and more difficult for John to maintain his positive attitude. He now saw the war as 'rather a nuisance' despite his determination to continue contributing to the Allied effort until final victory. It had certainly restricted his future; he had already served five years and there was more to come.

Without a doubt, revelations on the dark, inhuman acts of war also contributed to John's overall negativity. While he was at Ravenshoe there was a request for three IOs at brigade level to meet at MacArthur's Headquarters in Brisbane: 'We were put in a room. Material was brought to us in great quantities, reports from all over the Pacific area of all these bloody awful atrocities—beheading blokes, cutting them to pieces—it was gruesome. Reams and reams of reading. From all of that we had to prepare a lecture and present it to the whole of the AIF ... how to escape, evade capture, how to contact the natives, how to integrate with them, how to live with them, how to get them to help you and get back to your lines again. Hell of a job really.'

The task was daunting. John's half-hour talk was delivered to every unit of the 20th Brigade 'to frighten hell out of each and every soldier'. He spent weeks at the job. No one was to think that the Japanese were a pushover. 'Escaping was not half of it.'

John tried to keep his mind off the horrors exposed in his briefings. Particularly distressing was the story of the 1047 Australian and British prisoners who were sent through the jungle in January 1945 on three death marches, from Sandakan to Ranau, in northern Borneo. 'Of those who survived the march, all but six were killed at Ranau.'[7]

In early March 1945 a letter John wrote to Margie gave hints of his fading positivism:

> *Thanks for your letter darling—received it two days ago.*
> *This morning I packed Ruth off by train for Southport—she is going to spend a few days with Dick [her brother] near Murwillumbah and should be home on or about Friday next. So you can imagine I'm feeling a bit miserable and sorry for myself this morning.*

After reflecting on a few family matters he wound up:

> *Excuse this poor attempt darling—but it's just how I feel at the moment. I'll be OK after lunch and a few beers.*
> *5 March 1945*

To add to his concerns, by the end of March John's plans to get the family together on a farm seemed to be falling apart. His suggestion for the family to move north saw too many stumbling blocks, one being the fact that for Charlie the change would be a major one. There was now talk of John going out by himself:

> *... I should have at least 1000 pounds of my own when I get into civilian clothes. Even if Ruth and I have a child, then we can still keep ahead of things. We certainly won't go back.*

So therefore, the fact that any help for me from the rest of the family will not be available (except for Lorraine), does not worry me unduly. I know I will have enough to start on my own place if the Government sees fit to give me one.

It is certainly not fair to expect Charlie to live out west or anywhere for that matter if it does not suit him ... Don't worry darling if the family arrangement will not work out—all will be well eventually. Mine certainly will be one home and family where you would be perfectly happy at any time; Ruth loves you so much, for which I thank God ...
25 March 1945

Though he had admitted in a letter to Margie that without Ruth he felt miserable, he added that as a couple they both acknowledged that this was the way it had to be, that he would 'do exactly the same thing again if the clock were put back'.

But John was becoming fidgety, increasingly impatient to start a new life with his wife. The training sessions in the Atherton Tablelands seemed to stretch out indefinitely.

By 11 April, after a visit from a planning party, the dreaded confirmation of another move was announced. Embarkation orders were issued and preparations commenced. The battalion was to move offshore yet again.

Chapter Twenty-Two

Borneo

As for myself, I am very well but working hard and
have little time to do anything other than my work
for the army. It comes in rushes — sometimes nothing
much for a week or so and then all of a sudden
things go at a furious pace and I find myself almost
buried under a great heap of documents ... However,
it's interesting and I like it and the rest of the staff
officers on the HQ are a very fine lot indeed, which
makes such a difference.

—John Murray, 1945[1]

By then John had been mentioned twice in Despatches for his war efforts. Ruth was invigorated when she received one of the official citations, in which His Majesty the King was 'graciously pleased to approve of the Award'. Shortly afterwards she received a certificate detailing the two Mentions in Despatches, his stars and medals: 'For your services with the Armed Forces during the Second World War 1939/45 you have been awarded the undermentioned Decorations, Campaign Stars and War Medals:

> Decorations: You were mentioned in Despatches on two
> different occasions.
> Campaign Stars: 1939/45 Star. Africa Star and 8th Army
> Clasp, Pacific Star.
> War Medals: Defence Medal, War Medal.'

However this official recognition did not make it any easier for either Ruth or Constance to accept the fact that John was soon to leave the country again. A move outside Australia was imminent for the entire 20th Brigade.

John wrote to his mother:

> *Well darling one, please look after yourself because later on there is so much happiness in store for you, I know. The war has been a sacrifice for all of us in that regard …*
>
> *Never mind darling—we will be allowed enough years to have the happiness we all want and I feel so rightly deserve, of that I feel sure.*
> *19 April 1945*

It was 25 April 1945, ANZAC Day, the day that commemorated all the sacrifices made in World War I, and now the many lives already lost over the last six years. After a trip from the Atherton Tablelands to Townsville by train, the men set sail—this time on the *Frederick Lykes*—destination unknown. Three days later the men were looking at the familiar mountains around Milne Bay; in another two days they landed on Morotai, an island that had been captured from the Japanese in 1944 and would now be used for approximately three weeks of additional training.

The ultimate plan, soon revealed, was to capture parts of British North Borneo—Brunei and Sarawak—where the Japanese had seized vital oil fields in early 1942.[2]

After the usual sorting out of gear, cleaning weapons and settling into camp at Morotai, the familiar route marches and weapons training began for the men. John was otherwise occupied. One of his responsibilities as Brigade IO was the construction of a relief model, on a scale of 20 inches to a mile, which gave a clearer picture of the ground to be attacked and an explanation of battalion and brigade responsibilities. 'A very fine piece of work it was,' reported Tim Fearnside.[3]

On 30 May, the brigade was taken in trucks driven by US Army personnel to the embarkation point and in early June a silent convoy of nearly 100 ships escorted by US destroyers made its way west. Beginning a journey of 1600 kilometres (1000 miles), they headed for Borneo.

The landing at Brunei was considered 'a walkover'. The Japanese had been taken entirely by surprise. Some of the lookouts were not even manned.

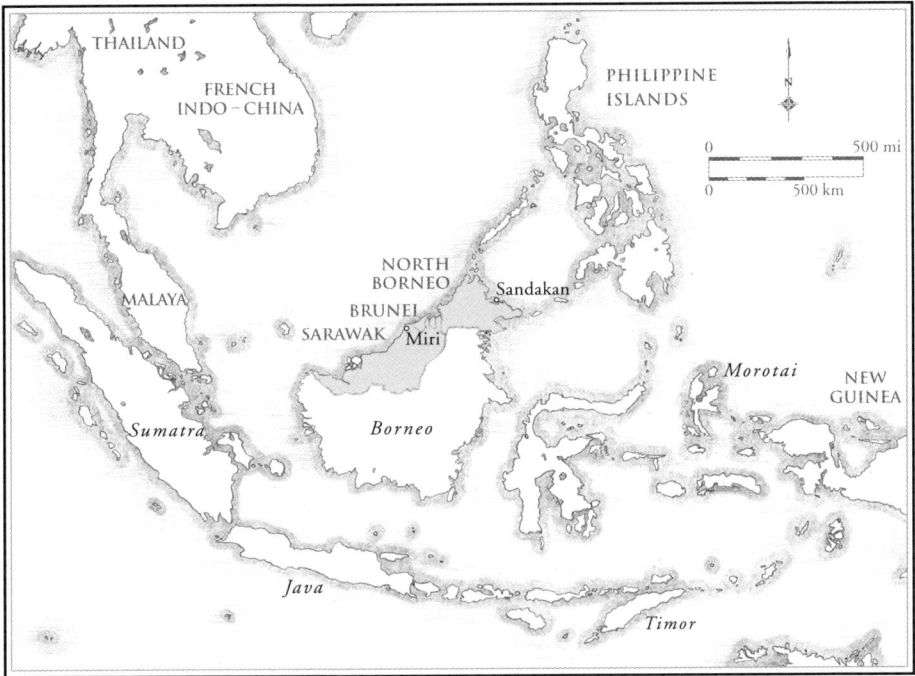

Presence in Borneo of the 20th Brigade from early June to October 1945.

The small numbers of Japanese soldiers disappeared into the thick scrub to their jungle hideouts when faced with direct contact. Allied patrols fanned out in widening arcs until most of the wanted areas were covered.

John was still obliged to write detailed reports of each day's activities. It was fortuitous that the fighting activity was comparatively slow, as there were refreshing distractions: 'The monkeys used to come down past my tent for bathing—they used to wash in the bit of a surf just like human beings—look at us curiously and disappear back into the scrub again.'

One phenomenon John reported on was the huge fires that burned. The Japanese had torched all thirty-seven oil wells in the area, destroying at the same time anything that could be used to put out the fires: 'The Japanese set them alight and did enormous damage. There were these great wells just burning thousands, millions of dollars worth of oil, burning like great Bunsen burners up into the sky. Amazing things, the flames—miles along the coast these oil wells were burning and we could read a letter five miles away from the glare ... But it was the damage that was being done, the cost.'

Though the fires were fierce, the opposition was not. The Allies now had numerical superiority on land and in the air and 'the overstretched Japanese forces [were] facing the inevitability of defeat in their recently occupied territories'.[4]

It was claimed later that the Australians had been placed in 'out of the way' destinations, 'where MacArthur wanted them to be'. Having ignored US Government directives to place senior Allied officers on his HQ's staff, and disregarded most of the advice Australia's General Blamey had to offer, MacArthur was able to take the easy step to isolate Australian forces from the direct offensive against Japan.[5] The US general wanted the personal glory of the capture of the Philippines and 'the final anticipated assault upon Japan'.[6]

John's memory of MacArthur's early visit to Borneo, accompanied by numerous war correspondents with cameras, was vivid: 'I don't forgive MacArthur. I think he was a lesser mind quite frankly … a showman. He demonstrated it in Borneo. We landed in Borneo early morning—captured the beachhead quick smart … Our troops went in … a successful thing.

'MacArthur was well out with his fleet waiting for the word to come in—so that he could put on his show … I had my interpreter, a young Australian officer questioning one of these Jap privates. I wanted a bit of information quickly on the names of a couple of Jap commanders … and MacArthur arrived on the beach just behind me …

'I was just in on the sand dunes under a palm tree with this little group with my batman making sure no one took a pot shot at me, and MacArthur arrived with his coterie … You should have seen it! He had to take his boots off, waded in, so ridiculous the whole thing—unnecessary, completely stage-managed. Once the filming was over, he left.'

The campaign continued on through July and August 1945. By now, the cleaning up of the Japanese was 'a pushover' for the men. They struck small pockets of resistance—especially in the swamps and mangrove islands—but many of the enemy surrendered, without further fuss.

Though Borneo was an easy assignment for John compared with those in North Africa or New Guinea, there were aspects that bore no comparison. It was activities there more than anywhere else that resulted in his increasing negativity. Speaking to witnesses, assessing hundreds of documents and compiling information forced him to face an ugliness far worse than he could ever have imagined. So horrific were the details of his investigations that at times John was forced to hand over his work 'for a break'.

When the oil towns were liberated by the Allies, it was discovered that there were still some British women and their families up in the hills—the wives and children of the oil companies' employees. Their men had gone off to fight the Japanese and had finished up in Singapore. In an attempt to hide from the invading Japanese, the defenceless women had fled, stumbling further and further back into the surrounding hills and from there into the mountains. The native Dayak tribes had attempted to shelter the fugitive women, but mostly to no avail:

> 'The Japs patrolled right up into the mountains and got most of them … They bayoneted the children; they threw little babies from one to the other. From bayonet to bayonet … They chopped women's breasts off … sliced their breasts off and then let them go … picked up a little baby by one leg and chopped it in half with their sharp sword.
>
> That was written … It came in on letters to me … You see, I was the Intelligence Officer for the Brigade. All that stuff came to me. The Dayaks fed me letters months old … You just got so sick … that you didn't want to listen any more. The stories you heard were just beyond belief … When the women finally came down into the coastal centres we'd set up, they learnt that most of their husbands were dead … [most likely interned in Changi, the notorious POW camp].
>
> I made notes and records … [which] went back to Divisional Headquarters and then back to Army Headquarters, to God knows where.
>
> It was a dreadful, dreadful story, never really published.'

In letters following there were hints that John's duties in Borneo were beginning to affect his perspective:

> *Well darling one … this war has shown me a lot of the world, some I wanted to see and other parts I wasn't so keen about … Just how much use it will be to me is rather doubtful, because we see lots of things which are beautiful associated with many things which war makes ugly. And all the experiences I've had, or most*

of them I can only share properly with someone who speaks the same language—a soldier who has experienced similar things.

The months slip past until they become a year and then before you know it a further year. Not only the best years of my life but the best years of my wife too. And we do so much want a family … Soon I'll be thirty, not old I know but I'm not as good a man as when I joined up. I am sure of it—I have lost so much energy and have not the desire to do things I loved five years ago.
11 July 1945

As though to obliterate the present, John turned all his thoughts to the future. He wrote that he knew Ruth would support any decision, even if it meant going way out west. 'Whither thou goest, I follow,' he repeated admiringly of his wife's loyalty and confidence in him. He was not sure what the government was going to do about giving land to returned soldiers. He could certainly go out to Peter and 'be okay'. It would be an eye opener for Ruth, but she wouldn't have to go right back to basics like Peter's wife Jane had. What an incredible job *she* did! He would have no difficulty getting a reasonably good job but definitely did not want to take a job involving physical work only. He had to get into something where he could have a balance of mental and physical—'more mental than the other'.

John repeated his concerns to his mother. There was now a sense of urgency. 'What lovely children they are,' he had written a few months before of Margie's two children. '[She] is very lucky indeed to have them. I hope Ruth and I are as fortunate:'

He continued:

This has been all me darling—but it's best for you to know how I'm thinking from time to time—you have a right to know. A bit confusing I admit.
11 July 1945

It seemed to John that the war was fast approaching its end. He knew 'something was in the air' when General Windeyer approached him in early August and requested that he look after the Commander-in-Chief of the Australian Army and Allied Land Forces in the South-West Pacific, who was coming to Borneo for a few days. Windeyer asked John to attend to General Blamey's every need whilst at Brigade Headquarters, including his penchant for a glass of whisky at night. Preparing the nightcap turned out to be one of John's easiest tasks.

A more taxing duty was taking receipt of a vital message for Blamey that would be dropped from the air at a particular time, on a certain day. Since there was no suitable landing area near Brigade Headquarters, it was to be dropped outside the forestry building that had been taken over by the brigade officials. It would be dropped 'from a fair height and land in the grassy area outside the building'. John would recognise it—a leather bag that had red, white and blue streamers attached to it.

There was one problem with these seemingly straightforward instructions. The designated area was covered in kunai grass—2 hectares (5 acres) of it—as tall as John himself. General Blamey needed to call out directions from the verandah once he saw the bag land. Louder and louder directions issued from the building. John was barely able to hear them as he struggled in the loudly crackling grass. 'No! No! Go further north! No! That's too far! NO! Come back again!' Still John failed to deliver. 'Oh, you bloody fool. You bloody fool. Can't you follow my directions?'

John had lathered up into a heavy sweat when he eventually stumbled onto the bag, quite by chance. He floundered back through 90 metres (100 yards) of kunai grass to Headquarters. Fuming, General Blamey grabbed the satchel without a word. John thought, 'Oh God, I'm finished,' then made his way into the building, where his blokes had been observing the debacle and 'laughing their heads off'. The image of the general shouting hysterically into the grass was impossible to erase. John could not live it down, though he too had a lot of good laughs 'once the commotion died down'.

It was not until a few days later that John discovered the significance of the unusually delivered message for Blamey. It was confirmation that an atomic bomb had been dropped on Japan. The Potsdam Declaration, signed by the United States, Britain and China, had been presented to Japan on 26 July 1945, threatening 'prompt and utter destruction' unless Japan surrendered.

Also enclosed in the package were the logistics for Blamey's departure from Borneo—which greatly relieved his keeper: 'A little reconnaissance plane landed for him on the beach and took him away … I didn't have to go groping around in the kunai grass to find anything else. That was the last I saw of him, thank God.'

When Japan's Prime Minister Hideki Tojo ignored the Allied warning, America was true to its word. Bombs were dropped on Hiroshima and Nagasaki, on 6 and 9 August respectively, which 'seared to death practically all living things, human and animal',[7] forcing Japan's capitulation.

The bombings had been persuasive. Emperor Hirohito stunned his people by broadcasting a message to the nation; his subjects had never heard his voice before and possibly did not understand its delivery in archaic court Japanese. He spoke of 'a new and most cruel bomb'. Continuing to fight would result in 'the ultimate collapse' of Japan and also, the 'total extinction of civilisation'.[8]

John heard the official announcement on 15 August 1945, broadcast on two old battered radio sets, brought back from Syria. Emperor Hirohito had surrendered unconditionally but had not accepted any blame: 'We declared war on America and Britain because of our sincere desire to ensure our safety and endeavour to carry out the stabilisation of East Asia …'[9]

This declaration was greeted with amazement and looked on with amusement. Just a month or so before, John had produced an operations report, covering the previous six months. In the foreword Brigadier Rogers, the Director of Military Intelligence, had given his opinion of the enemy. His sentiments, expressed with the full force of bombast and sarcasm, were quite different from the Japanese Emperor's. At the time, Rogers' views were accepted by most Allies as a true interpretation of the Pacific experience: 'The war is ended. The Nipponese castles … have crashed completely and irrevocably … Already perhaps, its leaders, using their peculiarly delicate means of departing this life, are joining their "honourable" ancestors …

'Not for many decades, however, will we forget the treacherous war waged by their evil hordes, nor the unspeakable sufferings and the atrocities committed against our men in Malaya, New Guinea, New Britain, British Borneo, and the islands of the Dutch East Indies. These, when eventually disclosed, will cause the decent people of the earth to stand aghast that a nation could sink to such baseness, cruelty and depravity.'[10]

Though undeniably relieved at the formal announcement of surrender by the Japanese Emperor, John was in no mood for celebrating:

It seems incredible that the war is over. There has been no reaction here, just life as normal because we are well past the stage of being excited over anything. I know it's a comfort for you to realise that I will soon be home again, at least within six months, and that I am well and fit and have suffered very little from the war ...

I feel I have done my part, Mother—my conscience is very clear and I feel also that I am now free of any obligations to my country. Although it's a terrific waste of years out of my life, I am glad I have done it—I would do the same again. I know also that you are glad I took the exact course I did. I have learnt such a lot Mother, and I know that whatever trials may lie ahead, in the end I will succeed in whatever I take on.
20 August 1945

Almost three weeks after the Emperor's announcement, General MacArthur formally accepted the Japanese surrender—on 2 September 1945, aboard the USS *Missouri* in Tokyo Bay. During the ceremony General Blamey signed the official documents for Australia and the Japanese generals handed over their swords—an act of ultimate shame. This surrender was followed by ceremonies throughout the Pacific.

Borneo was one of the last countries in which the Japanese conceded defeat and it was not until 9 September that John attended the official ceremony in Brunei Bay. Sitting on the left of Brigadier Windeyer, John was handed one of the Japanese swords. 'David [his oldest son] has it now.'

Being the Brigade Intelligence Officer and a senior HQ officer, John was responsible for the interrogation of senior enemy. Based on his experience in New Guinea where he had seen how some captured enemy either killed themselves or begged to be killed, John made sure, after the surrender, that Colonel Aikyo, the Commander of the Japanese troops in Sarawak, had nothing to kill himself with. All knives, sharp instruments and cloth of any kind were removed from the special tent in which the Colonel was to be interrogated after the ceremony.[11]

However John had not counted on the order the Japanese leader made to his own batman—to fill a water bottle with sand and beat his Colonel's head until he was dead. The fourteenth-century samurai tradition of suicide as an honourable death was still strongly entrenched in the twentieth century.[12]

After following his master's instructions the batman came out and called some of the 'I' fellows. He was 'grinning happily', having successfully carried out his orders. They were horrified to find the Colonel's head bashed to a pulp. 'The little batman fellow had just done what he'd been instructed to do.' John was flabbergasted: 'The Jap … we couldn't understand anything about them. They were just so different … You were dealing with a totally different culture—they would kill themselves readily—become victims. There were so many differences.'

Despite the official declaration of surrender, the Japanese soldiers were slow to cease hostilities in Borneo and remained hidden in the mountains, attacking sporadically. John shared the frustration and anger of the men who had survived up to five years of brutal war only to find themselves still at risk from this renegade remnant of the Japanese Army.

The native Dayaks offered their loyal support to the Australians' effort to 'clean up' the area. John concluded that two factors had motivated their pledge to assist: the treatment they had observed and received from the Japanese and their own cultural norms, involving rites performed before a marriage ceremony.

On asking for the hand of a young girl in the next village, the betrothed proved his masculinity by presenting the smoked head of an enemy to that village. When the Dayaks heard of the hunt for the remaining Japanese in the mountains, they had no hesitation. The logic was simple: Japanese heads were valuable. They could be traded for weapons, which could then be used to shoot more Japanese soldiers. John and his team were made responsible for the transactions, their orders being to gather as many heads as possible: 'If they brought heads—evidence of a Jap being killed—we would exchange weapons with them, captured weapons, we had stacks of them, big enemy dumps of weapons. So we were giving them weapons to go and shoot more Japs.'

The first time it happened John was decidedly uneasy. A chieftain arrived with his escort of warriors, all carrying huge knives and eager to begin the bargaining process. A native servant around Headquarters was called to assist in the translation. Soon John and the chieftain were 'getting on famously', talking about their customs and nodding in approval at the deal about to take place. The Dayaks laid newly severed Japanese heads on the table; in return rifles were handed over. The chieftain then gave instructions for the heads to be gathered up and taken away to be smoked.

But this was not the end of the transaction. Along with the heads, John could see live Japanese prisoners—strung up 'like pigs on poles', shoulder to shoulder along bamboo poles. After more weapons were exchanged, they were taken down from the poles and put into the POW camps. 'They were the lucky ones. You know they [the Dayaks] were pretty brutal … but they'd seen what had happened.'

John was told that such deals were 'against the laws and usages of war' and that the unit should have 'nothing to do with it'. At the same time he was instructed to mastermind the transactions. In practice, the higher echelons turned a blind eye: 'That's right. It was a very, very constant PR job as far as I was concerned … to keep onside with these [natives]. I went ahead and did it … and made the swap.'

Eventually there were signs that at last the surrender had been accepted. On 21 September, an Allied victory march was held; native victory songs and dances were performed on a stage with a triumphal arch stating in Chinese 'Celebrations of the Final Victory'. The Chinese National Anthem was sung repeatedly.

News of the surrender was broadcast through a PA system set up in the Miri marketplace, with advice on 'where to get food and medical attention' … and how to receive help in re-establishing an orderly society.

By then John had had enough. He was trained to be inured to the awfulness of war—toughened, seasoned, even cold-hearted—but by that time it was very hard. His companions had kept him sane, but 'I was getting towards the end of my tether.' Married for almost sixteen months, but in reality single, John's thoughts were increasingly of Ruth. He wrote to his wife:

My darling, have no fear regarding my desire to get home to you. I even turned down an offer today for a staff appointment, in my present job [Brigade IO] with the British Army in India … However … the only career I am interested in is you … It's terrible being parted like this when there is so much we have to give to each other and make up for all the lost years … I love you so much darling and want you in my arms. I think of you most lying beside me quiet and content—your warmth and sweetness and beauty. The months will soon slip by and it will all be over.
5 August 1945

Another career offer for John was soon to follow. After the surrender, Lieutenant Colonel Colvin accepted an invitation from the British to command one of the peace-keeping battalions in Japan. John was invited to assist him, but having gone through so much in the desert and then in New Guinea and Borneo, he acknowledged that his state of mind was 'too sensitive'.

The deaths in New Guinea were still fresh, in particular those of Alan Toose and the two officers of the 2/15th Battalion. Another 516 Australians had been killed in Borneo. 'To be truthful I was concerned about how well I would adapt to the peacetime scene.' There would be a lot of hatred—inbuilt hatred. The Japanese hated; the Australians hated. The mutual feelings 'would take a lot of sorting out'.

Once he made up his mind to return home, John was restless. He admitted to his mother:

> *Only a short note darling to let you know I'm well and fit and leading a pretty lazy life generally. Now that it's all over, every day seems a waste of time—in fact, it is—I could be doing so much more if I were home. However, it won't be long now, and after waiting all these years, a few months won't hurt. I still find it hard to realise that the whole rotten business is really over and done with and that it's now only a matter of waiting until I'm released and can get on a homeward boat. With a bit of luck, we may have blackout restrictions lifted for the trip—that would really make a difference. Travelling by boat through tropical countries all closed down is always sheer hell ...*
> *1 September 1945*

Most of the men from the 2/13th felt the same. They had all shown grim determination and loyalty through those hard long years, but few would have argued with the unequivocal sentiments expressed in one of the many verses written at that time:

> Oh! My military ambition
> Has vanished to perdition.
> I don't want to be a soldier,

I don't want to even try.
I just want to pick a possie
Right back in dear old Aussie
And I'll gladly be a civvie
Until the very day I die.[13]

John's first homecoming had been through Sydney Heads to his mother; his second would be to his wife. He was to come back to a happy, peaceful time—elated and relieved. After five-and-a-half years in the army, John Murray was ready to return home for good: 'Oh dear, oh dear, oh dear. I was starting to get too sensitive—and I was getting jittery—it was over five years by then … I couldn't do it any more … I was ready to hang up my boots. I was ready to have a sleep.'

Chapter Twenty-Three

Go west
young man

FELLOW CITIZENS, THE WAR IS OVER. THE JAPANESE
GOVERNMENT HAS ACCEPTED THE TERMS OF SURRENDER
IMPOSED BY THE ALLIED NATIONS AND HOSTILITIES WILL
NOW CEASE ... AT THIS MOMENT, LET US OFFER THANKS TO
GOD. LET US REMEMBER THOSE WHOSE LIVES WERE GIVEN
THAT WE MAY ENJOY THIS GLORIOUS MOMENT AND MAY
LOOK FORWARD TO A PEACE WHICH THEY HAVE WON FOR US.
LET US REMEMBER THOSE WHOSE THOUGHTS, WITH PROUD
SORROW, TURN TOWARDS GALLANT, LOVED ONES WHO WILL
NOT COME BACK ...

—Prime Minister Ben Chifley, 1945[1]

JOHN HAD PLENTY of time to think on his way home from Borneo by ship.
Apart from the fervent wish for a trip free from mishap and the desire to be
reunited with his wife and his family, he was consumed with immediate
plans for his post-war life. Positivity in letters to his mother returned:

*Land will be safety and security ... Never fear—things are
definitely going to work out for the best even though it may seem
to be taking such a long time. We all get rather impatient at the*

delay—I've been impatient for over five years now so I can stick
it out for a few more months.
13 September 1945

A more impatient man could not have been seen on the day of his return
to Australia in November 1945. John rushed to 8 Cecil Street, Gordon,
where Ruth was living with her Aunt Tess. It was about eighteen months
ago that he had left this house agitated and in love, determined to propose
to the beautiful young woman he had met up with on Wynyard Station.

However, relaxing with his wife would have to wait. She had handed
him some letters on that first day, one of which was to change the course
of their lives forever. Peter had written, informing his brother that *Gidgee*,
the property adjoining the one he was managing, was for lease. It was in
the far west of New South Wales, between the outback towns of Cobar
and Wilcannia. Quick action would be needed to procure it.

Abandoning ideas of the delayed honeymoon they had planned, John
set off with Ruth to inspect the property. John's official discharge from the
Army on 5 November meant that plans he had been dreaming about for
so long could now be realised. This trip was important to their future.

Inspecting the land and home at *Gidgee,* John felt there was much that
would suit them. Ruth looked around without comment. The November
day was blistering and the forecast predicted no relief. The flies were
interminable. She could count thousands of them on John's back.

The original Aboriginal name of the property—*Gidyea Golambo*—meant
gidgee tree by a waterhole. There *was* a waterhole that provided water from
Gidgee Creek for the dam, but the water was muddy and smelly. Drinking
water from the rainwater tanks at the homestead was in short supply
because of the drought. It could not even be used for washing hands.
How would she cook the vegetables? And how did the wood stove—the
old Aga—work? Ruth had never seen one before. She had never driven a
Ford utility and she had never gone droving.

To John, *Gidgee* seemed like a rather more acceptable proposition.
The property could carry 7000 sheep and on purchase of the lease there
would be 3000 full-woolled sheep on the place at one pound per head.
It was 41,000 hectares (101,000 acres), mostly covered with low to fairly
steep rocky hills and ridges, all covered with thick mulga, which would
provide vital nutrition in the leaves for sheep, goats and cattle when the

earth was bare. Paddocks ranged in size from small yards to 9000-hectare (20,000-acre) enclosures.

The facilities were hardly satisfactory. The shearers' quarters and cookhouse had been burnt out at some earlier stage. However, a reliable shearing contractor called Pearson—he had worked for Peter for years—could be brought in to manage the job in the old woolshed. His team, generally four shearers and an equivalent number of roustabouts were used to rough living. They could rig up tents and a tarpaulin. Their cook could roast and bake in the old stone and brick ovens that had survived the blaze. John would not have beds and baths to offer the men—just some beer and a few bottles of rum at the end of the day.

The deal for *Gidgee* was done within days, using the combined savings of John, Charlie and Constance, with additional backing from a small financial company. A week later the rural company Glanville and Murray was born.

With a secure job and salary but no capital, Peter was not a signatory. However, as a long-standing manager he'd had vast experience and was more than willing to advise on the particular rural circumstances in the far west. He was a very good bushman—a compassionate man who always put his men first and never asked anyone to do anything he would not do himself. 'Peter was an enormous help to me to start with. I'd never had identical conditions.'

John's promise to the owner to take a mob of cattle to Cobar about 95 kilometres (60 miles) away, and then arrange trucking to Young was Ruth's first droving experience: driving a Ford with no brakes and dripping petrol; sleeping on the ground at night; cooking by fire when she'd never cooked before; and staring at mobs of unsettled cattle through the filtered moonlight. 'She was at her absolute best when things were toughest.'

It was important to John that his mother and Charlie had as much comfort as possible. The original part of *Gidgee* homestead was made of stone—gathered and cut on the property—and an old set of stone stairs led down to a deep cellar, carved into the earth. This was converted into a large sized bedroom, which was perfect for escaping the midday heat. Temperatures could rise to 43 degrees Celsius (109 degrees Fahrenheit).

Ruth was in the modern section of the house with John, though she felt the conditions were ancient. A firmly shut gauze door supposedly kept out the flies from the kitchen, but however hard she tried to eliminate them, Ruth found more of the insects, ceaselessly buzzing around. Also humming incessantly was the telephone line. It was almost impossible to speak with anyone in Sydney. The mail arrived once a week.

The dry heat was unbearable. Drought was something they both struggled with in the early months. John used a push-bike around the property, carrying it on his shoulders up the ridges in the high country and riding it along the sheep pads—the little tracks made by the compliant animals, one following the other. There was not enough feed even to sustain a workhorse: 'At this stage we were leasing for 900 pounds a year—we didn't own it. He [the owner] left a couple of horses and a bike which I rode a lot in the early stages, when the drought was still on. I couldn't afford to feed the horses all the time. We were very pinched for money.

'I used to do all the mustering myself. It was a very slow business. Day by day I would take what I'd mustered down to a holding paddock, put them in and then go back the next day and muster again until I got them all.'

Ruth had never experienced anything quite like the whirling dust and dryness of the hot, drought-ridden landscape. 'There were tins of dust.' She quickly learnt that drought meant deprivation: washing her hands, hair and clothes in muddy water and looking every day at the fine covering of dust over the furniture. Mice dashed through the pantry, far too fast for her to catch, and gauze on the storage cupboards did not keep the weevils from the flour. These challenges did not help her condition—a few months pregnant with her first child, feeling nauseous morning, noon and night.

The old Ford utility they had was 'a beauty'. Because it had no fuel pump John had to set up a gallon tin of petrol to drain into the carburettor, which required filling, once depleted, from the larger petrol tank in the back of the truck. To start the thing they had to crank it. 'It was brutal of me to ask Ruth to cope with this but I was out all day—sometimes back late at night—and she needed a vehicle.'

One day, in the late afternoon, about six months after their arrival, the sky turned inky, almost black, and a dark quiet fell around them. Even the animals stopped. John and Ruth looked at each other in silent anticipation, waiting. They could smell the earth as large isolated drops began to spit. There was a breeze blowing; it carried the smell of fresh, wet dirt.

When the rain began to pelt down on the tin roof, they laughed out loud. Streams of water fell from the heavens. They wondered if the creek was running, and how much water was in the dam. It had been close to dry since their arrival.

'I think I'll go and see what depth of water there is.'

'I'll come too.'

They sloshed through the mud to the dam, in the dark, with only a hurricane lamp to guide them. As the rain soaked through to their skins, they stripped off—not a stitch on. Laughing and splashing they played in the water and then waded further and further in, chest deep, while the lamp spluttered on the side of the dam. They could hear the water rushing down the steep slopes—some 3 metres (10 feet) high—but could not see it. This primitive, unexpected sound was good reason for a strong embrace—two waterlogged bodies in celebration of water and the sodden earth. They walked home, hand in hand, naked.

The next morning, at dawn, John inspected the overflowing dam and the raging creek. Water was still running down from the hills. Just days later a green tinge covered the earth. The country had metamorphosed; it had come to life.

Within six months of their occupation, the drought of 1945–46 had broken. Luck was with them. The first shearing brought more than the 13 pence per pound they had budgeted for. They mustered 300 more wethers than they had paid for. And 1000 healthy lambs were produced in spring.

The good news of rain was followed just a few months later by an even more momentous event for John and Ruth—the birth of their first child, Jill, on 11 August 1946. Ruth travelled to Sydney for the confinement, and after a short period of care from Aunt Tess returned to *Gidgee* with John—proud parents with baby in tow. Just fifteen months later, their second daughter, Robyn, was delivered safely—this time in the town of Wilcannia, about 145 kilometres (90 miles) southwest of their property.

Meanwhile the rural holdings of the company continued to expand. It was agreed that Charlie, Peter and their wives would live on *Gidgee*, which had now been purchased outright, while John and Ruth would move to *Korreo*, the new property acquired more easily this time through assistance from the Returned Soldier Settlement Scheme. In any case, John was obliged to live on this government-subsidised holding.

A year or two later, in 1948, *Pinchinara* came onto the market. With a successful wool clip yielding 25,400 kilograms (56,000 pounds), Charlie, Constance and John were prepared to commit to the cost of £52,000 for this third property, which adjoined *Korreo*. With a loan of a small amount of money from Lorraine, Peter now became a member of Glanville and Murray

Brothers as an equal partner. It now made managerial sense for John to move to *Pinchinara,* Peter to remain at *Gidgee* and Charlie and Constance to move to *Korreo.*

John was happy that he had 'an ideal partnership' and he was more than content with his personal life. Two more children had swelled the family: Margaret-Jane (Janie) was born on 26 June 1949 and their first son, David, was born a year later almost to the day, on the third day of the sixth month, 1950. John's dream of a family of his own—so sharp and tenacious both in the desert and jungle—had at last come true.

The price for their wool had risen from 13 pence to 240 pence per pound between 1946 and 1950—an increase of 1746 per cent. The owners of Glanville and Murray Brothers agreed with the well-worn metaphor. Undeniably, Australia was riding on the sheep's back.

It was fortunate that things had moved along so quickly for John on his return from the war. More than likely he knew, even if only subconsciously, that constant hard labour was what his racing mind required. The pounding images had to be quieted. He needed to compose himself, to stabilise. Others, who returned from the battering of war without the benefits of counselling or at least a sympathetic listener, coped in their own ways. One battler reported: 'To settle back into civilian life was very tough for all of us. Blokes … were inclined to go a bit berserk and overindulge in things like grog. You don't have to come out of the war with an arm missing or a leg missing or a bullet wound. You come out with a mind that's been churned up.'[2]

And another observed: 'I think we felt that outsiders don't understand what we're talking about … there's some terrible bloody things happened, things that aren't in the history books, and you never forget, never. I still wake up at nights dreaming, it's still in your mind, the things that happened.'[3]

And so it was with John. He was settled enough during the day, able to control his thoughts. But he could not afford to relax. If he did, he found that the memories, buried deep, all too quickly emerged. Many who could not control their memories took their own lives.[4]

With John, the distress emerged at night. The nightmares that had started in the trenches continued for years after his return to Australia. 'Your subconscious—it was buried, but I couldn't control it at night … it went on for years.' Many nights he woke in a sweat, still squashed in a trench or unable to hide. He saw severed heads; mutilated bodies; flesh and guts. The piercing scream of the shell just before the explosion; bombs exploding in front of his eyes.

But he was not in a trench. Ruth put out her hand across the bed. He heard her whisper hundreds of times, 'What's the matter darling?' She would stroke him until he fell back to sleep. 'Many, many times she did that. It took a long time to wear out … She was wonderful.' In the morning he would throw himself back into his work.

John had never worked in such an unforgiving Australian environment before. He and Peter had to contact each other every day to discuss their tactics either by phone or in person. More often than not it was the latter, especially when the phone lines were knocked down by strong winds. The men had their days cut out for them—moving stock, crutching, hand feeding, shearing. Not a day went past when water was not mentioned. Wireless reports were invaluable for the news and for weather forecasts. Rarely was rain predicted.

To help him with the gigantic task of moving up to 7000 sheep, John made good provision. Having had experience with dogs at *Manfred*, he appreciated the advantages they gave a lone stockman. Before long he was planning to put a kennel together. Contact through an advertisement with a Captain J.L. Moore of the Kyneton Kennels in Victoria set him on a rewarding path. 'I told him exactly what our circumstances were and asked him if he had any dogs to lend or sell. This was the start of an extraordinary correspondence.'

The first of the pack—a black, white and tan border collie with a white ring around his neck, a white tip on the tail and a big, broad forehead— became his number one dog. 'Cap was a big, strong dog, my absolute ideal.' And then Lass arrived—'a beautiful little black bitch with grey markings on her'—all the way from Victoria in a box. Various people along the rail line had fed and watered the pup. Lass and Cap were the foundation for John's expanding kennel. Correspondence with another dog breeder, Dr R.B. Kelley, who worked at the Council for Scientific and Industrial Research (CSIR),[5] led to the acquisition of another excellent dog. John's purchase of a black, white and tan bitch named Gyp, from Kelley's litter of smooth-haired pups, produced, in time, half a dozen excellent working dogs—all crossed with his perfect sire, Cap.

Before long John had trained his dogs for paddock work. They kept the sheep in one position, did not let the mob get too big or small, and understood how to shepherd, 'just like a man did'. Driving mobs of 3000 to 4000 sheep at a time, 'saving the wages of two men', they knew exactly what their master wanted.

Having to leave the vehicles at the homesteads in case of an emergency, John found use for his dogs at night too. In the early days at *Gidgee*, during the relentless drought, the dogs' white-tipped tails were guiding lights as he rode his bicycle in the dark from one paddock to another, hand-feeding the stock.

John was constantly aware that his nightlife experience in the desert helped tremendously for this unusual duty on the dry, parched properties.

Entering little Gyp into the Novice Dog Trials at Hall, just outside Canberra, led not only to an exciting win, but also to an interesting introduction through Dr Kelley to Dr Jack Griffiths-Davies—another CSIR officer who was there for the trials.

Dr Davies was an advisor on pasture improvement. Eyes flashing, he immediately proceeded to talk about his research interest: the enormous impact that could be made with the introduction of legumes, north of the Tropic of Capricorn. He complained that the present situation was abysmal, that there was no nutrition for the cattle. Grass, which seeded and turned into 'rubbish' in the dry season, was the only available feed.

Kelley and Davies were also inspired by the idea of a different kind of cattle for the tropics. In 1933 they had been instrumental in importing significant numbers of Brahman cattle. Hailing from India, the Brahman had a distinctive hump on its back, a droopy neck and most importantly, was drought and tick resistant.

The two scientists invited John to accompany them on a trip, to examine their theories first hand. John saw farmers struggling with the coarse tropical pastures which grew in the wet but turned to cellulose in the dry. With no nutritional value at all, the harvest was not worth baling. The conditions were useless for the traditional English cattle; hundreds of them were dying. In contrast, John also saw the tough new breed—Brahmans—and some successful legume plantings. 'Kelley showed me the works—all of it. He was on a mission to make me his firm disciple.'

By the end of the observation period the grazier from the west was totally convinced. These new farming principles led him into deep thought.

John hated the idea of the dust and death of drought, convinced that the 'dreadful dry' in the 1930s had contributed to the death of his father. The seed of an idea developed and began to take over his waking hours.

How could their company protect itself against the killer drought? Why not take a first step, look at the Kidman model seriously?

In the 1930s Sidney Kidman ran a cattle and sheep empire out of a small South Australian town—a venture so vast, that at its height it covered an area from the Gulf of Carpentaria down through Western Queensland and into northern South Australia. He had bought the best properties along the big river chains of inland Australia and used the recently built railway system to take his meat to market in the new refrigerated transport. What would stop Glanville and Murray Brothers from doing something similar?

Soon John was organising family meetings. To date Charlie, Peter and he had conferred constructively on every property matter. There was a great synergy between the three. John and his brother worked together out west like they had in the early days at *Manfred* and *Kilfera*—an ideal partnership. Peter claimed that they complemented each other, John being 'the wonderful tactician that he was'.[6]

They listened as John laid his ideas on the table. Currently facing the one-name-one-property situation required by the Western Lands Division of New South Wales, they could not expand any further in their own state. This state government requirement stifled secure land tenure.

John felt strongly that it was sensible to diversify; a tax bill of £80,000 would surely indicate that it might have been just plain stupid not to do so. Surely the Kidman philosophy was worth exploring—owning a string of properties from north to south, with different latitudes giving different environments and rainfall patterns. They discussed the possibility of buying properties in central and southern Queensland and further south into Victoria, perhaps to the Murray irrigation areas—all on the one longitude. To add to their existing sheep interests, they could branch into cropping.

However, the ideas met with some resistance. Personally Charlie would have been happy to return to his beloved North Queensland where he had spent so many years in the Gulf country. Peter on the other hand was a sheep man through and through. 'He wasn't happy with us dabbling in farming.' John still held the view, however, that the Kidman philosophy would give them the security that irrigation and fodder provided.

Back to the table. Discussion now centred on a complete change of direction. Why not branch into the North Queensland beef industry? The broad plan would be to buy a rundown cattle property in the tropics where John could put into practice the ideas he had discussed with the CSIR scientists. It was agreed that if he found such a place he should secure it. Peter would run the NSW business with Charlie and Constance back on *Korreo*; and John would move north and start building the northern operation.

They had enough capital to invest; their record wool income had recently been bolstered by a massive sale at the right time of 6000 wethers off the shears. John suggested that Peter build himself a beautiful home, set up with an aeroplane, and run the three western NSW properties as one. He was convinced his brother could do it. Meanwhile he would develop properties in the north with the assistance of Dr Kelley who had said, 'You can't go wrong, boy!'

After much searching John found *The Orient* at Ingham in North Queensland. There were 800 head of cattle on the place, with about thirty-five bulls of British stock—Devons, Shorthorns and Hereford. Being suitably rundown, this property fitted the bill. However, when he made moves for the purchase, little prepared him for what was to follow.

Was it Ruth and Jane, the wives, who did not get on? Was Peter's wife not happy with the decision for Peter to have the added responsibility? Was it that Peter and Jane needed to be closer to medical services for their first son, John, whose health was worrying them? Was it that Peter, a successful manager for many years out west, was completely unconvinced by the theories behind the proposed expansion? Did the proposal not make economic sense?

Whatever the reasons, by the time John returned, his brother had sold *Pinchinara* and had made moves to buy *Nekarbo*, a well-known property situated between Ivanhoe and Cobar. John felt totally deflated: 'It was a massive blow. We laid the foundation for it [the expansion] and then destroyed it and watched it fall to pieces … NZL [New Zealand Loan] were ready to lend us the moon. They could see two young fellows ready to go. But … without the family network it fell to pieces. The foundation of the whole thing just collapsed.'

He was tremendously regretful, claiming that the strong relationship he had with Peter was reminiscent of another team of brothers who had also worked wonderfully well together—their grandfather and great uncle, William Benjamin and George Chaffey: 'They [the Chaffey brothers] were a brother team who worked wonderfully together, as Peter and I did … At *Manfred* we were a perfect team … we were often sent off together with a mob of sheep … we might be a week on the road with them going across the length and breadth of *Manfred*. It was a wonderful experience …

When we put together *Gidgee*, *Pinchinara* and *Korreo*, Peter and I were an extraordinarily strong partnership. We ran things so well together. We took notice of each other time and time again. We leant on each other for advice. Sometimes my vision was good enough, probably his [view] on management was better than mine … We'd come to agreement always.

'There was a magical chemistry between us … I think Peter had regrets too.'

Over fifty years later, Peter himself expressed intense disappointment: 'I was lost without John … he was wonderfully visionary. We complemented each other. He was probably a bit lost without me … maybe he wasn't, but I was definitely lost without him. We made a very good team the two of us together … He was just so wonderful at getting on with people.'[7]

Peter continued with his arrangements to make the move to *Nekarbo*, offering to look after *Gidgee*, and afterwards arranging for his wife's sister and her husband to live there and manage it. For better or for worse, John decided to go ahead with the purchase in the north, moving to Ingham. John and Peter both made sure that their mother and Charlie were well set up with stock and all the equipment they required at *Korreo*. A weatherboard cottage was purchased in Nowra, so that their mother had a home to go to when she visited Margie and her family, who were now living in that town on the NSW south coast.

The halcyon days were over. Once everyone went their different ways, the kind of success they had enjoyed together was never repeated. From then on, Peter's ventures were never as successful. Similarly, John did not achieve ultimate success. Possibly the chemistry between the brothers was a prerequisite for the fortune of large enterprises: 'Although Peter and I both had our moments of achievement and satisfaction … the potential of our partnership was never reached … That is my firm belief.'

Chapter Twenty-Four

Cattle and command

THE WEST WAS A DEAD END FOR ME. I COULD NOT
BEAR TO THINK THAT MY LIFE WOULD BE CONTROLLED
BY DROUGHT. NO HOPE OF PASTURE IMPROVEMENT.
WE COULD FINE-TUNE OUR MERINO FLOCKS BUT WOULD
LOSE THEM IN THE DROUGHT, AS SURE AS NIGHT FOLLOWED
DAY ... [MEANWHILE] THERE WAS AN ENORMOUS SHIFT
OF EMPHASIS IN CATTLE PRODUCTION IN AUSTRALIA ...
IT WAS SLOWLY MOVING—BUT BOUND AND SHACKLED BY
THE OLD TRADITIONALISTS WHO'D COME FROM THE SOUTH
AND GRADUALLY MOVED TO NORTH QUEENSLAND ... THEY
FOUNDERED ON THE ROCKS OF REALITY. THEY COULDN'T
BREED IN THE TROPICS WHAT THEY WERE BORN TO BREED
IN A TEMPERATE CLIMATE.

—John Murray, 2005[1]

WITH A FAMILY of four children John and Ruth made the move to North
Queensland. It was the second half of 1951. While the old shack at
The Orient was being rebuilt into a two-storey home to the specifications of
Ruth's architect brother Dick Stanton-Cook, they lived nearby, in the small
town of Ingham. Very soon after they settled into their new home, John
wrote to his mother, easing her fears about the separation:

*Distance is nothing. The very last thing you must have is any
heartache or thoughts that you may be losing me. I've learned too
many lessons over the years to ever allow that to happen ...*

*The family, which we have proved so strong in adversity over
the years, must not be allowed to drift apart in the crosscurrents
of success. I cannot believe we would allow it to happen.*
17 November 1951

With great energy John was now throwing himself into an entirely different
project—building up a herd of drought and tick-resistant cattle in the
tropical North. He needed mountains of patience for the job. The breeding
formula might have been intricate, based on percentages and mixes, but
the reason for it was simple. The more Brahman genes in the cattle, the
more tick resistant they were.

Ticks were the bane of cattle farmers' lives around the Tropic of
Capricorn and north of it. They led to loss of condition, loss of blood
and even fatal fever. The poor British cattle 'had to rub themselves almost
to death' to suppress the ill effects. It was the sweating mechanism in the
Brahmans that was important. These cattle sweated like a horse—through
the skin—an effective repellent to ticks. The British cattle by contrast
sweated like a dog—through the tongue. The ticks loved them.

Drs Kelley and Griffiths-Davies had fired John with enthusiasm
about the way to avoid this seemingly insurmountable problem. Kelley
had him 'hooked as his disciple', albeit an educated one. John had done
his own homework and by 1954 had made an investigative and purchasing
trip to King Ranch in Texas. His research showed that the Brahman
was most suited to his particular tropical environment of the north.[2]
Cattle needed at least 50 per cent Brahman blood; Santa Gertrudis had
37 per cent.

To this end he began to eradicate all traces of British breeding cattle on
The Orient. All the bulls were rounded up and castrated. 'There was not a
breeder left on the place.' After acquiring some Brahman yearling half-
breds and three-quarter-breds to begin the slow process of breeding with
full-bred British cattle, John's next step was to import a number of pure
Brahmans. He sent the expert Kelley to the United States, authorising him
to import twelve stud Brahman bulls to Australia, for vast amounts of
money. 'It took a bank to import them privately.'

John was to carry out award-winning pasture improvement at *The Orient*.

John also began his dream of pasture improvement. On *The Orient*, over 243 hectares (600 acres) of tidal salt swamps that had been drained and planted with guinea, centro and Molasses grasses, won a pasture improvement contest sponsored by the Royal National Association in 1960. The improved pastures were described as 'the equal of anything in the country'.

Representing his own company, Tropical Cattle Pty Ltd, and with constant encouragement from Dr Kelley, early on John set out to convince the farmers in Queensland that his views on a different kind of animal and pasture improvement had merit. He 'felt like a firebrand', attending all manner of gatherings and rallies to spread the word: Rotary, Graziers' Association and CWA members all heard his speeches. However, he had not counted on such rabid opposition from the conservative, wealthy cattle industry and was surprised at the vehemence directed at him. The conventional breeders made sure the 'new people on the block' such as the Atkinsons, the Frasers and J.W. Wright were derided; routinely the traditionalists referred to Brahmans as 'camels' or 'yaks'. Every opportunity was used to ridicule the research. The strongest opponent was well-known cattle breeder Arthur McCamley who took it upon himself to brand John as a traitor at a public meeting, accusing him of sabotaging the industry. The word got around. 'This bastard Murray is mad—stark raving mad.'

But John did not veer from his path. Totally convinced that his decision was the right one, he was proud of the fact that more and more animals on his place had evidence of a hump and a neck decorated with extended folds. The Brahmans were graceful animals with wonderful natures. His children climbed all over them: '149 was a beautiful cow—she came over as a yearling. She looked for the kids every day. She'd let the kids lie all over her. Beautiful quiet cow ...'

John tutored his children on how to handle the cattle. 'He used to let us lie on their humps as pillows. He would show us how to rub their rumps, to get around behind them and make them feel secure. It was so natural for him and I know he wanted us to be like that as well.'[3]

One day his daughter Janie sped towards a young Brahman bull resting on the ground, aiming to jump over him—surely sufficient provocation for the beast to stand up and charge—but it was as though the animal knew it was a game. The child jumped high; the bull did not move.

Gradually the government saw great sense in John's views. Having discussed the matter in detail with him, the Minister for Territories in the Menzies' Government, Mr Paul Hasluck, supported John's stance to the hilt, claiming that 'a transformation could be brought about in cattle-raising right across the north of Australia ... by applying the lessons of pasture improvement work by Mr John Murray ... and others'. He added that export of cattle from the Northern Territory to the Philippines and Hong Kong would only be increased by pasture improvement 'along the lines advocated by Mr John Murray'.[4]

Fifty years later John's views have been vindicated. No one in the north breeds English cattle now. The whole area is a successful Brahman breeding region. Once cattlemen saw the advantages of the tick-resistant, hump-backed creatures they gradually threw off the mantle of conservatism and listened to reason. The McCamley family is now one of the biggest Brahman breeders in the country.

When asked to think of his achievements, John pondered and then replied: 'I think that my greatest achievement was kick-starting that [the Brahman industry]. It was a national necessity.'

Although John was engrossed in Brahmans and pasture improvement at *The Orient*, towards the end of 1952 he took time off to attend the opening ceremony of the Tobruk Memorial Baths in Townsville, presided over by his former superior, Victor Windeyer. The brigadier had invited John to join him for dinner at the Queen's Hotel and during their get-together pressed him to visit the 15th Battalion Mess in Brisbane the following evening. Brigadier 'Bull' Monaghan of the 11th Brigade, responsible for three battalions in Townsville, Rockhampton and Cairns, would be there. Already a plan was being hatched.

After the Mess dinner the next evening, Monaghan asked John when he was joining up. The civilian Army needed him. John was adamant in his response. In the midst of developing *The Orient*, unfortunately he had no time for the Army now, to which the brigadier joked: 'I'll get you!' A week later the phone call came. If he wouldn't join, would he at least do one thing for the brigadier? There was 'a wreck of a company in Ingham'. Would he go and have a look at them in the Drill Hall at the local showground and report back?

John was shocked. Some of the soldiers were in uniform, some in shorts and singlets, yelling out to each other. There were three platoons of 130 men in total, 'an absolute rabble' without any sign of discipline whatsoever. One exception 'stood out a mile'—a warrant officer named Ernest Tarr who had been with the Ghurkhas in Malaya and was extremely capable—a fitness and drill crank.

It was the beginning of 1953. John spoke to Ruth—who was seven months pregnant with their fifth child. They both agreed that given the disastrous state of the unit it was important for John to take over command of C Company, 31st Infantry Battalion. The next day a stack of uniforms arrived at *The Orient* so that John could fit himself out appropriately as the commanding officer.

The following week he faced the mob. This time each man was dressed in uniform, according to instructions from Captain John Murray, conveyed through Warrant Officer Ernest Tarr. John inspected the first platoon, stopping in front of each man and introducing himself: 'Right Private Barlotti; thank you Private Brunini'. Eighty per cent of the population of Ingham were of Italian descent—sons of immigrants who had come out in droves to work in the sugar-cane fields.[5] John then addressed the entire company: 'I've learnt there is a drill competition—"The Brigadier North Shield". We will of course enter this competition. I understand it's a very, very tough competition. We will enter this year with Number 7 Platoon and we will win it. Next year we'll win it with Number 8 Platoon and the following year we'll win it with Number 9 Platoon.'

The men looked at their new commanding officer and at each other: 'Oh, the bastard's crazy.' But John had already talked to Ernie Tarr who had agreed that with rigorous training involving two or three extra nights per week, it could be done. For that type of company drill, Tarr was perfect.

With proper encouragement, the men threw themselves into the extensive drill routines. They knew that John was on their side and adopted the affectionate nickname of Giovanni Maggiore (Major John) for their new leader.

By the time the competition came along 7 Platoon was ready to perform. Their win rippled through the company; they had successfully competed in the drill competition against some 3000 men. They also did very well in all field exercises, including charging with a bayonet. John pushed them to further heights: '8 Platoon—you've got a year to do the same. You will emulate 7 Platoon. You'll be even better than them. There will be no mistakes next time. We'll be absolutely mistake free. No errors whatsoever. We'll have much more time to practise.'

Inspired by their success, John soon began jungle training in the tangled, tropical rainforest along the Herbert River, not far from *The Orient*. This developed rapidly into a national program after the brigadier recommended it as a demonstration area for the rest of Australia. Groups of officers and NCOs were taken down the trail and ambushed. John himself led them, pausing at a place where 'there were pairs of eyes everywhere', alerting them to the danger of camouflage and the jungle's sinister nature. They learnt escape and evade techniques.

On these missions John always had the same rifle. There was nothing strange about that except that this rifle—number 61739—had been issued to him in 1939, relinquished at the end of the war in Sydney, and turned up in a munitions cupboard at Ingham in 1953, among some military stock at the showground. John considered it to be a lucky omen.

Now settled into military activities and long hours on the property, John celebrated the birth of his fifth child. Susan was born at Ingham on 31 March 1953. A little over four years later, with the safe delivery of his youngest son, John, on 22 May 1957, John and Ruth now had a family of six children. 'I'd recommend a large family to anyone,' John mused. 'It keeps you young and informed'. How informed, John was to learn—on 1 January 1958.

New Year's Day was hot, still and calm. The frogs were croaking. It was going to be a sticky one. John and Ruth were lying down on long couches on the verandah listening to the news. The kids were all around them, playing and chatting: 'Suddenly one of them shouted, "We heard your name—Captain John Murray of Ingham! You've been awarded something." I said, "Don't be silly darling." "We *did* Daddy—we heard it!"

'And then the phone started to ring.

'They never let you know in advance for military awards. You're never given a choice. You can never refuse. Civil decorations—yes—but not military. You're just told. In this case I heard about the MBE from my children!

'I cleared out for the day—went out into the paddock somewhere and poor Ruth had to deal with the phone calls ...'

Some time later John received the official citation: 'Major John Murray joined the Australian Imperial Forces in May 1940 and served with the 2nd/13th Australian Infantry Battalion in the Middle East, New Guinea and Borneo campaigns. He was twice mentioned in Despatches. Immediately on taking up residence in Ingham in 1952, he joined the Active Citizen Military Forces. Since then he has commanded C Company 31st Infantry Battalion with distinction. His personal example has greatly enhanced the reputation of the Army in the Ingham district. By his untiring efforts, loyalty and devotion to duty, Major Murray has greatly improved the efficiency of this company. He is an outstanding leader of men and inspires confidence in all who come into contact with him. His readiness to give his utmost to the Service, without regard for his personal inconvenience, is far beyond what might reasonably be expected of him.'

Many of John's mates from the 2/13th Battalion contacted him with congratulations, including Jim Walsoe. Commander of C Company for most of the Tobruk Siege, Jim's serious countenance earned him the name of 'smouldering Swede' from Tim Fearnside—a name that stuck. He had supervised John's original Intelligence activities in Tobruk and

wanted to keep him in his company when the time came for the trainee
to return to his own.

A day or two after John's award was announced, Walsoe wrote a poem
and sent it to the *The Townsville Daily Bulletin*. John was chuffed to receive
the original—typed in blue, on the page of a child's lined exercise book—
now discoloured and tattered, but still treasured:

JOHN MURRAY'S MBE

John Murray is the very chap
To get that MBE,
He proved himself in Old Tobruk
So clear for all to see.

He hid with me in No-man's land
When Jerry put up flares,
We flattened out behind a bush
While tracers singed our prayers.

John proved that he could organise
In every kind of sport,
He never wasted precious time
Spine bashing on his cot.

Intelligence his specialty
(Not only with his dome),
But maps and plans, patrol reports,
That helped send Rommel home.

He knew the boys—the boys knew him
They liked him very much,
They liked him for his 'How do you do?'
And for his common touch!

The war was gone—he battled on,
Through Cobar's heat and dust,
He took the lead and went up north
Saying 'Ingham—or we'll bust.'

Santa Gertrudis soon he bought,
He gave the sheep away,
And still he found some time to spare
Tin soldiers for to play.

He marched 'em up—he marched 'em down,
He worked 'em cold or hot,
Not sun nor palm could do them harm—
What a colonel they have got.

Good on you John! You've earned it lad!
Remember the smouldering Swede?
'Tis he submits these humble lines
Because you're MBE'd.

The year 1958 proved to be demanding. While commanding C Company in Ingham, John's attention was divided. Brahmans and pastures filled his waking hours, but conversion to his ideas by members of the cattle industry was slow. Building up through cross-breeding was laborious work and personal finance soon ran dry: 'When we saw that we needed more money we approached George Bryant and Leo Tutt of Tutt Bryant [Ltd], who ran the Alice Chalmers empire in Australia—earth-moving—they lived in Wahroonga [a northern suburb of Sydney]—very wealthy, smart men.

'Kelley warned me that they would take over *The Orient* and I could see that they would, as long as they took it over on my terms. They didn't know anything about cattle but they liked the venture … If I could make sure this whole thing was on track—cattle breeding and pasture improvement—I could let go … ' John's decision early on to approach financiers to invest in Tropical Cattle Pty Ltd. had been successful, but educating Queenslanders about the advantages of Brahman breeding was painfully slow work. It came as a tremendous blow to him to admit his inadequacy: 'No one would take much notice of me as plain John Murray—a humbling lesson I learnt. It brought me down to earth very quickly when I realised.'

A self-admitted 'impatient young man', John had had enough. The next day he told George Bryant in a directors' meeting that there was nothing like politics to get a voice in what was going on. This opinion had been formed years before: 'Well the politics came out of the blue really.

We'd just had a good wool cheque—1948—and we bought a Citroën, a big 6, the first little group of them imported to Australia after the war. I had to go up to Bathurst to collect it. What a glorious trip we had driving this thing down [to Sydney]. It was the same kind of model as the German police used—those big black Citroëns they used in war films—with a running board, front wheel drive and pneumatic suspension. I was sitting in that thing outside Farmers waiting for Ruthie … and I turned the radio on and it was Canberra—a bloke name White. He was Minister for Air or something or other. God he spoke well this bloke. And that fired me up.

'I got into politics in 1958, but this was ten years before. When Ruth came out I said, "Sorry, darling, but this is what I'm going to do. I've got to get into that place. It'd be terribly interesting and you could really DO something."'

Chapter Twenty-Five

Coalition

I just love the Westminster system. I really believe …
it's a wonderful system … Of course it is ponderous.
Of course it has failings. It depends on how you view
these failings and the ponderous methods of getting
there … but my God what would you change it for?
Nothing at all … yet we try and ruin it.

—John Murray, 2003

With his mind made up, John joined the local branch of the Country Party, which at that time was made up of equal numbers from both the Liberal Party and the Country Party. 1958 was an election year. As the endorsed candidate of both parties, he would have to 'work like the devil' in the federal seat of Herbert, a true blue Labor seat, to break the mould. His brigade commander offered the services of two Army assistants—friends of John's and 'tough cookies. 'They're yours!' said the commander. Together they hatched 'a proper campaign': 'My blokes said, "Do you think you're known in Townsville?" I said, "I think I am." "Well, we'll test it. Walk up Flinders Street tomorrow morning and ask every third person or so, 'Could you tell me where I could find John Murray?'" And lo and behold, I hadn't gone two blocks before somebody said, "John Murray, who's he?" Nobody knew of me at all.' The advertising was clever. A number of images of John Murray looked out at the public, always with a different question. 'Have you met this man? Have you heard of this man?

Do you know this man?' They all projected someone who had come up the hard way; who had worked with sheep and cattle; who had interests in the North; who had served his country; a family man:

'Then on the Saturday it finished up: "The man is John Murray!"

"Now walk up Flinders Street," they said. And even the kids were saying, "There he is!"

The personal emphasis did the job.'

While his reputation was built up in newspapers and on radio, John drove thousands of miles over the 435-kilometre (270-mile) coastal strip of the electorate, attending every function possible, addressing every Rotary Club and every Country Women's Association. The intense exertion paid off. Later that night, on 25 November 1958, two workers in the electoral office looked hard at John. 'You're going to win this … these are the best figures we've ever seen coming in.'

As John was driving the 130 kilometres (80 miles) back to *The Orient* from Townsville the news of the election result filtered through on the car radio. Herbert was mentioned continually. He was close to home when he heard the announcement: the seat was almost certainly his, though it would not be officially declared for another week. It looked as though he had broken the pattern of over fifty years. Tired but overjoyed he woke his sleeping wife. 'Oh darling,' she replied groggily, 'where to now?' Ruth had always followed her husband. She knew she was in for another move.

The next day John wrote to his mother:

> *It's a feeling of great relief to have the campaigning behind me— it has been an interesting experience, but also in many respects, a very humiliating one too. It must surely be the worst side of politics or public life.*
>
> *I've worked terribly hard for this … The final build-up came with the visit of the Prime Minister and Dame Pattie. Ruth and I dined with them privately and then the big meeting in the Town Hall with Menzies and Dame Pattie and Ruth and I on the stage … Then came polling day—tense and difficult for me and of course, Ruth was also a bundle of nerves. She has been really rather wonderful, because I've hardly been home for months and always rather on edge with her and the children.*

On polling day, I told the electors I would visit every polling booth—quite a task in an electorate 270 miles long. However, I got a Bush Pilots' Cessna plane and did them all. Where I couldn't land I circled over low and dropped pamphlets and waved to all the good workers …

The poll won't be declared for a week or so. Therefore, I am not making any statements concerning my win to the Press—it would be wrong—just in case something happened and mistakes have been made in counting. And I'm not making any plans until the poll has been declared …
26 November 1958

Charlie and Constance Glanville were elated. However, just months after John's election success, Charlie died on 25 January 1959. John had written to him only a few weeks before:

Your position is extremely good. You have <u>NOTHING</u> to worry about. You have wealth and security and Mother to keep an eye on you—I wish I had the same!

I will be in touch with events and if there is anything which you, New Zealand Loan or I, think needs my attention, I will be down straight away.

If you want to make a clean swap of worries, I'll be in it any time!

My love to you both, and remember I'm always here to help.
7 January 1959

After Charlie's death, Constance continued living out the year at *Korreo*, alone. John and Peter had committed to assisting her with the shearing. She then moved to Nowra. However, her daughter's death from cancer in 1964, at the age of forty-seven, forced another move.

The family were overwhelmed with the news of Margie's death. Lorraine had travelled from London to be with her. A few days before she died, Peter and John visited Nowra. Knowing they were travelling from faraway places, she had 'willed herself to stay alive to say goodbye' to them.[1]

John described her as 'a golden gift'; Ruth referred to her as 'a very bright little soul'.[2] Peter said, 'Poor little thing. She was just absolutely sweet … There wasn't anyone like her you know, my little Margie. I loved her. She was just the be-all and end-all of all people … She was the most beautiful woman in her heart that has ever lived in this world.'[3] Constance was lost without her daughter. She soon moved north to live close to John and his family.

Once John began his life as a federal politician, life changed dramatically. He immediately set to work to put his electorate on the map. 'In the last triennium more influential visitors have been in this area than in any other similar period since Federation,' cooed the editor of the local paper.[4] At last Herbert was being promoted as its residents wanted it to be.

Work was not just confined to Herbert. John argued strongly for suitable pastures and cattle to be the number one issue in Queensland—not roads. He believed the flourishing cattle industry would pay for the roads.

In addition, John's hand went up almost immediately for committee membership in both Defence and Foreign Affairs. This led to an unusual experience.

Breaking his parliamentary briefing session in Malaya in February 1961, John joined an Australian military operation into the depths of the Malayan jungle—checking reports of communist infiltration. The terrain was rough, undeveloped, virtually uninhabited and infested with leeches. The men were forbidden to shave because of rat-borne disease spreading into any kind of cut. While patrolling, carrying Owen submachine guns, the regiment kept a look out for tigers, and even worse, death by blow pipes—accurate and lethal. 'The natives seldom miss. The poison on the dart is extremely deadly and kills a monkey in about one and a half minutes.'[5]

For a while, John tried to do it all—cattle, commanding, federal politics and family. His children remembered the strain it put on their family life. David was disappointed when his father arrived home from Canberra only to travel further north for more campaigning; Jill saw her father having to drive around his huge electorate, 'to the exclusion of us all'; Janie felt her father was 'always busy, always out of the house at meetings … almost to the disadvantage of family'; Susie remembered him 'only in the festive times'; and Johnnie recalled him 'as a visitor in the background of all my early recollections of Mum'.

Even Ruth, normally unruffled and 'getting through' balls, debutante presentations and gala functions, reached boiling point. David recalled:

'She was extremely loyal. But I do remember one time she threw a plate at him.'

Now that he had full-time political responsibilities, the cattle experiment for John was far too time-consuming. 'Time, time, time. You needed a long line of determined people.' Though Dr Kelley had earlier published a document detailing the mechanics of the cross-breeding program and John had continued to 'push the cattle idea flat out', there was still insufficient knowledge and interest in Australia for the venture to fly.[6] His decision had not worked out; it was 'just too much attempting two ventures at once'. He summarised his situation quite simply: 'We weren't making any money.'

With the decision in 1960 to sell *The Orient* to his backers Tutt Bryant Ltd and to hand over his immediate command of C Company, John moved to Townsville to throw himself fully into politics, stimulated by dealing with 'the lifeblood of the nation—defence, foreign affairs, the treasury'.

He could not have predicted the dreadful credit squeeze of 1961: in a massive swing against the Coalition Government, Menzies' majority was reduced from thirty-two seats to two. Though *The Townsville Daily Bulletin*'s editorial encouraged voters to support the incumbent who 'had not merely been the member but also the ambassador of the constituency … a man of action allied with ideas', John Murray lost the seat of Herbert. He was now without a job—neither cattle man nor politician.

On both of the occasions he went to *Coolibah* to help Peter—Peter had moved his family to the Northern Territory two years before, in 1958—he joined a mustering camp. During his second visit John received a bush radio message. Would he come to Brisbane to discuss standing for another seat—this time a state one—the safe Liberal seat of Clayfield in the city? John did not have to think too hard; he needed income. 'I was getting on and this way I could anchor my family—get them all into good schools.'

John won the seat of Clayfield easily with no need for military precision at all. He entered state politics on 1 June 1963. The win involved another move—this time to the suburb of Hamilton in Brisbane.

One night at a function attended by Sir Robert Menzies, the leader asked John how he was getting on in his 'degenerated circumstances'. John knew exactly what he meant; Menzies had been a state politician too. State affairs seemed less of the 'big picture'; at that level 'you were not moving nations'. The glamour and the stimulation of his former role was gone: 'I knew it would be a step down, going from federal to state … Just think about it. The House of Representatives—the Senate—and what were you doing in state?

You were dealing with all the broken down portions of that ... In federal politics good men went on and up; in state, good men were static or moved down.'

The children were the beneficiaries. Their father had more time. At *Yarrum Hills*, John's newly acquired property on the far north coast of New South Wales they were given opportunities for learning to ride, mustering sheep and cattle, shooting, camping around a campfire, driving a tractor, swimming in the creek and even becoming involved in the production and growth of a small stud of black-faced Suffolk sheep. In Brisbane John took David to the rugby games, Johnnie to the Moscow Circus in Brisbane and all of them to the Brisbane Exhibition Grounds Raceway on Saturday nights. Guy Fawkes night was always memorable, especially for Janie: 'Dad arrived home with bungers, crackers, Roman candles, sparklers ... you name it. We set them off under the stars ...'

Despite family treats, the children were all subject to a military discipline of sorts. Their shoes had to be polished during the week; they had to get up early on Sundays 'to help in the garden, pull those weeds, hoe the garden bed, sweep and tidy'.[7] Robbie remembers the stern voice of her father commanding his family. Obedience, discipline and politeness were expected.

After more than a decade of state politics, John retired from the seat of Clayfield, in February 1976.

His mother was now eighty-six and ailing. She had just enough energy for the occasional visit to *Yarrum Hills* which was close to the Tweed Heads Nursing Home. But her spirit and vigour were gone. Her once strong body was frail and she was confused. She died peacefully at the age of eighty-eight, and her ashes were laid in the Tweed Heads Crematorium.

Packing away her personal belongings—photos, books, clothes—brought memories flooding back. While folding her grey serge skirts and deep pink cardigans John recalled his children's name for her out west—'Granny Galah' and 'Granny Gidgee'—both names grounding her to the outback.

And then John opened a plastic bag filled with old letters, stored in the back of her cupboard. Hundreds of them. He recognised the handwriting immediately. Most of the letters were from faraway places—the Middle East, the Atherton Tablelands, New Guinea and Borneo. In detail they recorded five years of his life.

John now purchased another property, *Bellanboe*, a 2830-hectare (7000-acre) property at Tenterfield on the northern tablelands of New South Wales. Life here imprinted indelible memories. Grandson Cameron

Kerr wrote much later, upon John's death: 'I look back on the *Bellanboe* days as the most magical times of all. I always cried when we had to leave. It's a place that always brings a smile to my face and a feeling of safety and comfort. A place that represents a time when everything was perfect to me. I remember sitting up on the fender of the tractor as we ploughed away the fields, standing on the back of the truck or riding in the sidecar of the motorbike. I remember the electric fence and the irrigation system and the pump pulling from the river. Working with those amazing border collies. The time that Shep chomped my forehead—and you driving me to get stitches in Tenterfield. I remember the oily wool smell of the sheep shearing shed and the smell of freshly cut lucerne in hay bails. Whenever those smells flood my nostrils today I race back to those wonderful times. Watching you smoke your pipe ... cranking the handle on the telephone to get an operator … sleeping out on the verandah, listening to the hard rain pelting the roof. You telling me to throw a shoe at you if you were snoring and having really nice chats about what exciting adventures await tomorrow. But mostly I remember the warm feeling of us all being together with you and Granny.'

A bad back eventually prevented John from even lifting one of his beloved black faced Suffolks over a rail. 'The fun went out of it.' Following a spinal operation, he and Ruth moved back to their home in Clayfield, Brisbane where he set up his own woodwork business.

He would work for hours, designing, sanding, brushing and polishing round wooden bowls and more specifically, wooden verandah brackets. He was always on the lookout for new designs. Leaning over the lathe, shaping and cutting, filled in the long hours of his seventies and eighties. His products were much in demand for newly renovated Federation homes.

In early 2001, aged eighty-five, John opened a letter from the Australian Government—an invitation to attend the centenary commemoration of Federation on Wednesday, 8 May in Melbourne. John quickly rang his daughter Janie. Could she accompany him? Regrettably Ruth's painful arthritis would prevent her from attending.

The ceremony was attended by about 7000 official guests, including one of the biggest ever gathering of politicians in Australia. On the following morning, 9 May, the Federal Parliament assembled at the Victorian Parliament House, where it had sat for twenty-seven years beginning in 1901.

With the official functions at an end, Janie was already focusing on her father's past. She knew that she was now visiting the area he had travelled to as a sickly jackeroo. She had heard snippets of her father's story years before, but wanted to know more. What was to stop them visiting *Woodlands*—Ben Chaffey's home?

After many calls Janie found the information she wanted. Close to Melbourne's Tullamarine Airport, *Woodlands* was now owned and being preserved by the Victorian Government. The Friends of Woodlands, a community volunteer group, worked there to bring a greater awareness to the public and offered regular theatrical productions about the homestead's history. Sue Wright, then the convener of the Friends group, was particularly interested in the history of Ben Chaffey, looking on Ben's time there as the most significant era of ownership after the original settlers.

It was Sue Wright's number that Janie dialled from central Melbourne on the afternoon of 9 May 2001—a call that would give definite direction to John's next few years.

There was dead silence for what seemed like a minute at the other end of the phone. And then she said, 'I beg your pardon?' Sue Wright was cautious but hopeful. She knew that Ben Chaffey's only child, daughter Mavis, had died childless in 1968. She had also heard from reliable sources that Ben had fathered other children. Had a member of his second family finally made themselves known? Or was this some kind of practical joke?

After no more than ten minutes into the arranged meeting the following day, Sue Wright slowly looked up at John. She said quietly: 'You know more about Ben Chaffey than I do. You know more about *Woodlands* than I do.'

John then started to open up; to tell her everything. They talked into the small hours. John and Janie arranged to meet her at *Woodlands* the next day. Sue Wright would gladly break her school-teaching routine for them.

Next morning father and daughter were up early. They drove along Sunbury Road, past Tullamarine Airport, until a large sign, *Woodlands Historic Park, Woodlands Homestead,* directed them to turn right. Three hundred metres (330 yards) would take them to the home. They stopped the car. John would not go through the gate; it had to be gradual: 'We waited—just standing at the fence—having my first look since the 1930s.'

John then stepped into the homestead with Sue. He was silent. He could feel Ben Chaffey at the bedroom door; hear the kettle boiling in the kitchen; see the gleaming trophies in the room where he had stood in front of the fire and answered his father's question about his weight. Outside were the kennels where Mavis had kept her West Highland terriers, and the stables where he and his father had inspected the horses. He attempted to stay calm.

The meeting meant extensive historical revision of the theatrical production Sue Wright had written and performed in with other members of the Friends group. First produced in 1997, the play was based largely on the story of the Ben Chaffey era. It would have to be rewritten to include the astounding new information. Only since 2001 has the production incorporated, 'with permission', the story of the jackeroo. Its new title, *Journey to Woodlands*, reflects both journeys John made to the property—as a young boy and as an older man.

And then a third journey was undertaken—a grand pilgrimage that John Murray and his children arranged in April 2002. His extended family travelled from all corners of the country primarily for the rededication of Ben Chaffey's grave at Bulla Cemetery.

John bowed his head as his father's restored gravestone was consecrated. Ben Chaffey's grandchildren then returned to *Woodlands* to plant three small lilac trees, saplings grafted from an ancient lilac in the garden. The young lilacs were placed ceremoniously in the earth, in honour of Ben and Laura's three children: Peter, John and Margie.

Sue Wright had arranged an evening performance of *Journey to Woodlands* in John's honour. She played Bess McPherson, Cowra Chaffey's companion. The audience moved in a cavalcade of cars, from Ben's grave at the cemetery, along the *Woodlands* driveway to the home. They tip-toed through the main entrance of the homestead into the ballroom to watch the re-enactment.

The cold, hard facts of the June 1937 *Woodlands* auction were played out, Chaffey's problems emerging through the bleak, drought-ridden, post-Depression years. The property, a 'magnificent suburban country home … delightfully situated on a knoll, surrounded by 164 acres of land, with stables, garages, feed store, chauffeur's cottage, manager's cottage' was auctioned for a pittance; the homestead was 'ruthlessly stripped'.[8] John Murray's youngest son, Johnnie, was flabbergasted: 'I didn't know. I had no idea …'

At the end of the play the audience was invited to join the cast for supper in the Chaffey Room and 'partake in conversation'. John was moved by the performance and his surroundings. The photos of winning racehorses Whittier and Manfred had taken on a rich glow on the walls of the Chaffey Room. He found it difficult to speak in the *Woodlands* drawing room.

Cowra's words rang in his ears—her negative response when he had rung to ask permission in 1937 to visit his dying father. His acquiescence to her rejection hovered now. The older John Murray wondered once more, with painful self-doubt, if he should have reacted another way: 'I don't think I could have handled it any differently. What should I have done? Should I have done anything else? Turn up against her wishes?

'I think that would have been—no, not right.'

After leaving Melbourne, John and two of his children continued the journey, visiting the outback towns of Ivanhoe, Broken Hill, Cobar and Wilcannia. He lingered at some of the places he had known well—*Manfred, Kilfera, Beilpajah, Darnick, Pinchinara, Korreo.* Janie and David often saw his head shake from side to side, as he stood silently reminiscing, pale eyes absorbing his youth. They observed him swallowing, fighting the tug in his throat as he stared at the homes, paddocks, dams.

Some of the visits were disappointing. The old *Kilfera* house, previously so meticulously kept, was falling down. And the inland lake, where John used to sit and watch the birdlife with the sun setting over the water, was parched beyond recognition. *Beilpajah* was burnt to the ground; *Pinchinara* and *Korreo*, formerly in such good repair, were overgrown with 'rubbish timber'.

The owner at *Beilpajah,* Tim McKenzie, asked him hesitantly: 'Can you tell me one thing? Was Ben Chaffey your father?' 'Yes, he was,' John replied. 'Come and sit down and I'll tell you about it.'

In 2002 John was eighty-six years old, and Ruth eighty-five. On his return John wondered how best he could describe to his wife the emotions he was experiencing. His world was opening out; hers was closing in. It was around this time that their long relationship started to show signs of strain.

Ruth was suffering. Her bad hip was unbearably painful; signs of Alzheimer's were increasing in regularity. Frustrations abounded. Ruth blamed; John felt helpless. A wedge cut into the union and into family life. John acknowledged that he might have wrongly approached the pledge of secrecy to his mother, recognising how difficult it had been for his wife, who had grown up in a conservative Victorian household. 'She'd always realised there was something funny in the background. You see, I never told her. She probably never quite forgave me for that.'

John felt disheartened at his lack of ability to deal with the problem. For months he tried: 'It was the onset of dementia ... I found I couldn't lift her. She was too heavy for me. I couldn't countenance a nurse living in the place—it just didn't add up.'

And then their third daughter, Janie Kerr, came up with a solution that restored the balance.

Chapter Twenty-Six

Full circle

JANIE SAID, 'DAD THERE'S ONE DOWN HERE [IN NERANG, ON THE GOLD COAST]. COME AND HAVE A LOOK. I'D LOVE TO HAVE YOU HERE.' BY COMING DOWN AND GETTING A PLACE IN THE LODGE OF THE RETIREMENT VILLAGE I COULD GET A PRIORITY FOR RUTH INTO THE NURSING HOME HERE ... THEY SAID, 'A BED'S AVAILABLE — BUT WE WANT HER TODAY. WHAT CAN YOU DO ABOUT IT?' 'YES,' I SAID, 'WE'LL GO AND GET HER.'

—John Murray, 2003[1]

EARLE HAVEN IS set amongst manicured gardens, with a view of mountains in the background. It is a haven insofar as it is protected by a high wall from the noise and bustle of the outside world. Residents have a plastic card to operate the heavy iron gates that allow entry and exit. Inside the walls of the lodge one can find facilities such as a swimming pool surrounded by tropical gardens, a library and a hairdressing salon.

What particularly appealed to John was the workshop, where residents were producing and selling all manner of objects: wooden tables and trays, hand-painted boxes, magazine racks, dolls' houses and intricate sailing ships. John could continue with his woodwork there.

By July 2002 John and Ruth Murray were settled into the last 'home' of their lives. Different wings in *Earle Haven* catered for different stages of life. Though Ruth was restricted to one room, her children decorated it with her creations—painted porcelain, landscape oil paintings, crocheted blankets—a life in microcosm. And every evening after dinner her husband made the short walk back to the intensive care unit to present her with a red rose. The deeper the red the better, he told the local florist. A little over sixty years earlier, when the newlyweds were separated, he had written to his mother:

> *We're longing to see each other again, even just for a few moments, and we are very much in love ... Next Saturday the 17th is Ruth's birthday. If she has not left by then could you please arrange for some flowers to be sent to her? Dark red roses if possible—she likes them best.*
> *11 February 1945*

But initially at *Earle Haven* the roses were not enough. 'John, I've been in this hospital long enough. Please take me home.' While Ruth kept repeating her plea, John kept repeating his reasons for staying—that neither of them could look after each other. They were going to be much better off here—together. Where else could they go? Weren't they lucky?

Gradually Ruth started to accept it. In small but significant ways her personality changed. Each night in the nursing home it was an elementary equation that she repeated to the nurses as they admired her red roses: 'He loves me so much—and I love him.' The staff often commented, 'How could they love each other so much after all this time?'

Aged eighty-eight, John wrote to his granddaughter, Rebecca Durant, who married Peter Thompson in December 2004:

> *Lovely to know you are both settling into married life—there is no more wonderful state of affairs. After all these years—April 1944—I can say with the utmost truth and confidence, that Ruth and I love each other more than ever. Sitting beside her bed, holding her hand, looking deeply into her eyes and into her very soul, is the most rewarding gift we can give each other—replacing and transcending sexual satisfaction—whispering to each other 'I love you darling.'*

When you can truly say you like each other, then I know you have your feet on the first rung of the 'love ladder'—a great achievement. For Ruth and me it was a matter of learning how to be tolerant and understanding—it was not easy—there were obstacles on the path—they had to be dealt with, and deal with them we did. The reward is more than worth it.
January 2005

Though Ruth was immobilised by her arthritis, hip problems and increasing symptoms of dementia, John was still able to get around. While in his late seventies, arthritis, back pain and an anaemic condition necessitated quarterly blood transfusions, his ability to live a normal life remained, with the help of several aids: a walking stick, a motorised buggy and a regular dose of morphine.

However, John was more concerned with the health of his wife. To keep her mind active he would arrange for the children to tell her their stories of the day. He thought at times that his methods were working: Did I show you Ruth's scribbling? I gave her a piece of paper and a pen and said, "Write something for me." She looked at me and in her childish hand she wrote, "John, you are a stinker but I love you just the same." So I got hold of it and I wrote underneath, "And I adore you too." Then she wrote, "Are we both drunk?" ... So I wrote, "Yes, no, yes, no." A couple of months ago she couldn't do that at all.'

But then she took a turn for the worse. Her chest was bad. As her cough worsened she became weaker and weaker: 'Finally one of the girls said, "Dad, I think she's going." I didn't know what I was prepared for and nor did the kids ... She gradually, gradually let go. And we spoke to her and kept nuzzling against her. She knew we were all there. It was lovely, it really was. She died in our arms, you see.

'For me, that was the first and only peaceful death I had ever witnessed. Every other death has been associated with violence, war deaths ... Looking into a bloke's eyes, knowing he is going to die. That wasn't a peaceful death it was a dreadful, painful death.

'But this was peaceful. That was the lovely part about it—the touch, the warmth. And finally the stillness.'

It was 5 July 2005. Ruth Florence Murray was eighty-eight years old.

Hundreds of roses decorated the gardens, bent low with the weight of their blooms. This was *Allambe Gardens* where John had travelled in his car every week—along the same route on the same day at the same time—to collect his weekly standing order for Ruth. The gardens were now the venue for the commemoration of her life. She lay stretched out in a coffin. On its lid, amongst the profusion of deep red roses was a simple note:

> *To my darling Ruthie, mother of my six children,*
> *Thank you for a lifetime of love, happiness and support.*
> *See you in my dreams.*
> *All my love, Johnnie.*

Some of the petals after the funeral were transformed into an exquisite garment sewn by Tania Murray, the wife of John and Ruth's youngest son, Johnnie. It became known as The Rose Petal Wedding Dress. Tania had deconstructed the blooms and attached them to paper panels. The dried bouquet of long-stemmed red roses, hanging beside the paper dress, was the last bouquet John had given his wife.

Visitors to the chapel entered the area behind the heavy curtain. The children smiled at each graciously. Ruth's face was framed by the polished wood of the coffin—a still life, with neither wrinkle nor frown. Susie, the youngest, bent to kiss her mother, to hold her hands. Until then she had been strong.

John sat on a wooden pew in the front of the chapel, both hands on his walking stick, head to one side. He listened to the words about Ruth; that she was cheeky and humorous; that she was gentle and loving; that she was supportive, determined and indomitable, beautiful.

Tiredness around his eyes suggested a wretched wakefulness. Mourners bent to embrace him. He bowed his head, acknowledging each one.

John's thoughts about his own death were simple. He believed that while medical safeguards were necessary, no one should be allowed to suffer unduly. Both his children and his doctor were quite aware of his wishes. 'I'm totally relaxed about dying. Totally relaxed. Dying would be a very peaceful, lovely thing for me. I've feted ninety odd years of life but I'm still healthy. Maybe I'll hang on for a while'

In his last years John adopted a military routine to his life, albeit punctuated with interruptions that would have been unacceptable in army life. Emails, faxes and phone calls were part of his waking hours. Jokes for him to chuckle over; serious articles to ponder on.

His bookcase was crammed with books of all dimensions—chunky parliamentary manuals, history books, poetry, smaller wartime magazines, sporting articles, dog-breeding manuals, cattle reports—all of them distractions from the reality he faced. Life without Ruth.

At 5.30 am he awakened with the radio news. Then he spread out the pages of *The Australian*, which he read from cover to cover. His interest in politics and sport never waned. After an early breakfast in the communal dining room he would return to his room and settle himself at the computer to read several of the opinion pieces from other daily newspapers. 'There's a devil of a lot here … if you really browse through it you get a pretty rounded opinion. I like the computer. The news is selected for me … it's all there. Now Doug [son-in-law Doug Disher, married to Susie] wants me to get on to *The Times*—English and US … but I don't get up early enough to do that.'

The necessity to have regular blood transfusions was never discussed in more than a cursory way. 'I'm feeling on top of the world,' meant that the transfusion had been recent; 'I've been better,' indicated severe tiredness and an imminent treatment. When he was 90 years old, John's doctors ordered the procedure to be on a weekly basis. One of his children joked of the danger of his becoming 'a permanent drip'. His response was light-hearted: 'That cruel slur has been avoided—temporarily at least—by the clever boys deciding on a program of one bag of blood each week. So now I front up to Pathology each Monday morning to give a blood sample which is sent off to the Lab. for matching and processing—and on Tuesday morning I'm picked up by a Department of Veterans' Affairs car, delivered to an oncology unit in a private hospital in Southport, transfused over a couple of hours and then returned by the same transport to the bosom of my adopted family—at Orchid House.

'Half a day in the life of young Jackie Murray!'

After breakfast and the computer news John devoted his time to woodwork, continuing the production of finely turned cedar or maple bowls and intricately designed verandah brackets for Federation or Victorian homes. Dressed in his old overalls, his 'silly suit', he cut and shaped, ground and sanded, until the product was just right: 'I can get $1200 to $1500 a month.

It's very comfy. I brought the useful machinery with me [from Brisbane]. I've given it to the workshop. I'll just use it for as long as I can. If the brackets ease off then I'm still set up. All the timber that I order—I select the good bits and put them away. I can make bowls from them in my dotage.'

John occasionally sat still in his room and just looked around. Outside was a minuscule courtyard garden, big enough for one chair in the sun. The apartment itself was tiny: a kitchenette, a bathroom and a bedroom all flowing into each other. On his chair was a tapestry cushion, its message always prominent: *Attitude is the one positive choice we have each day.*

Under the table, beside the chair, was a brand new accordion. 'There is all my original music,' John volunteered, pointing to tattered sheets. 'I need to get that accordion out every day to practise… I went to use it [his old one] again and it's miles too heavy. So I bought a little new one …. Now I am going to practise it, practise it, practise it. I'll feel helpless, it's only a baby compared with that one … I've got the original instruction book and two big books [*Pietro Diero 12 & 6*]. That's what I learnt from years ago—those two books. They were purchased by me in 1932.

'I've got to get back to where I was … trying to work that thumb … it's very sore but I've got to work on that. I've got to practise every day—practise about half an hour every day—I must.'

In this little room was his life. There were reminders all around him. Ruth looked at him from every wall: a smartly dressed secretary, a laughing bride, a coy young woman. A grandmother. And her ashes rested in a small urn on John's mantelpiece. When his friend, Patricia Gardner, presented him with his portrait one day, she was taken aback with his response: 'Put it up there, next to Ruthie.'[2]

He bade Ruth goodnight without fail. Silently, as the past engulfed the small space, tears would well in his eyes. 'This happens rather often, alone together as we are. It seems to strengthen rather than weaken me.'

There was plenty to distract John from his loss. He would often look around at the mementos of life gone by, enveloped by the retrospective:

> See that mug. That's the drinking utensil I got from the
> hills in India. Beautiful thing.
> There are all my old pipes …
> That's the fax machine. It's probably Sue [his daughter].
> She's always faxing me these little jokes …

Any book you want on the war is there on those shelves. And there are all the books Mother left.

These are my medals … This one, the Polish Cross of the Armed Forces of the West … I value it enormously. The Polish Government led by Lech Walenska decided they would find those Australians who served with their little group in Tobruk … Walenska was the bloke who followed it right through … there were only a handful of us really—the investiture was lovely. The Polish Consul General came up from down south, and it took place at Government House in Brisbane. It's, in fact, an unofficial medal but is worn now by all the 9th Div blokes …

One year—maybe it was 1965—I decided to go to Sydney to march. We were living in Brisbane. I just woke up one Anzac morning and said to Ruth, 'Goodbye darling. I'm going to ring the airlines'. I got a seat, met them coming up George Street—wonderful feeling. George Colvin was leading and they gave me a nod and 'Ahoy!' … wonderful! I enjoyed it immensely—to see so many old friends.

After the luncheon George said, 'You can't just go off like this. Slim Somerville and Wooton the general and I, we've got a thing we do every Anzac day. We go off to a pub … ' I said 'I've got to get on to a plane.' He said, 'Oh I'll get you on to a plane'. So we went there and drank and drank and drank—and somebody did get me out to the airport—to the last plane, about 11 o'clock at night.

I remember the girls, the hosties as I came aboard— I was about the only one on the plane, wore my ribbons. They said, 'Oh, how absolutely lovely'. I said, 'Just let me sleep somewhere please'. Finally I woke up standing in the loo and of course in the male loos there's a head rest thing and I was standing there fast asleep … I came out and looked up and down and there was a bloke cleaning the plane out … He said, 'What the bloody hell are you doing here?' They'd forgotten me entirely. I somehow got to the terminal and got a cab. Ruthie rolled over and said, 'Oh, it's you again.'

In 1991, a little handful of us decided to march [in Brisbane]. See, it's a NSW battalion [the 2/13th] but there's a few of us living in Queensland. The Association had the old banner, lovely big green and gold with our battle honours on it, but it was pretty dilapidated. It needed repairing.

There was a sail company who had made some sails for the family … They went into the big sail loft and all volunteered to restore our flag for nothing. Made a beautiful job of it. It's a whacking great flag about ten feet across and six feet deep. I made new poles for it. My boys have been carrying it for years—David and Johnnie— they'd fight for it now … they love it. So we've all been marching together since 1992.

Just one moment while I take this call. It's [about] organising the annual Alamein dinner. In Brisbane. David will probably come up with me—and maybe Sue's husband, Doug. He'll be interested.

Oh, there's the phone again. She's saying she'll come here to collect the bracket [his woodwork]. Trying to stop my driving. There's a plot to do that. No one wants me to drive any more now that I'm in my nineties.

Will you have a sherry? Let's have something to eat too. I'll put these biscuits in one of my little wooden bowls.'

John's life was busy; his company interesting. He never once stopped to dwell on the maudlin.

It is questionable whether a person hears the words that are said in their favour at a funeral. Some believe that the body or perhaps its soul hovers above the church or the grave and that every word, action and thought is absorbed. Others say, 'Bunkum! Once you're dead, you're dead!'

Even before his death, John received numerous accolades from members of his immediate family, though not directed to him. In 2003, oldest daughter, Jill, commented: 'Even to this day Father is not quick to step forward to take the praise … I don't believe it is of tremendous importance to him to be showered with praise. … He just gets on and does it and encourages other people … He leads by example … firm and tough, but gentle … I always remember him saying "You should be able to get on your knees anywhere and pray to your God. It doesn't matter whether it's Jewish, Hindu, Catholic or whatever."

'His influence now is a very calming one, though we had a happy, idyllic life in the countryside [as children]...'

Robbie acknowledged her father's ability to keep the family close, always with a strong love for their mother. 'They worked together to make our family such a happy one. The closeness of the siblings ... we all hold very dear.' She appreciated her father's urging her to have the courage of her convictions, not to dwell on the past and to deal fairly in all things: 'He is principled and courageous in adversity. Dad has a good attitude. He's told us about the plot down in Bulla [the Bulla Cemetery], where we could all be laid if we wished and he's said: "We could all have such fun. All come out at night and have a great old time!" He's philosophical about it and I guess that helps him through.'

His search for inclusiveness through 'the harmonious action' was Janie's presiding memory of her father. He showed each child how to 'do unto others, to have humility, to think about those less advantaged in giving service to the community'. Tolerance, understanding and fair play were high on his agenda. 'He always used to say to us a simple little verse. I've only ever heard Dad recite it.' She recalled it by heart:

> Harmonious action always costs a little;
> sometimes a great deal.
> It costs self-control, courtesy and an effort
> to put yourself in another person's place.
> But it's always worth tenfold what it costs.

Janie's first memory of him was of a 'wonderful, tall, strong father coming home to the family—always positive, always full of life with this great sense of humour, of fun'. She remembered her father 'greeting people, communicating, organising, people coming to the property, people fascinated by him, always hovering around him. He is honourable and courageous ... brave and sensitive ... so soft. I can't believe how soft he is. There's a sense of always wanting to please others ...'

John's oldest son David was always eager to know more of what his father had done. They would sit up for hours talking, losing all sense of time. They were good mates. Like his sister Janie, David saw his soft side. Sensitive, the older son takes after his father. 'He's very loving and caring ... I've seen him cry. There's a really soft side. If I could do half the things he's done and the way he's done them ... he's a great person, truly.'

Susie remembered her father in the early days as someone she looked up to: 'I always remember his moustache and the games he played with it—the strength and character of that moustache. Dad is a very strong character.' She was convinced that her father's greatest influence on her had been to have tenacity—to keep going. 'Search for what you want in life and do it for yourself.'

Johnnie saw his father as 'a powerful father figure who guided our family through the battlefields and past the big bad monsters of life'. His father was someone who made each one of his children feel special—the parents being a magnet in their lives. 'Dad would never force his opinions on us, but we knew that his opinions and standards were to be respected and more often than not, were correct.' Johnnie felt that Rudyard Kipling's poem 'If' was probably the backbone of his father's philosophy on life: 'Dad could "fill the unforgiving minute with sixty seconds worth of distance run" ... and still can in many ways. The lasting principles of my father are to stand by your beliefs, to be kind and understanding, to reach out to others and be tolerant of others' beliefs. Look the person in the eye with a firm handshake, be punctual and stand by your word, be honest with yourself and all those around you. Walk with Kings but don't lose the common touch. And love and be proud of family.'

John was genuinely moved when he heard his children's evaluation of him. When asked subsequently to consider what kind of father he'd been, he sounded reflective and slightly questioning: 'Well, I *think* my children respect and love me. I think they do. And I suppose that's all ... you expect from your children ... you want their trust, you want their love, you want to be able to talk to them ... I think, I think so ...

'What is wonderful, my kids just love the family now. It's as it should be, in that you are surrounded by children, grandchildren and great-grandchildren. That's as it should be.'

When not surrounded by his six children, nineteen grandchildren and fourteen great-grandchildren, John found his attention focused more and more on a matter that had always dominated his solitary moments:

Geoff Ferguson, Secretary
Bulla Cemetery Trust
PO Box 119
Broadmeadows 3047
28 April 2003

Dear Sir

I have been advised by Sue Wright, Convener—Friends of Woodlands Historic Park, to forward you the attached Statutory Declaration to assist my application for a right of burial in the Bulla cemetery.

During April 2002 a large group of my family and relatives attended a service conducted by Reverend E. Cass in the Bulla Church. Visiting Ben Chaffey's grave after the service, I asked the minister for advice on what may be involved in securing the burial site alongside my father. He replied that it was not an unusual request, and that if I felt it in my heart I should certainly pursue it. He was aware of the relationship and gave me encouragement. It is certainly in my heart.

Sue Wright has, I understand, given you a broad sketch of my background, during which I have been privileged to render considerable service to my country—some sixteen years army, both peace and war—and another sixteen years in parliament, both House of Representatives and Queensland Legislative Assembly. Otherwise grazing and farming. And further, I have been made a Member of The Most Excellent Order of The British Empire (Mil), awarded The Cross of The Polish Armed Forces in the West, twice Mentioned in Despatches, WW2, and am a Justice of the Peace for Queensland.

It was not until my early teens, in the early 1930s, when my elder brother and I were employed by our father on one of his western NSW properties, that I had an opportunity to get to know him. And although the circumstances did not allow the normal father–son affection to develop, his care and concern for his extra-marital family as a whole, marked him as one of unusual character and integrity, for whom I personally felt a great respect, which has never diminished.

The revelations of time and research have given us a very extraordinary story, for which Sue Wright is so largely responsible. It is clearly true that Ben Chaffey and my mother, Laura Treweek, had a remarkable, enduring love affair.

It is my heartfelt and sincere wish, and that of my family, that my mother's ashes can be allowed to finally rest close to the grave of my father, Ben Chaffey, and that mine, when time ordains, can join her.

Yours Sincerely

John Murray MBE

This was not a letter from John to his mother. It was written twenty-seven years after her death. But had his mother read it, she would have furrowed her brow, swallowed to rid her throat of the constriction, and considered the letter repeatedly, with full concentration.

John Murray's mother had spent her waking hours sheltering the four children from her past actions. She had created an imaginary father for them, fought to provide them with an education, and fiercely protected them against the consequences of her unconventional circumstances. A certain pride and distance in her demeanour prevented the uncovering of her heavy secret. Yet by her very model she had taught her children strength and courage.

The truth emerged in the end. In 2004 John removed her ashes from the Tweed Heads Crematorium where they had rested for almost thirty years, and placed them next to Ben Chaffey's at the Bulla Cemetery, in Melbourne.

Her simple gravestone reads:

Laura Constance Glanville
1890–1978
Fortiter et Fideliter
In Loving Memory of a
Wonderful Mother and Grandmother
An Example of Courage and Fortitude to us all.
From Lorraine, Peter, John and Margie
And their Families.

On 25 January 2009 John died peacefully at 10.40 am. His wish to die in his own small *Earle Haven* room was observed; photos of his mother, Ben, Ruth, his children and his children's children would smile upon him. For several hours after his death, family, friends and residents grouped around his bed. Some touched his cold face. A single red rose was laid on his pillow. There were sniffles, photos, sobs, whispers, the notes of a piano, a rare hush; people arriving, departing. He would have enjoyed the attention, the vigil, the tranquillising classical recessional.

John and Ruth's favourite piece, 'Rustle of Spring' by Norwegian composer Christian Sinding, played in the background as the chapel in Allambe Gardens swelled with mourners. They could barely see John's officer's cap and military medals for the abundance of red roses on the coffin. Eulogies honoured his life; the Lord was his Shepherd. Captain Jacob Costello, a uniform-clad protégé of John's, stood to attention and saluted the flag-draped casket while the plaintiff notes of the 'Last Post' symbolised the end:

'Come home! Come home! The last post is sounding for you to hear.'

Had John's mother ever dreamt that her son's ashes would lie beside those of Ben Chaffey, the man she loved? And had she ever dreamt that her ashes would lie there also? That her gravestone at Bulla Cemetery would be grand in its simplicity: solid, strong and constant? And that John and Ruth's would be too?

Just as she was proud of all her son's achievements, so too would she have been unbearably proud of his military-like precision that had arranged for this tender funeral arrangement.

To look beyond the travails and achievements of John Murray's life is to observe the completion of a journey. Everything is orderly now, in its place. A full circle in one's life is difficult to achieve.

– Acknowledgements –

MANY PEOPLE HAVE helped me in the writing of this book. I am deeply indebted to them for their valuable assistance.

Sue Wright was unfailingly helpful in checking information about John Murray's early life, particularly his relationship with Ben Chaffey. As the author and convenor of Friends of Woodlands Historic Park, she was motivated to delve into the life of John's mother, writing a commendable report entitled 'Looking for Laura'.

John Searle (former honorary secretary and public officer of the 2/13th Battalion Association, and editor of the battalion's publication, *The Devil's Own Despatch*), painstakingly read the section covering the war years and then generously offered suggestions to improve its accuracy. He also gave me materials including maps that were to prove a useful addition for my writing, and has been unfailingly helpful providing information ever since.

John Gardner, MBE, ED, (former Officer Commanding C Company 31st Battalion, (the Kennedy Regiment) the Royal Queensland Regiment), is convenor of the 31st Infantry Battalion Association's annual Kennedy Regiment Commemorative Service and editor of the Association's news bulletin, *The Whispering Boomerang*. He and his wife Patricia shared with me their many memories of John Murray and searched for photos from the 1950s.

I would like to pay tribute to John Murray's family. All the siblings recounted vivid memories of their father. My cousin Robbie Murray and her daughters Rebecca, Ruth and Sarah spent many hours typing up over one hundred of John's letters, for which I am extremely grateful. Special thanks go to my cousin Janie Kerr who, living close to her father, was able to act as a most competent go-between. She was unfailingly helpful in thinking of ways to bridge the distance gap between author and subject.

For the transcribing of the many hours of tapes, I owe a huge debt to Barbara Buhagiar. In commenting on the final manuscript I sincerely thank Chris Chaseling, Claire Hammond and Bill Hunt—all so generous with their time. Consultant Stephen Wilson from MarlooMedia (M²) was a marvellous source of creative suggestions; and Angela Damis and Catherine Hammond gave me most useful advice and direction through their meticulous checking. Jody Lee was an editor everyone wishes for. I warmly thank her for the strength and extra focus she gave to my story.

In addition, I would like to sincerely thank my son Ben Austin and his wife Rachel, my daughter Lucy Watts and her husband Stuart, my sisters Sue-ann Makeham, Julian Shepherd and Gina Oldham and my niece Louise Shepherd, all of whom offered most constructive comment and encouragement. Finally, I would like to praise my husband Terry Austin who firmly reassured me throughout the years of writing. He was commendably patient.

For information about the war I relied heavily on reference material, much of which John Murray lent to me. I have acknowledged this dependence in the Endnotes and Bibliography.

One book that stands out is the 2/13th Battalion's unofficial history—*Bayonets Abroad*—written by the ex-members of the 2/13th Battalion and edited by Lieutenant G.H. Fearnside, who became a close friend of John's during their time together in the Middle East. I found the detail in this book to be invaluable.

Another excellent book was Hugh Gillan's *We Had Some Bother*, compiled by the 2/13th Battalion Association. Initially a copy was lent to me by one of John's fellow battalion members, John Searle; a second copy was later collected in a mercy dash, from another battalion member—Don Ashe (now deceased). The book contains extracts of Les Clothier's diary of the war and other fascinating personal reflections. I was extremely grateful for the lending generosity of the owners, as the book is now virtually unprocurable.

Bibliography

LETTERS AND INTERVIEWS

Letters from John Murray to Constance Murray/Glanville, May 1932–January 1959

Letter from Constance Glanville to Lorraine Murray, August 1935

Letter from John Murray to Margaret Oldham, undated 1942

Letters from John Murray to Ruth Murray, July 1944–August 1945

Letter from Ruth Murray to Constance Glanville, August 1944

Letters and emails from John Murray to author, March 2002–June 2007

Email from John Murray (Jnr), 24 July 2005

Letter from Tania Murray to author, 26 July 2005

Email from Robyn Murray to author, 28 September 2006

Telephone interview with Sue-ann Makeham and the author, 30 September 2002

Letter from John Murray to author accompanying Peter Murray's interview tapes, September 1989

Interviews (taped) between John Murray and author:
October 2003
15 August 2005
17–19 October 2005
4 June 2006

Interview (taped) between Peter Murray and author:
September 1989

OTHER MATERIAL DIRECTLY RELEVANT TO JOHN MURRAY

Australian Corps Summary, Part VI, Miscellaneous, 29 July 1945

Certificate from the Commonwealth of Australia, listing awards for Captain J. Murray NX20884, signed by Records Officer, Army Headquarters (undated)

Copy of advertisement for *Woodlands* auction, dated Tuesday 22 June (1930)

Kelley R.B. Dr, *Zebus (Brahmans) in America: an Importation. Proposal for Use in Australi*a, Wilmett & Sons (Pty) Ltd, Townsville, Australia, 1951

Letter from Lieutenant Colonel H.J. Bennett, Australian Military Forces, to Mrs Ruth Murray, 14 April 1945

Lieutenant John Murray, IO, *War Diary, 2/13th Battalion, Finschhafen Operation, 21 Sept–25 Oct, 1943*

Parliamentary Records, Parliament House, Darwin, June 2006

Poem written by Jim Walsoe, on hearing of the MBE award to John Murray. Dated 3 January 1957

Speech given by Lieutenant General John Coates at the Anzac Day Reunion of the 2/13th Battalion, 25 April 1996

Text of Citation for the Award of MBE to John Murray

The Devil's Own Despatch, October 1979 edition

BOOKS

Blainey, Geoffrey, *A Shorter History of Australia*, William Heinemann, Melbourne, Australia, 1994

Bowden, Tim, *The Way My Father Tells It*, ABC Books, Sydney, Australia, 1997

Brune, Peter, *A Bastard of a Place*, Allen & Unwin, Sydney, Australia, 2004

—— *Those Ragged Bloody Heroes*, Allen & Unwin, Sydney, Australia, 1991

Carroll, B., *The Engineers: 200 Years at Work for Australia*, The Institute of Engineers, Canberra, Australia, 1988

Caulfield, Michael, (ed.), *Voices of War*, Hodder, Sydney, Australia, 2006

Coates, John, *Bravery above Blunder*, Oxford University Press, Melbourne, Australia, 1999

Cochrane, Peter, *Australians at War*, Department of Veterans' Affairs, Australian Broadcasting Corporation, Sydney, Australia, 2001

Day, David, *The Politics of War*, HarperCollins, Sydney, Australia, 2003

Department of Conservation and Natural Resources, *Red Gums and Riders: A History of Gellibrand Hill Park*, Melbourne, Australia, 1993

Dodkin, Marilyn, *Goodnight Bobbie: One Family's War*, UNSW Press, Sydney, Australia, 2006

Dornan, Peter, *Nicky Barr: An Australian Air Ace*, Allen & Unwin, Sydney, Australia, 2002

Fearnside, G.H. (ed.), *Bayonets Abroad*, Success Print, Perth, Western Australia, 1993

—— *Half to Remember*, Haldance Publishing Co. Pty Ltd, Sydney, Australia, 1975

FitzSimons, Peter, *Kokoda*, Hodder, Sydney, Australia, 2004

—— *Tobruk,* HarperCollins, Sydney, Australia, 2006

Fogarty, John P., *Great Australians: George Chaffey*, Oxford University Press, Melbourne, Australia, 1967

Fraser, Bryce (ed.), *The Macquarie Book of Events*, Macquarie Library, McMahons Point, Australia 1983

Gibney, Frank (ed.), *Senso: The Japanese Remember the Pacific War*, Sharpe, United States, 1995

Gillan, Hugh (ed.), *We Had Some Bother*, Hall & Iremonger, Sydney, Australia, 2001

Glassop, Lawson, *We Were the Rats*, Australian War Classics, Angus & Robertson, Melbourne, Australia, 1944

Gregory, F.H., *Rommel*, Wayland Publishers Ltd, London, UK, 1974

Hall, Timothy, *Tobruk 1941: The Desert Siege*, Methuen, Sydney, Australia, 1984

Ham, Paul, *Kokoda*, HarperCollins, Sydney, Australia, 2004

Harrison, Frank, *Tobruk—The Great Siege Reassessed*, Arms & Armour, London, UK, 1996

Hill, Ernestine, *Water Into Gold*, Robertson & Mullens, Melbourne, Australia, 1958 (Revised Edition, 10 reprints from 1937)

Johnston, Mark, *That Magnificent 9th: An Illustrated History of the 9th Division 1940–46*, Allen & Unwin, Sydney, Australia, 2005

Maddrell, Roslyn, *Braidwood, Letters from the Front,* self-published, printed Hypercet Printing, Goulburn, Australia, 2001

Maughan, Barton, *Tobruk & El Alamein: Australia in the War of 1939–1945*, Series One, Volume Three, Australian War Memorial, Canberra, 1966

McDonald, Neil, *Chester Wilmot Reports: Broadcasts that Shaped World War II*, ABC Books, Sydney, Australia, 2004

Neale R.G., *Documents on Australian Foreign Policy*, Vol. 2, Australian Government Publishing Service, Canberra, Australia, 1986

Penglase, Joanna and Horner, David, *When the War Came to Australia*, Allen & Unwin, Sydney, Australia, 1992

Pitt, Barrie (ed.), *Excerpts of the History of the Second World War,* Phoebus Publishing Co., London, UK

Redesdale, Lord, *Tales of Old Japan*, Macmillan and Co Ltd, London, 1908
Soames, Mary, *Clementine Churchill*, Cassell, London, UK, 1979
Sublet, Lt Col Frank, *Kokoda to the Sea*, Slouch Hat Publications, Melbourne, Australia, 2000
Swain, Bruce T., *A Chronology of Australian Armed Forces at War 1939-45*, Allen & Unwin, Sydney, Australia, 2001
Wiest, Andrew and Mattson, Gregory, *The Pacific War*, Spellmount Ltd, Staplehurst, Kent, UK, 2001
Wilmot, Chester, 'Desert Siege', part of the compilation *Australian War Classics*, Penguin Books, Melbourne, Australia, 2003 (originally published as *Tobruk*, Angus & Robertson, Sydney, Australia, 1941)
Withers, Maxine, *Bushmen of the Great Anabranch*, self-published, Adelaide, Australia, 1989

UNPUBLISHED REPORTS
Nixon, A., 'Woodlands Homestead—Chaffey Era: 1917–1937 A Preliminary Report', unpublished report, Department of Conservation, Forests and Lands, Melbourne, Australia, 1986
Wise, Brian, '*History of 2/6th Australian Field Ambulance, Australian Imperial Forces, World War II, 1939–45*' Australian War Memorial, 1990
Wright, Sue, 'Looking for Laura', Friends of Woodlands Historic Park, Melbourne, Australia, 2006

INTERNET SOURCES
'Battle of Britain', http://www.the-battle-of-britain.co.uk
'Brahman', http://en.wikipedia.org/wiki/Brahman
'Calendar for 1939', http://en.wikipedia.org/wiki/1939
'General Erwin Rommel', http://en.wikipedia.org/wiki/Erwin_Rommel
'Samurai History', http://www.paralumun.com/asamurai.htm
'The Siege of Tobruk', http://www.diggerhistory2.info/army/1941/chapter03.htm
'Spanish Flu', http://en.wikipedia.org/wiki/Spanish_flu
'The Forgotten Force', Chapter One: World War II—the Legacies, http://www.defence.gov.au/Army/Ahu/books_articles/html
'The Fox', http://www.time.com/time/magazine/article/0,9171,818519,00.htm

'Three Theatres of War', http://www.warandidentity.com.au
'What is History?', http://www.history.ac.uk/ihr/FocusWhatishistory/
  evans10.htm>www.history.ac.uk/ihr/Focus/Whatishistory/evans10.
  html

NEWSPAPER ARTICLES

FitzSimons, Peter, 'The Fitz Files', *Sun Herald*, 23 October 2005
Hawley, Janet, 'Once Were Soldiers', *Sydney Morning Herald, Good Weekend*,
  25–27 April 2008
Levett, Connie, 'Retracing the March of the Dead', *Sydney Morning Herald*,
  19 April 2006
Marien, William, 'Too Many to Count Killed in Hiroshima', *Sydney
  Morning Herald*, 18 April 2006
McInnes, William, 'A Nasty, Dirty Nightmare', *Sydney Morning Herald*,
  22–23 April 2006

SPECIAL THANKS

I thank the many publishers who generously gave me permission to use
quotations from their books and feel deep gratitude to the following
individuals who kindly gave me their time and permission to use material
from their books:

Tim Bowden (*The Way My Father Tells It*)
Lieutenant General Coates (*Bravery Beyond Blunder*)
Jane Crane (daughter of Chester Wilmot, *Tobruk*)
Marilyn Dodkin (*Goodnight Bobbie*)
Timothy Hall (*Tobruk 1941*)
Neil McDonald (*Chester Wilmot Reports*)
Maxine Withers (*Bushmen of the Great Anabranch*)
Sue Wright (*Looking for Laura*)

~ Endnotes ~

PREFACE
1 The introduction is available on the website of the Institute of Historical Research at *What is History?*, http://www.history.ac.uk/ihr/Focus/Whatishistory/evans10.html

CHAPTER ONE — CHILDHOOD CUT SHORT
1 Peter Murray, taped interview with author, September 1989.
2 It was known as the 'Forsythe Cup'—named after the family who offered it. John's win was doubtless influenced by Arthur Ernest Henry, a King's schoolmaster known as Hoppy Henry because of his limp, who took a paternal interest in John's development. He was considerably hurt when John's mother rejected his offer to adopt her son.
3 Jane Lennon, *Red Gums and Rider—a History of Gellibrand Hill Park,* Department of Conservation & Natural Resources, Victoria, 1993, p. 46.
4 Peter & John Murray, interview and letter, September 1989.
5 Peter repeated to the author Laura's story that her grandparents, the Deans, were wealthy graziers who had disowned their daughter, Rebecca, for marrying 'beneath her'. However, certificates and other references differ in detail to this version of her past. Laura's grandfather, Thomas Dean (b. 1829 or 1830), came to Australia and married Caroline Artus, already here, in 1856 (see website, http://users. pipeline.com.au/~gd37ph45/deanweb.html). Upon their marriage they apparently selected land in Pooncarie NSW. Their cottage was made from wattle and daub, with pressed tin ceilings and was built on the banks of the Darling River, south of Pooncarie and was called "*Peaka Station*". Thomas worked as a butcher at *Wolverton,* also on the Darling River adjacent to *Moorara.* Later, he established a successful business in Pooncarie. (Sue Wright, *Looking for Laura*, p.3.)
6 Less than a month after Rebecca's death, on 18 September 1897, the newborn baby was registered by William as Mabel Rebecca Treweek.
7 Maxine Withers, *Bushmen of the Great Anabranch*, self-published, Adelaide, 1989, p. 178.
8 Peter Murray, interview with the author, September 1989.
9 Peter Murray, interview with the author, September 1989. Cowra was the daughter of Elliot Crozier of *Kulnine Station*, near Mildura, Victoria. Her unusual name was an Aboriginal place name. The Croziers had named their other two daughters similarly; Moorna and Keera. (Maxine Withers, p. 35).
10 Peter Murray, interview with the author, September 1989.
11 Wright, p. 6.
12 Withers, diary entry 1/4/16, p. 180.
13 Withers, p. 175.

14 Wright, p. 9. While living in the second property Constance paid rent to a real estate agent called Baillieu Allard. Mr Gordon Allard was a partner of the company and a good friend of Ben Chaffey's. His name later appeared on the auction notice for *Woodlands*, after Chaffey's death.

15 Peter thought that Laura might have asked if she could take Lorraine for a walk and then 'kept on walking', though this was just supposition.

16 *Red Gums and Riders*, p. 42.

17 Withers, p. 193. Instructions to Murray Forster, manager of *Tolarno*.

18 *Red Gums and Riders,* p. 1. *Woodlands* is now owned by the Victorian Government and is being preserved 'as a remnant of the initial European 1840s pastoral settlement'. It is open to the public.

CHAPTER TWO — LAURA'S DOMINION

1 Ernestine Hill, *Water Into Gold*, Robertson & Mullens, Melbourne, Australia, 1958, p. 50.

2 Hill, p. 128. The region now produces a high percentage of Australia's dried fruit, as well as over three million bushels of citrus a year and a large percentage of Victoria's winemaking grapes. Memorials in Mildura acknowledge the pioneering presence of the Chaffeys: the George Chaffey Bridge; a statue of William Chaffey (elected mayor in 1920); the Chaffey triple expansion steam engine; the revolutionary Chaffey pump (designed by George); and *Rio Vista*, the Chaffey mansion now a museum.

3 Withers, p. 177. Letter written to his friend Eli Barnfield, 'Barney', in May 1907.

4 Peter 'surmised' that this is what had happened to Lorraine. Interview with author, September 1989.

5 Peter Murray, interview with the author, September 1989.

6 Lord Byron 1788–1824: *Childe Harold's Pilgrimage: Canto the Fourth*, part of stanza x.

7 Sue-ann Makeham, conversation with the author, 30 September 2002, reporting a comment made by John Murray.

8 Peter Murray, interview with the author, September 1989.

9 Taken from a letter written by John Murray to the author, 27 March 2002.

10 Great Public Schools, made up of mostly private schools in New South Wales.

11 Geoffrey Blainey, *A Shorter History of Australia*, William Heinemann, Melbourne, Australia, 1994, p. 175.

CHAPTER THREE — EARLY TRAINING

1 John Murray, interview with the author, October 2003.

2 Peter Murray, interview with author, September 1989.

3 *Ibid.*

4 *Ibid.*

5 *Ibid.*

6 *Ibid.*

7 Even before the US stock market crash on Wall Street in October 1929 unemployment in Australia was around 10 per cent. The crash led to a depression for the entire industrialised world. During 1930 unemployment in Australia more than doubled to 21 per cent and by mid-1932 almost 32 per cent of Australians were out of work.

CHAPTER FOUR—WOODLANDS

1 *Red Gums and Riders*, pp. 71–2. Quoted from the plan of the Department of Conservation and Natural Resources, Victorian State Government, 1992.

2 *Red Gums and Riders*, pp. 41–2. 'Prior to the purchase of *Woodlands* in 1917, Ben Chaffey asked Miss Bess (Monty) McPherson if she would live with them as a paid companion to Mrs Chaffey. Miss McPherson, the sister of Alec McPherson, Chaffey's property manager from 1913 to 1924, agreed but on condition they moved from *Moorna*, west of Wentworth, which she considered too isolated and dry.'

3 Peter Murray, interview with the author, September 1989.

4 *Ibid.*

5 *Ibid.*

6 *Ibid.*

7 Letter from John Murray to his mother, dated 1941, exact date indecipherable. Charles Glanville was in the 2nd Light Horse Brigade, AIF.

8 Letter from Constance to Lorraine written from Rutland Hotel, dated 12th, Monday [August 1935].

9 *Red Gums and Riders*, p. 46.

CHAPTER FIVE—AUSTRALIA AT WAR

1 Michael Caulfield (ed.), *Voices of War, Stories from the Australians at War Film Archive*, Hodder Australia, Sydney, 2006, p. 302. Words of veteran Walter Wallace.

2 Broadcast message by Prime Minister Robert Menzies, 3 September 1939, reproduced in R.G. Neale (ed.), *Documents on Australian Foreign Policy*, Vol. 2, Australian Government Publishing Service, Canberra, 1998, ('Neale'), pp. 221–6.

3 Neale, pp. 221–6.

4 Under the secret protocols of the Nazi-Soviet Non-Aggression Pact of 23 August 1939, Stalin and Hitler had agreed that western Poland was to be Germany's if eastern Poland went to Stalin. Neither would encroach on the other's territory.

5 Peter Cochrane, *Australians at War*, ABC Books, Sydney, 2001, p. 98.

6 The Dingo Fence or Dog Fence, the longest fence in the world, stretched 5310 kilometres (3300 miles), beginning about 80 kilometres (50 miles) northeast of Toowoomba in Queensland and running through thousands of miles of arid country to the Eyre Peninsula on the Great Australian Bight. It was first used as a rabbit-proof fence during the 1880s, but it was more successful at keeping out pigs, kangaroos, emus and brumbies. In 1914, it was converted to a dog-proof fence—to keep dingoes out of the south-east part of Australia and to protect the sheep flocks of southern Queensland.

7 *Bugilbone* was owned by a Mr Thompson, whose son, 'Boy', was at King's with John. A branch of the Thompson family was also involved with the *Widden Stud*—a horse stud established in 1867 in the Hunter River Valley.

8 Pelmanism was a system of training to improve the memory, named after the Pelman Institute, founded in London in 1898.

9 John was witness to Peter's marriage to Jane Moore at Broken Hill on 27 June 1939. As the war progressed Peter also tried to enlist, but, suffering from emphysema, he was declared unfit. In John's opinion, Peter's ill health was a result of his work in the mines.

CHAPTER SIX — A NEW KIND OF TRAINING

1 Joanna Penglase and David Horner, *When the War Came to Australia,* Allen & Unwin, Sydney, 1992 (Penglase & Horner), p. 10. Words of Sally Bowen, hotel cook, Wollongong, New South Wales.
2 Hawley, Janet, 'Once Were Soldiers', *Sydney Morning Herald,* 25–27 April 2008, p. 30. Words of officer, John Watch.
3 From a speech delivered in the House of Commons, 4 June 1940, reproduced in Mary Soames, *Clementine Churchill,* Cassell, London, 1979 ('Soames'), p. 288.
4 G.H. Fearnside, *Bayonets Abroad,* John Burridge Military Antiques, Success Print, Western Australia, 1993 ('Fearnside, *Bayonets Abroad*'), p. 5.
5 Fearnside, *Bayonets Abroad,* p. 6.
6 Recorded in Hugh Gillan (ed.), *We Had Some Bother,* Hale & Ironmonger, Sydney, 2001 ('Gillan'), p. 76. Collated with the assistance of the 2/13th Battalion Association, this book contains extensive extracts from the diary of Private Clothier, of 11 Platoon. A dixie was a metal pot used by the soldiers for cooking or brewing tea.
7 Recorded in Gillan, p. 76.
8 Ruth Stanton-Cook was a friend of John's sister, Margie. They had attended the same school, PLC Pymble, and Ruth had spent much of her girlhood at the Murray residence, as her own mother had left her husband and travelled to England, taking Ruth's sister with her.
9 Hawley, Janet, 'Once Were Soldiers', *Sydney Morning Herald,* 25–27 April 2008, p. 24. Words of Joe Madeley.
10 Penglase & Horner, p. 7. Paraphrased words of Sandy Rayward.
11 Fearnside, *Bayonets Abroad,* p. 376. Burrows had commissioned Sgt Cyril Huggert 'to haunt the recruiting centres' in order to direct any musical talent towards the 2/13th Battalion.
12 G.H. Fearnside, *Half to Remember,* Haldance Publishing Co Pty Ltd, Australia, 1975, ('Fearnside, *Half to Remember*'), p. 14.

CHAPTER SEVEN — GETTING STARTED

1 Penglase & Horner, p. 3.
2 Recorded in Gillan, p. 75.
3 Fearnside, *Bayonets Abroad,* p. 23.
4 *Ibid,* p. 25.
5 *Ibid,* p. 26.
6 Tim Bowden, *The Way My Father Tells It,* ABC Books, Australia, 1997, p. 188.
7 Recorded in Gillan, p. 76.
8 *Ibid,* p. 77.
9 In January 1939, even before the men had left Australia, Hitler had referred in the Reichstag to the 'annihilation of the Jewish race in Europe'; anti-Semitic legislation and actions before this year had demonstrated his serious intent. Kristallnacht— the Night of Broken Glass—was a massive coordinated attack in late October 1938 on Jews throughout Germany. The full extent of the extermination program would not be known until much later.
10 Timothy Hall, *Tobruk 1941: The Desert Siege,* Methuen Australia Pty Ltd 1984, p. 97.
11 Mark Johnston, *That Magnificent 9th: An Illustrated History of the 9th Division 1940– 46,* Allen & Unwin, Sydney, Australia, 2005, p.12. 'The (9th) Division was terribly

short of equipment … Because its field regiments lacked guns and its cavalry lacked carriers, only the infantry brigades and some divisional units were sent to Cyrenaica (in Libya).'

12   David Day, *The Politics of War*, HarperCollins, Sydney, Australia, p. 122.
13   The end result of this move was ruinous. Not only were the 6th Division Australians in Greece forced to make a fast retreat after horrific slaughter, losing all their valuable heavy equipment, but their previous gains in Libya were almost all lost over a short period of time.
14   Bruce T. Swain, *A Chronology of Australian Armed Forces at War 1939–45*, Allen & Unwin, Sydney, 2001 ('Swain'), p. 25.
15   Johnston, p. 12.
16   *Ibid*, p. 42.
17   John Coates, *Bravery above Blunder*, Oxford University Press, Melbourne, 1999 ('Coates'), p. 11.

CHAPTER EIGHT — THE FIRST DEADLY EXPERIENCE

1   Fearnside, *Bayonets Abroad*, p. 41.
2   *Ibid*, p. 42.
3   Before the outbreak of World War II, Italy had enjoyed a long-term presence in Africa—Abyssinia (now Ethiopia), Libya, Eritrea, Somaliland. In September 1940, Mussolini pushed forward to expand his African Empire. Annexing Egypt, then under British control, would give him almost total control of an area reaching from Libya to the eastern shores of the Red Sea. Mussolini had decided to go it alone, rebuffing Germany's offer of assistance. He would regret his decision. After the fall of France, Britain was isolated and battling for survival. However, to lose control of Egypt and the Suez Canal would herald disaster. With all possible Allied power garnered—40,000 men at most—Britain successfully protected her interests in Egypt, with Commonwealth forces driving the Italian armies back across Libya by February 1941.
4   Recorded in Gillan, p. 79. The men regularly referred to Italians as 'Eyeties' (or 'Ities').
5   F.H. Gregory, *Rommel*, Wayland Publishers Ltd, London, 1974, ('Gregory') p. 47.
6   Barton Maughan, *Tobruk & El Alamein, Australia in the War of 1939–1945*, Australian War Memorial, Canberra, 1966, ('Maughan'), p. 21.
7   Fearnside, *Half to Remember*, p. 29. Bren guns were air-cooled gas-operated submachine guns taking 303 calibre ammunition, used in World War II.
8   Hall, p. 30.
9   John did not correctly spell his niece's unusual name—Sue-ann—in any of his letters. It was most likely he did not have ready access to Margie's letters for reference.
10   Recorded in Gillan, p. 79.
11   Hall, pp. 29–37.

CHAPTER NINE — FACE TO FACE AT ER REGIMA

1   Hill, 'Er Regima', *Wartime*, Issue 26, 2004, p. 38.
2   Hall, p. 48. Rommel desperately needed Tobruk Harbour as a supply base. His forces in North Africa needed about 50,000 tons of supplies each month in

order to cross the frontier into Egypt. The Germans could only lift about 29,000 tons a month from Tripoli Harbour, the only other possible port.

3   Gregory, p. 41.
4   The three battalions were the 13th, 23rd and the 24th, with another battalion on the southern flank. The 2/13th Battalion (the only one from the 20th Brigade) was short of one whole Company, previously detached to Headquarters in Barce. 'On arrival in Cyrenaica, the 2/13th had been required to detach its C Company for duty at Barce (where Cyrenaica Command was located) for guard duties, including duties at a camp which enclosed some 1000 prisoners of war, captured in the earlier advance, and not yet transported back to Tobruk.' Information supplied by John Searle to author, 24 May 2005.
5   Fearnside, *Bayonets Abroad*, p. 54.
6   Fearnside, *Half to Remember*, p. 29.
7   Lawson Glassop, *We Were the Rats*, Australian War Classics, Angus & Robertson, Melbourne, Australia, 1944, p 137.
8   Recorded in Gillan, p. 80.
9   Fearnside, *Bayonets Abroad*, p. 63.
10 Fearnside, *Bayonets Abroad*, p. 64.
11 Gillan, p. 80. See also Fearnside, *Bayonets Abroad*, p. 71.
12 Chester Wilmot, 'Desert Siege', part of the compilation *Australian War Classics*, Penguin Books, 2003, ('Wilmont'), p. 82.

CHAPTER TEN — THE SIEGE OF TOBRUK BEGINS

1   Neil McDonald, *Chester Wilmot Reports: Broadcasts that Shaped World War II*, ABC Books, Australia, 2004, ('McDonald'), p. 218.
2   The pits were constructed at angles and criss-crossed so that if a projectile from the air or a shell landed on one it would do less damage.
3   Fearnside, *Bayonets Abroad*, p. 88. Words of Bluey Dessaix.
4   Glassop, p. 153.
5   Maughan, p. 125.
6   Recorded in Gillan, p. 81.
7   Gregory, p. 45 (quoting from *The Rommel Papers*).
8   Swain, p. 33.
9   'Bomb Alley' was the name for the last 40 miles of ocean route from Alexandria to the harbour of Tobruk – always bombed when the Allies were trying to take out the injured or bring in reinforcements and/or supplies.
10 Corporal J.H. Edmondson's VC was presented to his mother by Governor-General Lord Gowrie, on 27 September 1941. In 1969 Mrs Edmondson gave her son's medals and some of his personal belongings to the Australian War Memorial. They are still on display there.
11 Maughan, p. 146.
12 Being on the flank, he and the men were able to employ enfilade fire, for which they had trained endlessly. John described this fire as 'not straight across the enemy line of penetration, but more to the openings of the perimeter that the enemy had used to come in'.
13 Fearnside, *Bayonets Abroad*, p. 93.
14 Words of Sister Ivor Helen, reproduced on http://www.diggerhistory2.info/ army1941/chapter03.htm.

15 Wilmot, p. 228.
16 Frank Harrison, *Tobruk—the Great Siege Re-assessed*, Arms & Armour, London, 1996, ('Harrison'), p. 27., p. 42.
17 *Ibid*, p. 301.
18 *Ibid*, p. 49.
19 Hall, p. 108.
20 Fearnside, *Bayonets Abroad*, p. 94.
21 McDonald, p. 207.
22 Winston Churchill, during the debate in the British Parliament over a censure vote against him for his failure to defeat Rommel. The vote failed. http://www.time.com/time/magazine/article/0,9171,818519,00.html.

CHAPTER ELEVEN — THE RATS DIG DEEPER

1   Cited in *The Devil's Own Despatch*, October 1979 edition, p. 6.
2   Wilmot, p. 125.
3   Maughan, p. 186.
4   Fearnside, *Bayonets Abroad*, p. 256.
5   Altogether, monies and goods were collected to the value of £4600 by the Ladies' Auxiliary for the benefit of the 2/13th Battalion. Men were given free issues from the canteen on several occasions, often during prolonged battle, 'to boost morale and … break the monotony of hardship'. Fearnside, *Bayonets Abroad*, p. 16.
6   Recorded in Gillan, p. 82.
7   Hall, p. 130.
8   Recorded in Gillan, p. 82.
9   Fearnside, *Bayonets Abroad*, p. 98.
10 Wilmot, p. 131. Diary of Lieutenant Schorm, 5th Tank Regiment.
11 *Ibid*, p. 124.
12 *Ibid*, p. 250.
13 Recorded in Gillan, p. 82.
14 Fearnside, *Bayonets Abroad*, p. 101.
15 Hall, p. 179.
16 Glassop, pp. 213–14.
17 Fearnside, *Bayonets Abroad*, p. 94.
18 Wilmot, p. 64.
19 Information supplied by John Searle to author, 24 May 2005.
20 Hall, p. 206.
21 Wilmot, p. 64.
22 Gregory, p. 43.
23 Maughan, p. 235.

CHAPTER TWELVE —   …AND DEEPER

1   Peter FitzSimons, *Tobruk*, HarperCollins, Sydney, 2006, pp. 401–2.
2   Fearnside, *Half to Remember*, pp. 57–8.
3   Fearnside, *Half to Remember*, p. 60.
4   Caulfield, pp. 320–1.
5   Hall, p. 105.
6   Fearnside, *Half to Remember*, p. 81.

7   Wilmot, p. 195.
8   Recorded in Gillan, p. 84.
9   Caulfield, p. 309.
10 Fearnside, *Half to Remember*, p. 61.
11 Wilmot, p. 182.

CHAPTER THIRTEEN — RELIEF GONE WRONG

1   Hall, p. 175.
2   Hawley, Janet, 'Once Were Soldiers', *Sydney Morning Herald*, 25–27 April 2008, p. 28. Words of John Dickson.
3   *Ibid.*
4   Each individual's water supply was increased to 3.25 litres from 19 June 1941.
5   Part of a poem written by Hugh Paterson—a ballad writer of the 20th Brigade HQ—cited in Fearnside, *Bayonets Abroad*, pp. 133–4.
6   Hall, pp. 191–2.
7   Hall, p. 27.
8   Hall, p. 102.
9   Gregory, p. 55.
10 Prime Minister Menzies had gone overseas for four months in early 1941 and during this period Arthur Fadden, head of the Country Party was Acting Prime Minister. On his return, Menzies faced dissension from within his own party and was forced to resign. Fadden stepped in on 29 August as Prime Minister, an office that lasted approximately five weeks until Labor leader John Curtin won office on 7 October 1941.
11 Swain, p. 93.
12 *Ibid.*
13 Recorded in Gillan, p. 88.
14 Hawley, Janet, 'Once Were Soldiers', *Sydney Morning Herald*, 25–27 April 2008, p. 24.
15 Fearnside, *Half to Remember*, p. 92.
16 Part of a poem written by Hugh Paterson; cited in Fearnside, *Bayonets Abroad*, p. 160.
17 Fearnside, *Half to Remember*, p. 98-99.
18 Poem written by Hugh Paterson; cited in Maughan, p. 421.

CHAPTER FOURTEEN — LAST STAND AT ED DUDA

1   Johnston, p. 61.
2   Day, p. 164.
3   *Ibid*, p. 162.
4   Recorded in Gillan, p. 89.
5   Wilmot, p. 294.
6   Recorded in Gillan, p. 89.
7   Fearnside, *Half to Remember*, p. 101.
8   Swain, p. 105.
9   Wilmot, p. 300.
10 Fearnside, *Half to Remember*, p. 101.
11 Maughan, p. 470.
12 *Ibid*, p. 477. Words of Cpl Thompson, 2/13th Battalion, Intelligence Section and John Murray.

13　Fearnside, *Half to Remember*, p. 109.

14　*Ibid*, p. 110.

15　John still has the binoculars, though sub-standard repair work at one time after the war ruined the superior lenses.

16　Poem by Matt Kirby of C Company, 2/13th Battalion; cited in Fearnside, *Bayonets Abroad*, p. 160.

17　Maughan, p. 210.

18　Fearnside, *Bayonets Abroad*, p. 159.

Chapter Fifteen — Leave at last

1　Fearnside, *Bayonets Abroad,* p. 162.

2　Day, p. 206.

3　The date was 11 November 1918, when John was almost three years old.

4　Fearnside, *Half to Remember*, pp. 123–4.

5　'The Fall of Singapore' http://ourstory.asia1.com.sg/war/headline/church.html. This article refers to *Operation Matador*, Dr Ong Chit Chung's book in which the military plan, Matador, is discussed.

6　Day, p. 258.

7　Maughan, p. 293.

8　Penglase and Horner, pp. 82–3. Words of postal worker Murray Fletcher.

9　Marilyn Dodkin, *Goodnight Bobbie: One Family's War*, UNSW Press, Sydney, 2006, p. 157.

10　Penglase & Horner, p. 76.

11　Swain, p. 149.

12　Penglase & Horner, p. 76. *Bulletin* entry 11 March, 1942.

13　Fearnside, *Half to Remember*, p. 128.

14　Undated letter from John Murray to Margie, probably March, 1942.

Chapter Sixteen — Shattering news

1　Fearnside, p. 193.

2　Day, p. 422.

3　Fearnside, *Half to Remember,* p. 129.

4　Soames, p. 315.

5　Day, p. 320.

6　Maughan, p. 696.

7　Recorded in Gillan, p. 94.

8　Fearnside, *Bayonets Abroad,* p. 194.

9　The Royal Military Academy at Sandhurst (commonly known as 'Sandhurst') is the prestigious British army officer initial training centre.

Chapter Seventeen — El Alamein

1　Peter Cochrane, *Australians at War*, Department of Veterans' Affairs, Australian Broadcasting Corporation, Sydney, 2001 p. 163.

2　Gillan, pp. 96–8.

3　Day, p. 391.

4　Gillan, p. 98.

5　*Ibid*, p. 99.

6　Caulfield, p. 317. Words of Walter Wallace.

7 Maughan was later transferred to Headquarters as the 20th Brigade Intelligence Officer.

8 Hawley, Janet, 'Once Were Soldiers', *Sydney Morning Herald,* 25–27 April 2008, p. 24.

9 Recorded in Gillan, p. 99. Clothier's short sentence was to become the title of editor Hugh Gillan's future book, *We Had Some Bother.*

10 Scorge, Martin K., *The Other Price of Hitler's War,* Greenwood Press, London, 1986, p. 43.

11 Maughan, p. 706.

12 Fearnside, *Bayonets Abroad,* p. 287.

13 Maughan pp. 745–6.

14 Maughan, p. 745.

15 Maughan, p. 742.

16 In winning the victory, the British 8th Army lost 13,560 men—killed, wounded or missing; the Australian '9th Division's casualties were about one-fifth of the total casualties of the Eighth Army'. Maughan, p. 742.

17 John Murray's report formed the basis of Barton Maughan's history of the battle; see indexed references in Maughan under Alamein, El.

18 Day, p. 417. Advice from Churchill dated 5 November 1942.

19 Fearnside, *Bayonets Abroad,* p. 300.

20 Day, pp. 407–42.

21 New Guinea was divided into three major regions. After World War I the Dutch controlled western New Guinea and the responsibility for eastern New Guinea, divided into the two provinces of New Guinea and Papua, had been transferred to Australia.

CHAPTER EIGHTEEN — SO NEAR AND YET SO FAR

1 John Murray, interview with the author, April 2003.

2 Fearnside, *Bayonets Abroad,* p. 411.

3 Recorded in Gillan, p. 102.

4 Taken from a letter written by John Murray to the author, 27 March 2002.

5 Recorded in Gillan, p. 102.

6 Fearnside, *Half to Remember,* p. 168.

7 Recorded in Gillan, p. 103–4.

8 Recorded in Gillan, p. 103.

9 Coates, p. 3.

10 Swain, p. 269.

11 The official name was gazetted as 'Kokoda Trail' by the Australian administration of PNG in 1972. However, the *Australian Macquarie Dictionary* states that while both terms are in use, Kokoda Track 'appears to be the more popular of the two'.

12 William McInnes, 'A Nasty, Dirty Nightmare', *Sydney Morning Herald,* 22–23 April, 2006, p. 14.

13 Brian Wise, *History of 2/6th Australian Field Ambulance, AIF, World War II, 1939–45,* Australian War Memorial, 1990, p. 32.

14 Paul Ham, *Kokoda,* HarperCollins Australia, 2004, p. 201.

15 Peter FitzSimons, *Kokoda,* Hodder Australia, 2004, p. 401. The Regimental Medical Officer of the 2/25th Battalion wrote in a report: 'I have examined two portions of flesh recovered by one of our patrols. One was the muscle tissue with a large piece of skin and underlying tissues attached. I consider the last as human.'

16 Recorded in Gillan, p. 103.
17 Fearnside, *Bayonets Abroad,* p. 329.
18 Caulfield, p. 323. Words of Walter Wallace.

CHAPTER NINETEEN — THE JUNGLES OF NEW GUINEA
1 Letter from John Murray to his mother, 17 October 1943.
2 Penglase and Horner, p. 226. Words of Nola Bridger.
3 FitzSimons, *Kokoda,* p. 108.
4 Windeyer had led the 2/48th Battalion in Tobruk. He was promoted to command the 20th Brigade after Tobruk, leading it during the El Alamein fighting, and later in New Guinea.
5 Coates, p. 105.
6 *Ibid,* p. 78.
7 *Ibid,* p. 3.
8 *Ibid,* p. 79.
9 Lieut. John Murray IO, *War Diary, 2/13th Battalion, Finschhafen Operation, 21 Sept–25 Oct 1943,* p. 4.
10 Fearnside, *Bayonets Abroad,* p. 343.
11 Coates, p. 102.

CHAPTER TWENTY — JUNGLE LIFE GOES ON
1 Coates, p. 7.
2 *Ibid,* p. 110.
3 *Ibid,* p. 282.
4 *War Diary, 2/13th Battalion, Finschhafen Operation, 21 Sept–25 Oct 1943,* in possession of the author.
5 Coates, p. 110.
6 Johnston, p. 159. From the diary of Private A Armstrong.
7 FitzSimons, *Kokoda,* p. 435, quoting from the Australia/Japan Research Project, Australian War Memorial.
8 Hawley, Janet, 'Once Were Soldiers', *Sydney Morning Herald,* 25–27 April 2008, p. 28. Words of John Dickson.
9 Penglase & Horner, p. 220. Words of Bill Graham.
10 Johnston, pp. 230–1. Instructions from Lieutenant General Katagiri of the Japanese 20th Division.
11 Poem in possession of the author.
12 Fearnside, *Bayonets Abroad,* pp. 355–6.

CHAPTER TWENTY-ONE — SECURITY AND SURVIVAL
1 Letter from John Murray to his mother, 22 February 1944. A 'Sam Brown' was a combination of gun belt and shoulder strap.
2 Fearnside, *Bayonets Abroad,* p. 200.
3 Swain, p. 240.
4 Letter from John Murray to his mother, 23 May 1944.
5 Report reproduced by John Murray in a letter to his mother, 21 July 1944.
6 Fearnside, *Bayonets Abroad,* p. 419.
7 Connie Levett, 'Retracing the March of the Dead', *Sydney Morning Herald,* 19 April 2006, p. 12.

CHAPTER TWENTY-TWO—BORNEO

1 Letter from John Murray to his mother, 19 April 1945.
2 British Borneo lay along Borneo's northern seaboard. It consisted of: the two states of British North Borneo and Sarawak; the small protected State of Brunei; and the Crown Colony of Labuan Island. One oil field was at Miri, close to the northern boundary of Sarawak, and the other 51 kilometres (32 miles) north, at Seria, in Brunei. The crude oil was pumped from both fields to a refinery at Lutong on the coast.
3 Fearnside, *Bayonets Abroad*, p. 385.
4 Day, p. 622.
5 'The Forgotten Force', Chapter One: World War II—the Legacies http://www.defence.gov.au/Army/Ahu/books_articles/html.
6 Peter Brune, *A Bastard of a Place*, Allen & Unwin, Australia, 2004, p. 614.
7 *Sydney Morning Herald*, 18 April 2006, p. 10, quoting an article published in the *Sydney Morning Herald* on 19 August 1945, entitled 'Too many to count killed in Hiroshima', written by war correspondent William Marlen in Guam and distributed by AAP.
8 Swain, *Chronology*, p. 409.
9 Communiqué from the Far Eastern Liaison Office, dated 10 August 1945.
10 Brigadier J.D. Rogers, Director of Military, *Australian Military Forces Weekly Review*, No 148, July 1945, Foreword.
11 Gibney, p. 161. In a letter written to the editor of a Japanese newspaper (the *Asahai Shimbun*) in the 1990s, Fujimata Masayoshi, a corporate officer in the Pacific War, wrote about the final days of many sick and wounded Japanese soldiers. He commented that he had seen many place where a small number of Japanese soldiers had sat in a circle to commit suicide—by exploding a hand grenade.
12 'Samurai History', http//: www.paralumun.com/asamurai.htm.
13 The last verse of a wartime poem by an anonymous author, cited in Gillan, p. 156.

CHAPTER TWENTY-THREE—GO WEST YOUNG MAN

1 The Prime Minister of Australia, Ben Chifley, speaking on radio on 15 August 1945.
2 Penglase & Horner, p. 231. Words of Alan Low.
3 Penglase & Horner, p. 231. Words of Hilary Hughes.
4 Penglase & Horner, p. 234.
5 Later to become the CSIRO (Commonwealth Scientific and Industrial Research Organisation).
6 Peter Murray, taped interview with the author, September 1989.
7 Peter Murray, interview with the author, September 1989.

CHAPTER TWENTY-FOUR—CATTLE AND COMMAND

1 John Murray, interview with the author, 17 September 2005.
2 *Herbert River Express*, 'New Major Extension Planned in Improved Pastures at The Orient', 11 October 1960.
3 Robbie Murray, email, 28 September 2006.
4 *The Townsville Daily Bulletin*, 30 July 1959.
5 The Australian cane fields were not mechanised for years after those of other nations. When John went to the United States in 1952 to purchase Brahmans, he stopped by in Fiji to see the mechanised cane fields for himself

CHAPTER TWENTY-FIVE — COALITION

1   Sue-ann Makeham (née Oldham), in taped interview with Peter Murray and Oldham girls, September 1989.
2   Ruth Murray to author, in taped interview, October 2003.
3   Peter Murray, interview with the author, September 1989.
4   *The Townsville Daily Bulletin*, editorial, 8 December 1961.
5   *The Townsville Daily Bulletin*, 22 February 1961.
6   Dr R.B. Kelley, *Zebus (Brahmans) in America: An Importation. Proposal for Use in Australia*, Wilmett & Sons (Pty) Ltd, Townsville, Australia, 1951.
7   John Murray Jnr, email, 24 July 2005.
8   *Red Gums and Riders*, p. 46. Description of *Woodlands* cited in copy of auction advertisement dated Tuesday, 22 June 1930.

CHAPTER TWENTY-SIX — FULL CIRCLE

1   John Murray, interview with author, October 2003.
2   John Gardner was former Officer Commanding C Company 31st Battalion (the Kennedy Battalion) The Royal Queensland Regiment, Patricia was his wife.

Index

(page numbers in *italics* indicate illustrations)

Published in 2009 by Pier 9, an imprint of Murdoch Books Pty Limited

Pier 8/9, 23 Hickson Road, Millers Point NSW 2000
Phone: +61 (0) 2 8220 2000   Fax: +61 (0) 2 8220 2558
www.murdochbooks.com.au

Murdoch Books UK Limited
Erico House, 6th Floor
93–99 Upper Richmond Road, Putney, London SW15 2TG
Phone: +44 (0) 20 8785 5995   Fax: +44 (0) 20 8785 5985
www.murdochbooks.co.uk

Publisher: Diana Hill
Project Editor: Sophia Oravecz
Designer: Melanie Young, InHouse Creative
Cartographer: Ian F Faulkner & Associates

National Library of Australia Cataloguing-in-Publication Data
     Author: Austin, Louise.
     Title: Journey to Tobruk : John Murray—bushman, soldier, survivor / Louise Austin
     ISBN: 9781741965063 (pbk.)
     Notes: Includes index.
     Subjects: Murray, John, 1915–2009. Australia. Army—History—World War, 1939–1945.
     Tobruk, Battles of, Tobruk, Libya, 1941–1942—Biography.
     World War, 1939–1945—Participation, Australian—Biography.
     Politicians—Queensland—Biography.
     Dewey Number: 940.542312092

A catalogue record for this book is available from the British Library.

Printed in 2009. PRINTED IN CHINA.